Marcel Siegler
Needful Structures

Edition panta rei

Marcel Siegler (né Müller) is a philosopher of technology and an alumnus of the research training group KRITIS, Technische Universität Darmstadt, on networked urban infrastructures. His research focuses on the dialectical interrelation between human agency, technology, and society, as well as the transformation of sociotechnical systems.

Marcel Siegler

Needful Structures

The Dialectics of Action, Technology, and Society
in Sartre's Later Philosophy

Extended PhD thesis, originally titled *Needful Structures: The Dialectics of Practical Ensembles and their Significance for Understanding Urban Mobility*
Supervisors: Alfred Nordmann and Christoph Hubig (TU Darmstadt)

Bibliographic information published by the Deutsche Nationalbibliothek
The Deutsche Nationalbibliothek lists this publication in the Deutsche Nationalbibliografie; detailed bibliographic data are available in the Internet at http://dnb.d-nb.de

Cover concept: Kordula Röckenhaus, Bielefeld
Copy-editing: LexAcademic

https://doi.org/10.14361/9783839462829
Print-ISBN 978-3-8376-6282-5
PDF-ISBN 978-3-8394-6282-9
ISSN of series: 2702-9034
eISSN of series: 2702-9042

Contents

II The Dialectic of Practical Ensembles

Introduction

Needful Structures

It is a constant of the human condition to be intricately situated amid other people, material things, and systems that are structured in myriad organizational forms—some of which are incredibly complex and others of which are simpler. Every human being is born into structures that contextualize and scaffold how humans act, and why they do so. These structures include their place and time of birth, their sex and gender, their sociocultural and economic background, the general constitution of their material environment, and so on. The interplay of these structures enables human beings to realize certain possibilities of their existence while constraining the realization of others.

It is also a constant of the human condition to be burdened with both basic and more complex material and immaterial requirements, wants, and wishes that need regular satisfaction. These requirements, wants, and wishes are due not only to the organic materiality of the human body but also to the position people adopt in the constellations of society. Humans are inherently *needful* beings. They require, among other things, water, clothing, shelter, food, the possibility to move around, and a caring community. They may also desire individual meaning, fairness, and a societal purpose. Paradoxically, these *constants* of the human condition are fundamental for understanding the *process-based*, or *processual*, character of human existence. Through these requirements, wants, and wishes, as well as through people's actions to satisfy them, humans can be understood as inherently goal-directed beings. How people may get whatever they require or wish for themselves strongly depends on the contexts and structures in which they are situated, as well as on their exact place within them. The requirements for water or mobility, for instance, can be rather easily tackled in the confines of one's own home or an urban environment. However, in a deserted area, or without the necessary means—instrumental, financial, and infrastructural—the satisfaction of physical requirements and other more complex wishes can be a somewhat intricate matter.

The relation between what humans need, on the one hand, and the structures giving rise to both possibilities and constraints to fulfill those needs, on the other hand, is an intriguing one. This fascinating relation is particularly evident in the large-scale provision of infrastructure services in urban spaces. Enormous structures, such as drinking water and waste-water disposal, roads, traffic, and transit systems, as well as information technologies and other facilities with similar importance for individual and societal thriving, are considered by some to be the indispensable lifelines of modern societies (BMI 2009, 3).

Urban infrastructures represent structured constellations of people, material things, norms, regulations, and practices that enable societies to address some of their basic and more complex needs in the long run. Simultaneously, infrastructures seem to be inherently *needful* themselves, in the full range of the term's meanings. Infrastructures are "precarious achievements" (Graham 2010, 10), full of demands, technical requirements, and practical constraints. These structures require constant maintenance to ensure proper functionality. Furthermore, critical events such as technical malfunctions, extreme weather, natural disasters, and also health crises like the COVID-19 pandemic, may disrupt the provision of infrastructure services. Hence, operating these structures on a large scale requires the employment of various preparedness and prevention measures to avoid or at least mitigate potential harm (Crespo et al. 2018). The war in Ukraine and the concomitant energy crisis further highlight the needfulness of modern societies and their infrastructures.

Infrastructures are not only full of demands and requirements—they are also rendered necessary by the essential services they provide to society, which is another aspect of their inherent needfulness. In light of the provision of these services, one way to understand infrastructures is in terms of their functional criticality. Infrastructures can be considered critical when the disruption of their functionality affects the functional interrelations of the larger form of organization of modern societies in which these infrastructures are situated (Lukitsch et al. 2018, 16–17). The inherent connection between infrastructures and society is also the root of infrastructural vulnerability. Because the continued existence of modern societies and the provision of critical infrastructure services depend on each other, these infrastructures represent vulnerable points in the larger organizational form of societies (Eifert et al. 2018).

Urban infrastructures may be exceptional examples of inherently needful structures, but this particular form of needfulness seems to pervade all of the human sociality in its myriad organizational forms. The exact composition of larger constellations between people and things may take many forms, but they are all grounded—in one way or another—in people's material and immaterial requirements and wishes, as well as in the inability of these people to satisfy them on their own. Whether in the case of families, political parties, factories, or urban spaces, all these constellations are permeated by goal-directed human actions to satisfy these requirements and wishes.

This work seeks to explore the close relationship between human needs and desires, their material and immaterial requirements, wants, and wishes, the demands and requirements of the built world, and the forms of organization that hold both humans and the built world together. The central claim is that the complexity of societal constellations must be understood through the requirements, wants, and wishes of individuals, as well as through the actions that these individuals perform to satisfy them. Such an understanding allows one to understand the practical constraints that pervade these constellations as a result of human action itself. Eventually, this understanding will also allow for the reassessment of the inseparable relation between human existence, technology, and forms of organization throughout human history. To achieve its aims, this work reconstructs the foundations and inner workings of social organization that Jean-Paul Sartre explores and outlines in his philosophical writings, and, in particular, his theories on practical ensembles.

Research Problem

In his later work *Critique of Dialectical Reason*,[1] Sartre concerns himself with the situation of historically situated individuals and the claim that these individuals are both products and (re-)producers of their sociocultural and material situation (Sartre 1978, 97). Sartre's later works, especially *Critique*, represent a fusion of his existentialist philosophy with Marxist thought. Although the later Sartre advocates a material monism, he objects to the dominant Marxist beliefs of his time, especially those that claim the world to be subject to materially dialectical laws of nature. Opposed as he is to the belief that matter is dialectical in itself, Sartre claims that free, individual human action, in confrontation with the physicochemical world, to be that which manifests a dialectical progression of history in the first place. Consequently, to understand history, it must be examined based on human action and experience (Sartre 1978, 40–43). To analyze this entanglement, Sartre undertakes a complex argument about the dialectical character of human existence and the products and structures that arise owing to humanity's engagement with their material surroundings. He applies a specific mode of dialectical thinking, which, at its core, seeks to depict processes in which initially contradicting, incompatible, or categorically different aspects of a certain thing in question are brought together toward a more holistic and actionable understanding of the said thing. He

---

1   The current work relies mostly on Volume I of *Critique of Dialectical Reason*, because it is there that Sartre outlines his theories on practical ensembles. For this reason, Volume I will simply be referred to as *Critique*. *Critique II*—subtitled *The Intelligibility of History*—remains unfinished but has been edited by Elkaïm-Sartre (1991). Although it contains other insights into practical ensembles, its unfinished status means that quotations and passages from the second volume are used sparingly throughout this work.

advocates a processual understanding of human existence, reality, and history as driven by the dialectical character of human experience and action. Both must be understood as inherently dialectical and synthetic interrelations between humans and their surroundings.

Throughout his philosophical oeuvre, Sartre conceives human action as ontologically free and intentional. At the same time, human action is fundamentally driven by how basic and more complex requirements, wants, and wishes project toward certain intended ends; these ends somewhat abstractly outline how courses of action are to be realized. Sartre's understanding of these requirements, wants, and wishes changes across his works. In *Being and Nothingness*, Sartre conceives of them as *desires*, whereas in *Critique* he conceives of them as *needs*. However, the distinction between *desire* and *need* must be understood in terms of neither a difference between immaterial wishes and material requirements nor a more conscious or more affective relation to a certain object. Rather, in Sartre's case, the difference between needs and desires is one between the level of abstractness or concreteness in how human beings relate to their material surroundings based on what and how they require, want, or wish for something. In this understanding, *desires*, translated from Sartre's French term *désir*, represent concrete and socially structured modes in which human beings relate to their surroundings based on their material and immaterial requirements, wants, and wishes. Needs, based on Sartre's French term *besoin*, represent abstract and initially unstructured ways in which human beings make these relations. Through peoples' active and practical membership in societal constellations, their abstract needs (as *besoins*) are transformed and concretized into desires (as *désirs*). This means that human beings are fundamentally adapted to the societal constellations they are situated in, and the adaptation occurs by how these constellations enable them to relate to and satisfy their requirements, wants, and wishes through actions. Performing such actions is a synthetic act that unites materially physical aspects—requirements, wants, bodily activity, instrumental means—and mental aspects—wishes, intentions, ends—by causing effects in the material surroundings to transform them following some intended result.

Due to its synthetic character, Sartre claims human action to be an instantiation of a rather abstract dialectical principle which he refers to as dialectical *totalization*. A totalization represents a synthetic activity in which individual (physical or mental) aspects of a thing or moments of a process are actively brought together as parts of a whole—a so-called *totality*—thus giving rise to this totality in the first place. Totalization proceeds in a dialectical three-step of *position*, *negation*, and *negation of the negation*, also known as *sublation*. Sartre derives this principle by questioning the process of how human experience and action come to their respective results. These results are totalities comprising different aspects. In the case of experience, it is sensory input, expectations, practical aspects, etc. In the case of action, these aspects are an agent's intentions, bodily requirements or wants, attitudes, etc. Owing to its totalizing nature, action must be understood as situated in socioculturally and materially structured constellations that co-constitute the frame in which this action takes place. These situated actions can be understood as structural moments in the overall processing of human existence and history. Although human beings might thus not be practically free to do as they please, they are nevertheless ontologically free. This freedom cannot be taken from them, as it is the abstract foundation they use to realize themselves by conducting concrete, totalizing actions for themselves as ends in themselves in the first place.

Sartre claims that to understand the full extent of human existence and reality, the larger constellations and historical transformations in which human action and existence are situated must themselves be understood to mirror this totalizing process. Through this understanding, human reality in its entirety becomes intelligible as a dialectical totalization that is fundamentally driven by the ontologically free and goal-directed actions of human beings to satisfy their requirements, wants, and wishes; they do so by concretizing their abstract needs into desires. In the course of *Critique*, Sartre further outlines this understanding.

In this later work, Sartre analyzes societal constellations of human and non-human elements in dialectical interrelation with each other—such as societal classes, revolutionary groups, national economies, or people at a bus stop—and scrutinizes the dynamics of their formation and transformation from what is now known as a *praxeological* perspective. Despite the subtitle of *Critique* (Sartre 1978)—*Theory of Practical Ensembles* (French *Théorie des ensembles pratiques*)—, Sartre does not use the pair of terms *practical ensemble* very often to describe such constellations. He frequently uses pairs of terms such as *social ensemble* or *serial ensemble* (e.g. 55), *human ensemble* (e.g. 65), society as *complex ensemble* (e.g. 121), the world as *ensemble* (e.g. 128), *material ensemble* (e.g. 185), and *technical ensemble* (e.g. 193). He does so depending on the elements and interrelations he intends to foreground. Since this work explores the conditions of possibility for the formation of such constellations, it uses the general term *practical ensemble*. Understanding societal constellations as practical ensembles reveals two facts: first, these constellations are permeated by human actions and, therefore, by needful individuals; second, these constellations consist of at least two elements in practical interrelation to each other. In this regard, any ensemble in the Sartrean sense, whether social, serial, communal, technical, natural and so on, must be understood as a practical ensemble.

This praxeological and dialectical perspective can be applied to the central claim of this current work. Understanding the dialectical interrelation between human existence and practical ensembles reveals both the conditions, possibilities, and constraints of goal-directed human action, and the inner workings, demands, and requirements of the forms of organization in which this action is situated. However, three factors complicate the understanding of Sartre's theories on practical ensembles. The three factors must be discussed in detail.

First, despite the subtitle of *Critique*, Sartre himself does not provide a systematic theory of practical ensembles. The main reason for Sartre's analyses of practical ensembles is to uncover the very conditions of possibility by which a dialectical progression of human history becomes intelligible in the first place. Sartre claims that this basis must be sought in the dialectical processes that pervade human action and experience. Consequently, he is much more concerned with the significance of human action and freedom than he is with the actual composition of practical ensembles. Despite his broad perspective on societal constellations and his nuanced descriptions of formation and transformation processes, individual action represents Sartre's methodological lens and his principal subject of inquiry. For this reason, Sartre's *Critique* can only with reservations be called a social ontology. Rather, it can be more properly understood as a dialectical and praxeological philosophy that examines the conditions of individual human existence in larger constellations by accentuating the social aspects of the practical relations between the elements of these constellations. Thus, the dynamics of social constellations such as social groups, societal classes, institutions, and society as a whole, as well as their role in historical processes, are at the heart of *Critique*.

Second, Sartre's early works have received much more attention than his later philosophy. Discussions on the implications of Sartre's later social thought can be found in Hartmann (1966), Young (1994), Boyle (2005), Rae (2011), and Richter (2011). The role of things in the constitution of social groups has been analyzed by Blättler (2012) and Kleinherenbrink and Gusman (2018). Sartre's general approach in *Critique* is analyzed by Flynn (1997; 2005), and by Simont and Trezise (1985). Approaches toward more specific aspects of Sartre's later philosophy, such as action, value, totalization, and counter-finality, can be found in Catalano (2007), Tomlinson (2014), Turner (2014), and Boria (2015). A broader conception of the practico-inert is provided by K. S. Engels (2018). More general approaches to Sartre's thoughts on technology can be found in Bonnemann (2009) and Weismüller (1999), to name but a few. Cannon (1991; 1992) provides an extensive psychological reading of Sartre's later philosophy. This work draws on Cannon's previous work on Sartre's conception of needs and desires. Ally (2012; 2017) applies Sartre's theses to ecological processes and understandings.

This list of authors is in no way complete; it is merely intended to illustrate the wide variety of topics covered by Sartre and his exegetes. Although some literature deals with various aspects of Sartre's later works, nothing specifically highlights Sartre's theoretical considerations about the fundamental structures of practical ensembles. This may be a result of the inconsistency of his examples. The underlying principles of Sartre's structural considerations about practical constellations are obscured by the social focus and by the general use of the term *ensemble*. The fact that a systematic theory of practical ensembles remains largely unexplored by Sartre and his scholars presents both a major challenge and a great opportunity for the current work.

Third, Sartre's often multilayered philosophical ideas and concepts can be hard to grasp, which complicates an understanding of their interplay within practical ensembles. Practical ensembles must be understood as historically transformational processes, as permeated and fundamentally driven by the free actions of individuals, and as inherently mediated by technology in the form of material objects and structures. Therefore, a full understanding of the inner workings of practical ensembles requires insight into their historical, action-theoretical, and technico-philosophical foundations. These foundations, however, have to be built up first, especially in the case of Sartre's different conceptions of action and his dialectical conception of technology.

Research Approach

This work aims to explore and systematize the theoretical foundations, principles, and dynamics of practical ensembles in Sartre's philosophy, to outline a theoretical framework about them, and to apply that framework for an understanding of societal constellations—in this case, urban mobility—as *needful structures*. To achieve this goal, this work will examine three fundamental aspects of Sartre's philosophy.

First, it is necessary to understand and reconstruct Sartre's general philosophical outlook, as well as the development of his ideas throughout his works. This work advocates for a complementary reading of Sartre's philosophical oeuvre and for the fact that a more complete understanding of his philosophical concepts requires a reconstruction of how certain concepts change and other concepts mutually complement each other. Borrowing Sartre's words, this means that the totality of his philosophy must be understood by reconstructing its totalization. This complementary reading and reconstruction is of central importance. In *Being and Nothingness*, Sartre lays down the existentialist foundations of his philosophy. Here, he introduces his idea of ontological freedom and develops a general conception of human action. Although the early Sartre already uses the concept of *totalization* to refer to the synthetic character of human existence as a unity of being and nothingness, he is much more concerned with the question of why this unity can never become a completed *totality*. In *Critique*, he builds on these thoughts and elevates the concept of *totalization* to the materially dialectical basic principle of human existence, experience, and action. According to Sartre, human existence is a constant mediation of internal and external dialectics. He claims that understanding this constant mediation makes it possible to understand history. History, in this regard, is ultimately understood to progress through material transformations of socioculturally and materially structured constellations that consist of practical relations between humans and non-human elements in a certain environment. It is here one finds Sartre's thoughts on practical ensembles.

However, before addressing Sartre's thoughts on practical ensembles, the second fundamental aspect of his philosophy, namely his view on the structures of human action and existence as a *praxis*-process, must be explored and further developed from an action-theoretical point of view. The reason for this perspective is the importance Sartre gives to human action in general, and to instrumental means in the formation of practical ensembles in particular. Despite the fundamental role of human action throughout Sartre's philosophy, and his general remarks about human action and history, there is no unified action-theoretical conception in his philosophy or in that of his exegetes that provides a structural understanding of action as both a mediation of internal and external dialectics and a goal-directed and totalizing endeavor driven by the dialectic of need and desire. The reason for this conceptual lack may be attributed to the fact that Sartre proposes two seemingly irreconcilable action concepts in his philosophy—the free action as self-projection in *Being and Nothingness* and the materially constrained, historically situated *praxis* in *Critique*. Only an action-theoretical understanding that unifies these action concepts based on the dialectical principle of totalization can provide the foundation for outlining the inner workings and overall structure of practical ensembles. Furthermore, Sartre provides many examples of how instrumental means mediate human actions and how this mediation, in turn, affects the larger structure of societal constellations. Thus, to understand the intricacies of human-technology relations in Sartre's philosophy, this action-theoretical approach is also needed.

Practical ensembles are societal constellations in the constant process of totalization. This process is driven by the structured relations between individual historical agents, other agents, and instrumental means. These agents engage in constellations to satisfy their requirements, wants, and wishes. How agents are motivated to take up goal-directed behavior stems from how these agents totalize themselves and their world through their needful interrelation with their environment and how their abstract needs are concretized as desires. This again returns to the overall form of organization of practical ensembles as needful structures. To develop an understanding of practical ensembles, it is not enough to state that human beings have certain physical or mental necessities and urges, or that they act in specific ways to satisfy them. Rather, the exact role of these needs and desires in the motivational structure of action, as well as the concrete course of these actions, must be demonstrated. Although this exposition eventually has some thematic overlaps with Sartre's broader historical account of action, it approaches the structure of action from a different angle. This does not just render the very course of action intelligible as a mediation of internal and external dialectics; it also lays the foundation for the third fundamental aspect of Sartre's philosophy.

That third fundamental aspect is his dialectical conception of technology. Throughout his works, Sartre concerns himself with the relationship, similarities, and fundamental differences between human beings and things. Here, Sartre has a dialectical understanding of instrumentality: he claims that a thing only becomes an instrumental object in the totalizing relation between agent and end. Furthermore, he says that human existence is technologically mediated. However, this form of mediation only becomes intelligible through an action-theoretical understanding of human existence.

Despite the social emphasis of Sartre's later work, reflections on the relationship between human action and technology, such as tools, machines, and consumer goods, provide the theoretical background for his philosophy. Insofar as material entities are manufactured, they must be considered *practico-inert*. As such, they must be understood as results of former actions. Practico-inert objects have specific material properties by virtue of which these objects not only signify possible options for action but also mediate and manifest human interrelations—and thus mediate and manifest the structure of societal constellations as well. According to Sartre, "these heavy, inert objects lie at the basis of a community whose bonds are, *in part*, bonds of interiority. It is through this interiority that one material element can act on another from a distance [...] social facts are things in so far as *all things* are, directly or indirectly, social facts" (Sartre 1978, 179).[2]

Foregrounding and further developing Sartre's reflections on human-technology relations from a philosophical perspective on technology helps to better capture some of his fundamental insights and to apply them to understanding practical ensembles. This is especially true for the multifarious ways in which human agency and technology interrelate and influence each other in these systems. Rather than accentuating social dynamics and understanding practical ensembles primarily as social ensembles, this work highlights the interrelations of humans and technology in these ensembles and demonstrates that technological artifacts must be given equal significance for the totalizing processing of practical ensembles.

Based on a general notion of these fundamental aspects, one can engage Sartre's understanding of societal constellations as practical ensembles. Such an understanding has deconstructive and reconstructive aspects. First of all, it reveals societal constellations to be in the constant process of totalization based on human actions. Therefore, this understanding allows one either to examine the function

---

2   Sartre comes to this conclusion by accepting both Durkheim's maxim to *treat social facts as things* and Weber's response according to which *social facts are not things*. In recognizing that social relations represent material interactions that are always mediated by matter, either in the form of the human body or material objects, he takes a middle position between Durkheim and Weber. However, a comparative analysis of these views cannot be provided in this work.

of the organizational form of societal constellations and scrutinize the structural elements—i.e. *partial totalities*—, which this organizational form consists of; or to reconstruct the nature of interrelations between these partial totalities as structural moments in the overall totalization. In this regard, a practical ensemble resembles a system (Ropohl 2009, 75). Furthermore, conceiving such constellations as practical ensembles allows one to understand how the partial totalities in these constellations become mutually adapted to the overall form of organization the constellations take over time. According to Sartre, such adaptations take place through material change, technological development, habit formation, and habituation. Eventually, the formation of habits and concomitant attitudes towards actions entails an as-sociation of instrumental means with the continued existence of human beings within these constellations. Therefore, when analyzing them, it is paramount to not lose track of the fundamental significance of human requirements, wants, and wishes, the way abstract needs are concretized into desires, and the way human action is technologically mediated.

Eventually, the general framework of practical ensembles can be applied to societal constellations of human and non-human elements to reveal their struc-tural interrelations. A factory, for instance, when conceived as a practical ensemble, presents itself as a constellation of laborers, directors, machines, and work routines, among other things. The overall function of this constellation is to produce goods. Scrutinizing the partial totalities as structural elements of this overall totalizing process, it becomes obvious that human requirements, wants, and wishes, as well as the dialectic of need and desire, pervade this organizational form. Laborers work for wages to reproduce themselves as laborers. Directors employ laborers for profit when selling goods for a higher price than their production required owing to the surplus value of the laborers' work. These goods themselves are needed or desired by others who are willing to pay for them. Machines and work routines support, manifest, and stabilize these labor processes by material inertia, both in the fea-tures and characteristics of machines and in the habituated and thus incorporated institutional rules and labor processes within the laborer's bodies. In this regard, a practical ensemble resembles a system in which the interaction of subsystems (laborer, director, machine) define the mode of operation of the system (factory) in relation to the system's environment (a societal system in demand for goods).

The fundamental tenet of this research approach is comparable to the one men-tioned by Ally (2017). He writes that the task of his book *Ecology and Existence*—a fu-sion of Sartrean thought and ecology—is not so much to think *about* Sartre but "*to think with and beyond him,* and even to stretch and bend his thought here and there, without breaking it" (5, emphasis in original). The same also applies to this work, insofar as it advocates for a novel reading of Sartre as a praxeologist, an action the-orist, a philosopher of technology, and a quasi-system theorist.

Motivation and Research Context

The personal motivation for this work is a long-standing interest in the conditions of human existence, the bonds and boundaries of human freedom, the potential for self-realization, and the possibilities and constraints of a technologically mediated life. Against this motivational background, it stands the question why Sartre's thoughts still have relevance for the contemporary challenges of the human condition. Current global, social, and technological developments—global warming, increasing social conflicts and disparities, and the rise of digital technologies and AI—make it necessary to take a particular look at the mechanisms by which the social systems in which one is situated come into being, the role that technology plays in them, and whether the ways in which these systems are organized actually meet one's underlying needs. Sartre's decidedly existentialist perspective on technology, society, and history allows one to understand and reassess one's position and role within social dynamics and systems and to reorient how one may engage with the world to make a change.

Academically, the work itself is situated within the research training group KRITIS at TU Darmstadt and represents an extended version of the author's PhD thesis that was titled *Needful Structures: The Dialectics of Practical Ensembles and their Significance for Understanding Urban Mobility*. KRITIS is concerned with a general understanding of networked urban infrastructures, the critical significance of these structures for modern societies, and the potential challenges and risks resulting from their composition. Concerning the research program of KRITIS, this work emphasizes the *construction* and *transformation* of the conditions of possibility for critical infrastructures. However, this must not be understood in a purely technical way. Within the research program of KRITIS, urban infrastructures are considered sociotechnical systems, or *systems of systems*, that comprise a functional interplay of people, things, large built structures, rules, regulations, and so on (Engels et al. 2021).

Sartre's approach lends itself to such an understanding. It too conceives of societal constellations as structured interrelations between partial totalities, which can again be scrutinized for their composition. Furthermore, it emphasizes the fundamental role of material and immaterial requirements, wants, and wishes in the dialectic of need and desire for understanding the inner workings of these constellations. Lastly, Sartre's conception of the practico-inert allows one to conceive of urban infrastructures as materially inert residuals of former actions, which manifest certain strategies of tackling supraindividual needfulness by concretizing abstract needs into desires.

This work intends to make a theoretical contribution to the study of Sartre's philosophy by providing new perspectives on various aspects of Sartre's works and promoting interest in Sartre's historical and theoretical ideas on action, his philosophical thoughts on technology, and his understanding of societal constellations.

Beyond that, this work is also located in the larger field of approaches toward the study of science, technology, and society (STS). It is especially applicable to approaches that assume a dependence between practice and materiality (Schatzki 2010) or a sociomaterial interweaving of practice, materiality, and forms of organization (Pickering 1995; Orlikowski & Scott 2008), or that deal with the research of infrastructures (Shove 2016; Shove & Trentmann 2019). In terms of the philosophy of technology, the work is situated in debates about a dialectical philosophy of technology (Hubig 2006) and the supposed power of and through technology (Hubig 2015), as well as postphenomenological approaches toward technological mediation (Ihde 1990; Rosenberger & Verbeek 2015). In addition, problems of habit formation are taken up as well (Sparrow & Hutchinson 2013). This work intends to make a practical contribution to infrastructure research, as it seeks to develop a sociomaterial understanding of larger forms of societal constellation from a philosophical and anthropological perspective. It is also meant to sharpen views on usually obscured modes of structuring that affect human existence and action.

How Sartre conceives of structured compositions of human and non-human elements, which practically interrelate to perform actions, has thematic overlaps with other approaches, such as Foucault's analyses of *dispositifs* and Latour's conception of hybrid action in actor-network constellations (Richter 2011; Hubig 2015) and other approaches that investigate the relation between *agents*, *action*, and *structure* (Giddens 1986). However, this work does not engage in comparative discussions about these approaches. Another related line of research that will not be examined here is assemblage theory (Deleuze & Guattari 2005; DeLanda 2006). However, the current work aims to be a foundation for future research in this regard.

Structure of this Work

This work is divided into two parts. Part I, containing the first three chapters, deals with the dialectical foundations of practical ensembles. Part II, in Chapters 4 and 5, then deals with the theory and *praxis* of practical ensembles.

Chapter 1 approaches the first fundamental aspect of Sartre's philosophy. It explores the core themes of Sartre's works *Being and Nothingness*, *Search for a Method*, and *Critique of Dialectical Reason* to reconstruct Sartre's philosophical development. The chapter leads chronologically through Sartre's works and demonstrates that Sartre consistently concerned himself with the dialectic of human existence. Whereas Sartre's early works lean more toward internal dialectics (section 1.2), his later works represent approaches to examine (section 1.3) and even unify the internal and external dialectics of human existence (section 1.4). The last section of the chapter examines some of Sartre's thoughts on the dialectical progression of history to illustrate the fundamental significance of human action in that process. The first chapter as a whole, therefore, aims to clarify the fundamental role of human action in Sartre's philosophy by reconstructing the complementary nature of his works. However, merely a historical account of the significance of action is provided at this point. This account lays the foundation for Chapter 2.

Chapter 2 turns the focus from the significance of human action for the progression and intelligibility of history to the structural characteristics of the action itself. The different foci of Sartre's works mean that a unified conception of action can hardly be identified on the surface of his philosophy. In *Being and Nothingness*, Sartre provides a relatively technical definition of action as the realization of ends through the employment of means, both in the form of the body and in the form of instruments. In his early work, individual action represents the situated realization of individual existence. In *Critique*, the *praxis* of historical human beings is emphasized as a socioculturally situated activity that takes place within a mediating material milieu. However, in *Critique*, Sartre also points toward totalization as the underlying principle of action. Therefore, the chapter is preceded by a technical reconstruction of Sartre's concept of *totalization* as the basic principle of human-world interrelation, and *totality* as the (temporal) outcome of totalization (section 2.2). The remainder of the chapter brings together action-theoretical thoughts from *Being and Nothingness* and *Critique* to develop a conception of situated action based on the dialectic of need and desire. The analysis begins with a closer look at the existentialist roots of Sartre's action-theoretical thoughts. Here, human existence becomes comprehensible as an existential lack that seeks completion. Based on this existential foundation, a Sartrean conception of situated action is developed. According to this conception, human action is an ontologically free, intentional, yet inherently need- and desire-oriented endeavor (section 2.3). This conception will be further developed and integrated into Sartre's understanding of human existence as an ongoing, autopoietic, and totalizing *praxis*-process (section 2.4).

Chapter 3 explores Sartre's philosophical thoughts on technology. The chapter proceeds less chronologically than it does thematically. From the dialectical character of action in Sartre, it follows that the use of instrumental means must be understood as a dialectical totalization as well. In this context, Sartre's understanding of the body as the center of an individual field of possibilities and how he links his thoughts to Heidegger's concept of *equipmentality* are introduced and scrutinized (section 3.2). According to Sartre, manufactured objects and body techniques not only serve as instruments but also signify certain forms of conduct by virtue of their materiality. They also refer to larger supraindividual forms of organization and history (section 3.3). The chapter concludes with a technology-focused exploration of Sartre's understanding of the practico-inert (section 3.4). The *practico-inert* is a fundamental concept in Sartre's later philosophy. It is significant for the formation of practical ensembles. It describes the fact that certain forms of conduct become materially inert in instrumental means.

Chapter 4 forms the thematic focus of this current work. Here, the theoretical framework of practical ensembles is developed based on the previous findings. The chapter begins with an examination of Sartre's conception of humanity's struggle against *scarcity*. This concept is rather important in Sartre's later work, as it represents the fundamental condition for humanity's needful relationship with its surroundings. According to Sartre, all forms of societal organization arise in a scarce material milieu. This means that societies emerge in an attempt to deal with the fact that there are not enough resources for everyone's survival at a given time. Therefore, resources must be gathered, rationed, and distributed in a certain socially organized way. Furthermore, access to certain resources must be secured (section 4.2). The analysis of this conception is followed by more focused analyses of processes according to which practical ensembles coalesce through serial modes of structuring (section 4.3), and of how these serial modes transform into communal modes of structuring (section 4.4) based on how individuals can satisfy their requirements, wants, and wishes. Following this, the persistence of practical ensembles is examined through Sartre's conception of *hexis*. This concept is neither well developed by Sartre himself, nor is it well researched in Sartre studies. Its significance is shown, however, for understanding how societal constellations stabilize and persist over time (section 4.5). This is followed by a more thorough examination of how the workings of practical ensembles generate external effects that act back on them in the form of *counter-finalities* (section 4.6). The chapter concludes with a discussion about the general understanding of the practical ensemble framework (section 4.7).

Chapter 5 applies Sartre's theories to urban mobility systems. It explores how urban mobility systems can be understood as practical ensembles, how the flow of urban mobility results from the structured interrelations between different users of urban infrastructure systems, how their interrelations are mediated by each other, and how urban dwellers escape the serial structuring of their practical ensembles through desire paths (section 5.2). In light of this, anthropogenic climate change is re-read as a Sartrean counter-finality (section 5.3). After this, infrastructures are scrutinized regarding their critical function for society among others (section 5.4). The chapter concludes with a more focused analysis of urban infrastructures as needful structures with the help of three key concepts in infrastructure research: resilience, criticality, and vulnerability.

I Dialectical Foundations

1. From Individual Project to Historical Praxis

1.1 Introduction

In this chapter, fundamental lines of thought from Sartre's early and later philosophy are introduced as foundational for his theoretical conception of practical ensembles. This is done to generate a general understanding of Sartre's philosophy and to introduce some of the considerations to be further developed in this work. The reason for the broader scale of this analysis lies in the fact that this work considers Sartre's early and later works to be complementary. To understand his later concepts, some earlier ones must be clarified first. In this way, conceptual transitions between Sartre's works can be reconstructed. Moreover, Sartre gives the theoretical basis for some of his earlier concepts in his later works, while changing his general perspective toward the social, cultural, and, most importantly, material conditions in which human beings find themselves.

Considering the specific focus of his philosophical writings, Sartre's philosophy can be divided roughly into his early, more existentialist works, which are more focused on human existence as an individual and free project, and his later, more Marxist works, which are more focused on the interplay between individual *praxis* and dialectical history. Throughout them all, Sartre takes an anthropocentric and deeply humanist view. His principal interest lies in the scope of human reality, freedom, and action. In an interview with *New Left Review* in 1969, Sartre stated that the quintessential problem at the heart of his philosophy is "how to give man both his autonomy and his reality among real objects, avoiding idealism without lapsing into a mechanistic materialism" (Sartre 1969, 46). Although Sartre approaches different aspects of this problem throughout his work, his principal methodology consists in analyzing the nature of human-world relations while taking ontological, phenomenological, dialectical, and praxeological considerations into account.

His two major works, *Being and Nothingness* and *Critique of Dialectical Reason* (in connection with *Search for a Method*), represent attempts to depict two apparently mutually exclusive aspects of human life—the internal perspective *of* an ontologically free agent and the external perspective *on* this agent as a needful material being in interrelation with sociocultural and material factors. These aspects, however, represent two interconnected planes of the existential reality of human beings. Human existence unites the lived experience of oneself as a free agent and of oneself as a socially dependent, material being. By reconstructing the changing foci of Sartre's philosophy and how he develops his philosophical concepts, this work intends to demonstrate how Sartre mediates between these two aspects.

1.2 Being and Nothingness

This section deals with the philosophical outlook of Sartre's first major work, *Being and Nothingness*. The main focus of this work lies in what can be called the internal dialectic of human existence, namely the fact that human existence is a dialectically synthetic relationship between being and consciousness. His later works are more focused on the external dialectic of human existence, or, rather, on the fact that human existence itself represents a mediation of the internal and external dialectic—a constant and mutually affecting interplay of these dialectical processes.

To understand the dialectically synthetic relationship of being and consciousness, "the *moments* of this synthesis" (Sartre 2021, 34, emphasis in original)—namely being and consciousness—have to be examined in the various ways they interrelate. Concerning being, Sartre explicitly differentiates between humans as exceptional beings that constantly relate to themselves and their surroundings and non-human entities. Ontologically, both humans and non-human entities *are* in the sense that both are *existent* by virtue of their ontological foundation in the materiality of being (Sartre 2021, 24). This being, Sartre claims, must be understood as follows: "Being is. Being is in itself. Being is what it is" (Sartre 2021, 29). However, Sartre identifies a difference in how humans and things relate to being. This is a differentiation of their respective *modes of being*.

Sartre refers to the human mode of being as being-for-itself, or just for-itself (French *pour-soi*). He refers to the mode of being of those non-human entities that comprise the physicochemical world as being-in-itself, or in-itself (French *en-soi*). Although his philosophical thinking is deeply influenced by Hegel, Sartre deviates from Hegel's concept of *ideality* in this regard (Bernstein 1980, 130).[1] Sartre justifies his distinction between modes of being with the claim that there is "an ontological chasm that cannot be mediated" (Bernstein 1980, 131) between being and human consciousness. Phenomenologically, according to Sartre, the consciousness of being can never be identical with being, because consciousness is characterized by relationality. He claims that the being of consciousness is to exist "*at a distance from itself*" (Sartre 2021, 128, emphasis in original).

---

1   A more thorough examination of Sartre's modes of being follows in section 2.2.

As a consequence, Sartre agrees with Heidegger on the fact that human existence is *being-in-the-world* (German *In-der-Welt-sein*). In Sartre's case, being-in-the-world must be understood as an ongoing, dialectical synthesis of being and consciousness. To exhaustively represent the nature of human existence, the fundamentally dialectical relation between humans and being must be the basis for all analyses. From this fundamental relationship, Sartre examines various aspects of human existence, such as *bad faith*, the conditions of the possibility of intersubjectivity, the situation of the individual, and the effects of the *look* or *gaze* of others. He does so by focusing on the internal perspective of a situated human existent. Such a perspective accounts for what it means to act in, experience, and engage the world based on a synthetic relationship of being and consciousness. Out of all the themes analyzed in *Being and Nothingness*, the most important ones for this work can be found in Sartre's conception of the nature of human agency, and his considerations about the quality of human freedom.

Action and Existence

Human action plays a central role in Sartre's philosophy. Sartre states that "being, in its case, is acting, and to cease to act is to cease to be" (Sartre 2021, 623). Action is decisive for being and not-being; it is an activity in which humans realize the possibilities that arise from their existential situation. Any human possibility not realized through action simply does not exist. Sartre gives three express conditions of action, namely *freedom of the acting being*, the *intention to act*, and the *discovery of the world as a lacking state of things* (Sartre 2021, 569–573). The *freedom of the acting being* represents the fundamental condition for action from which the other two conditions are derived.

Sartre locates the freedom of the *acting being*, i.e. the human agent, in the aforementioned fact that human beings exist in relation to being, or, more precisely, exist as a dialectical relating of being which is just given, or posited, as it is on one side and negating consciousness on the other. This dialectical relating must be understood in a rather practical way. Qua being, humans are material, organic, and necessarily social. They have basic and more complex needs and requirements that derive from physicochemical and psychological processes within themselves and their mediating milieu, i.e. their material surroundings, as well as from how these surroundings are socioculturally structured within forms of societal constellation.[2] Section

---

2   In *Being and Nothingness*, Sartre uses terms like *entours* (e.g. Sartre 1943, 549) and *milieu* (e.g. Sartre 1943, 618) to refer to a person's surroundings, whereas the terms *environnement* (e.g. Sartre 1960, 167) and *milieu* (e.g. Sartre 1960, 196–199) are more prominently used throughout *Critique*. According to Petit and Guillaume (2018), there is a somewhat clear distinction between the terms *milieu* and *environnement* in French intellectual discourse: "The French term 'milieu' designates (i) the middle or center and its surroundings; (ii) the 'in-between two

4.2 discusses what it means for the materiality that surrounds human beings to be *socioculturally structured*. Sartre's understanding of the *structure* of forms of organization between human beings and non-human things refers to the set of rules, regulations, and expectations that mediates and thus shapes how a person's possible options for action are enabled.

All these factors—physicochemical, psychological, sociocultural—which culminate in a human's corporeality and lived experience, belong to what Sartre refers to as *facticity* (Sartre 2021, 133). Qua consciousness, however, human existence does not coincide with its facticity, but, rather, relates to it (Sartre 2021, 622–628). Although this relational gap between being and consciousness is practically nil, Sartre claims it to be the decisive factor for the fundamental freedom of human existence (Sartre 2021, 128). Sartre refers to this fundamental freedom as *ontological freedom*. It describes the fact that human existence represents the dialectical mediation of being and consciousness. Human existence is a relation to and not an identity with being. This fundamental relationality of being and consciousness is the condition of possibility for recognizing that all forms of human conduct are, at their core, intentional and goal-directed actions. These actions are based on the inherent needfulness of human existence, i.e. the fact that human existence always strives for something

---

places' (mi-lieu); (iii) the ambient atmosphere; and (iv) the medium (middle-term, intermediate or mediator) [...] The term 'milieu' says both more and less than the term 'environment.' It says more, because it is not on the outside, but between the inside and the outside. It says less, because it refers to the unique experience of a living organism in a place, whereas the 'environment' is identical for all beings which find themselves in a place, and it stays outside the living beings. While the environment is objective, the milieu is 'trajective.'" (88). Petit's and Guillaume's first and second glosses for the term *milieu* can be found in the French phrase *au milieu du monde*, which Sartre often uses. This phrase does not at all refer to a supposed milieu of the world. It simply means *within, in the midst of*, or *in the middle of* the world. Their fourth understanding of *milieu* can be found in Sartre's conceptualization of totalization as a synthetic activity through which humans and what surrounds them become what they are in their interrelation in the first place. Agents interiorize the things, structural features, and people that surround them and totalize them as their world. However, this totalization is again shaped by the way the material surrounding is socioculturally structured, which again mediates and thus shapes an agent's actions. In *Being and Nothingness*, Sartre explicitly states: "My 'surroundings' [French *mes entours*] should not be confused with the place I occupy [...] My surroundings are the implement-things that surround me, with their coefficient of adversity and their equipmentality. Of course, by occupying my place I am founding my discovery of my surroundings [...] Thus I am thrown, from the moment I exist, in the midst of existences that differ from me, and whose potentialities are unfolding, for and against me" (Sartre 2021, 657; Sartre 1943, 549). In this regard, in Sartre's philosophy there is a conceptual equivalence between *surroundings* as the whole of people, things, structures, and systems, and *milieu*, in the sense of a mediating milieu that predisposes the conditions of possibility for action in the first place.

it requires, wants, or wishes (section 2.3). Dialectically speaking, material requirements or mental wants and wishes represent positings that are negated through an
active engagement between agents and themselves, or between agents and their milieu. Under the *freedom of the acting being*, i.e. ontological freedom, human beings can
be understood as agents. In Sartre's understanding, the *freedom of the acting being* thus
represents the necessary condition of possibility for human agency.

At this stage, the two other express conditions for action, namely the *intention to
act* and the *discovery of the world as a lacking state of things*, come into play. For Sartre,
human action must be conceived as an intentional and ontologically free undertaking that modifies the "way the world is *figured*" (Sartre 2021, 569, emphasis in original) according to certain ends arising within concrete situations. The condition of
intention to act refers to the motivational and directional aspect of human action,
namely the fact that human beings have certain ends that they intend to attain. The
condition *discovery of the world as a lacking state of things* refers both to the ontological
and to the epistemological aspect of human action, namely the fact that the concrete
outline of those ends is relative both to how agents apprehend their action situation
based on what their surroundings provide them, and to how this provision is assessed regarding an agent's requirements, wants, and wishes at the onset of action.
Both conditions, however, dialectically interrelate. The ends that agents intend to attain through their actions are relative to the attainability of these ends as provided
by the agents' capabilities on the one hand, and environmental factors such as the
right means and other action conditions on the other.

The early Sartre explains the dialectical nature of action most evidently through
the concept of *désirs* (Sartre 1943, 123), which can be translated simply as *desires*. In
Sartre's dialectical understanding, a desire in the form of thirst, for instance, initially makes itself known as a complex of physical symptoms like a dry mouth or a
slight headache (Sartre 2021, 139). As mentioned above, in Sartre's dialectical understanding, these physical symptoms represent positings of human being that express
themselves through the body. However, owing to the fact of ontological freedom, human beings do not coincide with their being. They relate to their being. This means
that they, for instance, examine what they feel and how they feel it. They try to explain
why they feel the way they do or how to rid themselves of certain feelings. In this
way, they relate to their physical symptoms rather than purely *being their symptoms*.
By questioning and challenging these symptoms, by attempting to understand and
even change them, these human beings engage with their facticity and temporality.
They refer back to their existence, their experiences, and past actions in similar situations and discover their symptoms as uncomfortable in relation to a possible but
as yet unrealized future self that is relieved of these symptoms. These human beings
thus discover themselves to be in a *lacking state of things* that simultaneously outlines,
anticipates, and projects toward a potentially satisfied future state of things (Sartre
2021, 511). Furthermore, these human beings recognize themselves as the very ones

who intend to transform their uncomfortable symptoms through action. They thus have the *intention to act* for themselves as ends in themselves. They are *autotelic*, in that they always, in some form or another, represent the end of their actions; their self (Greek *autos*) is their end (Greek *telos*).

Within this process of projecting toward a future state of things, together with the intention to act and the discovery of lacking something for themselves, the uncomfortable physical symptoms are disclosed to them as the desire of thirst. Sartre states that "[d]esire is a *lack of being*, and is haunted in its innermost being by the being that it desires. In this way, desire testifies to the existence of a lack in human-reality's being" (Sartre 2021, 140, emphasis added).

Desires bestow a fundamental directedness upon human existence because they project toward something that a human being lacks. For Sartre, desire is somewhat *attached* to an object of desire (Sartre 2021, 508–509). However, Sartre states that it would be "quite wrong to say that what is desired, in desiring, is our 'physical possession' of the desired object" (Sartre 2021, 508). Rather, a desire has a concrete direction toward an already familiar thing or toward a process in the world that represents the general context of its satisfaction. Thirst, as a desire for a glass of water or a cup of tea, for instance, represents a particular mode in which a specific, sociocultur-ally situated, human subjectivity transcends toward and engages with the world for themselves in very specific ways (Sartre 2021, 510). In desiring, human beings not only simultaneously exist as what is lacking and as what is lacked; they also project toward themselves as a potential future self that is the end of their actions (Sartre 2021, 146–149).

Sartre's thoughts on desires render more clearly his conception of what it means to act. Acting, according to the early Sartre, "is to modify the way the world is *figured* [French *la figure du monde*], to arrange the means in view of an end" (Sartre 2021, 569, emphasis in original; Sartre 1943, 477). The term *figure* here refers beyond the material shape of the world and the things it comprises to the way these things are phenomenally given based on their being. To act based on the ends projected toward by an agent's desires thus means to modify the materiality of the world in such a way that the *lacking state of things* may become a *satisfied state of things* for these agents. In this way, acting does not merely mean acting based on one's desires. Rather, acting means to realize a subject-dependent, potential future state of the world in which one is involved for oneself. This realized state can be satisfying, but it does not have to. What is important is that such a state has been realized through action. By inte-riorizing said state of the world, agents may assess whether they realized their in-tended ends or not. An action, in this regard, is more than a goal-directed activity. It is also the realization of individual existence, understood as a free self-projection toward the future, which is directed through desires. Although Sartre emphasizes ontological freedom as a basis for human existence, he is not ignorant of the var-ious interferences between an individual's action and their surrounding sociality, culture, and materiality. Sartre mentions the role of other people, for instance, the abstract sociocultural structures of the societal constellations in which individuals are situated, and the *utility and adversity coefficients* of the things that may be used as means to an individual's ends. All of these factors potentially shape an individual's course of action. Nevertheless, although the facticity and the situation-dependent outline of desires mean that human beings are not the originators of their existence, they are the authors since they decide how they realize themselves through their actions.[3]

1.3   Search for a Method

This section deals with topics from *Search for a Method*, a work that marks the transition between Sartre's early, more existentialist works and his later, more Marxist ones. Sartre's *Questions de méthode*, translated as *Search for a Method* in English and *Fragen der Methode* in German, was released as a standalone work in 1957, three years before *Critique de la raison dialectique*. Although it was reprinted as the introductory essay to *Critique de la raison dialectique* in 1960, Sartre himself mentions a thematic shift of perspective between this essay and the main text of *Critique* (Sartre 1978, 15).

In *Search for a Method*, and even more so in *Critique of Dialectical Reason I and II*, Sartre not only shifts the tone but also the general focus of his philosophy. He begins to concern himself mostly with what can be called the external dialectic of human existence, namely the fact that human existence is a dialectically synthetic relationship between individuals and history. History, in this regard, is understood as the common actions of other individuals, groups, and collectives in relation to sociocultural and material factors. In the interview with *New Left Review*, Sartre states that the reason for the fundamental change in his philosophical outlook lies in the fact that life has taught him *la force des choses*, which can be translated as *force/strength/might/potency of things*. In this interview, Sartre also refers to *la force des choses* as the "power of circumstances" (Sartre 1969, 44).[4]

Compared with his earlier philosophy, the later Sartre is much more aware of the practical necessity of materiality and the individual's place in societal constellations that constrain and enable individual action. This is mostly a result of ongoing debates between Sartre and other French intellectuals on the role of Marxism in philos-

---

3   Section 2.4 expands this earlier conception of action in Sartre's philosophy by incorporating the dialectical principle of totalization, the relationship of forms of need and desire, and the instrumentalization of means to ends.

4   This term already implies that in Sartre's understanding, things develop a certain force or power under specific conditions and circumstances; the alternative would be primarily conceiving of things as having or exerting this power on their own. This idea is further developed in section 4.3.

ophy and society, the principal relationship between Western Marxism, Stalinism, and the Soviet Union, and basic questions surrounding the significance of the individual in historical processes (Jay 1984, 347–350). Jay also reconstructs the impact of Heidegger's *Brief über den 'Humanismus'* from 1947 on Sartre's philosophy. In this text, Heidegger principally critiqued French philosophers, especially Sartre, for misunderstanding and misrepresenting his existential philosophy. According to Jay, the fact that Heidegger pointed toward Marx's understanding of history as one way of recognizing the historical in being led to Sartre's engagement with Marxist thinking, which again paved the way for incorporating materiality and history into his philosophy (Jay 1984, 346–347). Whereas Sartre's early philosophy is an expression of his experience of heroic individuality in Nazi-occupied France, his later works express his confrontation with societal collectivity and the processes of upheaval, revolution, and transformation that took place in the aftermath of World War II. Sartre claims that his earlier focus on individual freedom, paired with his negligence regarding *la force des choses*, is rooted in his emphasis on an "interior experience, without any coordination with the exterior experience of a petty-bourgeois intellectual" (Sartre 1969, 45).

To account for the fact that things and circumstances can develop a certain *force*, in his later works Sartre seeks a deeper understanding of the historical situation of individuals and the inner logic of historical processes. He does so by examining the various ways in which individuals, through their actions, practically (re-)produce the very historical situation that produced those individuals in the first place (Richter 2011, 198). The main point of Sartre's later works is that human existence is an expression of society and that history is a constant circle of liberation and necessitation, propelled by the actions of individuals within larger groupings. Nevertheless—and despite the implications of his later philosophical outlook—Sartre still defends his conception of human freedom. He claims that everyone "in a period of exploitation is *at once both* the product of his own product and a historical agent who can under no circumstances be taken as a product" (Sartre 1963, 87, emphasis in original). In this regard, Sartre's early and later works are complementary. The externalities of human existence become comprehensible based on the internalities of human existence, whereas the functional principles of the internalities become clearer based on the general dialectical conditions of historical human existence. Similar to his approach in *Being and Nothingness*, to understand the externalities of human existence, the later Sartre focuses on the moments of a dialectical synthesis: individual and history, as well as the nature of their interrelation. Sartre believes this examination to be possible by fusing his existentialist philosophy with Marxist thought.[5]

---

5   For discussions about whether Sartre can be called an existential Marxist, see Betschart (2019) and Aronson (2019).

Regressive-Progressive Method

Search for a Method marks this transition between early and later Sartre. In this work, Sartre fully agrees with Marx's materialism, according to which "[t]he mode of production of material life generally dominates the development of social, political, and intellectual life" (Sartre 1963, 33–34). However, according to Sartre, Marxist theory in his time had become dogmatic. Rather than attempting to represent the reality of human life as a materially dialectical struggle driven by individuals, Sartre laments that Marxist philosophers conceive human life to be subject to supposed dialectical laws of nature and history. Sartre claims that Marxism itself had become a tool of oppression, especially in the U.S.S.R., rather than a tool of liberation (Sartre 1963, 21–22). He complains that the dogmatic reduction of human life to a mere expression of historical totalities undermines the significance of individual action and existence. As an existentialist philosopher, Sartre affirms:

> the specificity of the human act, which cuts across the social milieu while still holding on to its determinations, and which transforms the world on the basis of given conditions. For us man is characterized above all by his going beyond a situation, and by what he succeeds in making of what he has been made—even if he never recognizes himself in his objectification. (Sartre 1963, 91)

With his strong emphasis on individual action, Sartre reinterprets Marxist materialism. Using his later works, it could be said that for Sartre, materially conditioned action is the primary *mode of production* of human reality and history. Sartre claims that human existence can only be understood as an expression of history when history itself becomes understandable as an expression of human existence (Sartre 1963, 57). To account for his claim, Sartre borrows Lefebvre's methodology and further develops it into what he calls the *regressive-progressive method* (Sartre 1963, 51–52). He employs it to dialectically de- and reconstruct all relevant factors constituting the progression of history based on individual action (Simont & Trezise 1985, 109).

Rather than conforming to dogmatic Marxism, and anchoring human beings within dialectical laws of nature, *Search for a Method* stays in line with his early works and emphasizes the significance of individual action as self-projection and self-realization. However, because this self-projection is situated in sociocultural and material conditions, the *historical situation* of the individual(s) in question must be analyzed as well. This means that "[f]or any *given period*, we shall attempt to determine the field of possibles, the field of instruments, etc. [...] we shall determine (among other things) the area of intellectual instruments" (Sartre 1963, 135, emphasis in original). All these factors structure the historical situation according to which the actions of individuals and their role in the progression of history can be understood in their entirety. The regressive-progressive method is thus "at the same time an enriching cross-reference between the object [...] and the period" (Sartre 1963, 148).

Sartre's method can be understood as a back-and-forth between historical and existentialist analyses that inform each other.

The regressive, analytical moment of this method is the analysis of certain historical, i.e. temporal, sociocultural, and material conditions. According to Sartre, these historical conditions scaffold the actions of individuals in meaningful ways (Hubig 1978, 127). In this regard, however, Sartre is careful not to postulate an insurmountable past and does not wish to make human beings a mere expression of their class (Dahlmann 2013, 139). Rather, he illustrates the fact that sociocultural and material factors are constitutive elements of human existence understood as a dialectical synthesis in progress.

The analysis of this progression is the subject of the progressive, synthetic moment of Sartre's theory. Here, Sartre intends to examine the interplay of constraints and possibilities, along with their significance for how individuals realize themselves as practical and sense-making beings. In this way, he claims himself able to depict the reality of an individual human not as stable, but as "a perpetual disequilibrium, a wrenching away from itself with all its body" (Sartre 1963, 151). Human existence is a free but historically situated, dialectical progression. From each individual's confrontation, overcoming, and reconciliation, in one way or another, with seemingly overpowering and all-encompassing processes and structures, these processes and structures not only derive their power and significance but are also instantiated as such in the first place. Unsurprisingly, a complete analysis depicting the entirety of an individual's existence would be extensive. Sartre's studies on Gustave Flaubert are a testimony to this extensiveness. In *Family Idiot*, Sartre meticulously studies the life of Flaubert, as well as his family and class relations. Sartre then tries to explain how Flaubert's literary oeuvre came about, which as Flaubert's life's work throws light on Flaubert's existence. With four books and over 2500 pages, Sartre's Flaubert studies remain unfinished.[6]

1.4 Critique of Dialectical Reason

This section aims to introduce the essentials of Sartre's *Critique of Dialectical Reason*. The methodology Sartre lays down in *Search for a Method* serves as the theoretical point of departure for *Critique of Dialectical Reason*. In the latter work, Sartre's thoughts on the scope of human freedom, the significance of individual action and experience, and his claims about historical situatedness culminate. His theoretical considerations about practical ensembles can be found here as well.

---

6   A more theoretical and phenomenologically grounded analysis of Sartre's regressive-progressive method can be found in Smith (1979).

Whereas the internal dialectic of human existence was at the heart of Sartre's early works, especially regarding change and development in the course of practical self-projection and self-realization, in *Search for a Method* his main concern is to emphasize the necessity and possibility of addressing the external dialectic of human existence. Although *Critique* thus represents a logical development of those earlier works, it is not the case that Sartre merely adds to or further develops his earlier philosophy. With *Critique*, Sartre fundamentally shifts his philosophical perspective, going from ontological and phenomenological questions surrounding being, freedom, action, and existence to the conditions of the possibility for understanding what it means to be a material human organism both among other such organisms and in engagement with spatiotemporally structured materiality.

The Foundations of Dialectical Reason

To engage with these conditions of possibility, Sartre stresses the tension between human existence and history. This history, according to him, becomes comprehensible only through a dialectical mediation of the internal and external dialectic; or, more concretely, through the dialectical and mutually affecting interplay between interiority and exteriority. Sartre not only adds a material, social, and historical component to his research but also underpins his earlier thoughts with a theoretical analysis of the conditions of possibility for dialectical science and experience in general. At its core, *Critique* represents Sartre's attempt to provide a critical theory of society in the form of a social ontology that takes a dialectical conception of human existence, action, and experience as its theoretical point of departure. Consequently, the human perspective remains front and center in Sartre's philosophical thought. What changes, however, is Sartre's focus on the internal perspective of a situated human existent.

The later Sartre is less interested in what it means to act, experience, and engage the world based on a synthetic relationship of being and consciousness, and more interested in how individual action, experience, and world engagement, based on a synthetic relationship between individual and history, are both constituted by and constitutive of their social, cultural, political, and, most importantly, material conditions. Consequently, Sartre alters slightly his analytical perspective. In *Critique*, he focuses on human existence as a mediation of internal and external dialectics. For Sartre's philosophical endeavor, this change of perspective means that the internal dialectic of human existence that renders human beings ontologically free and goal-directed must be reconciled with the external dialectic of human existence through which human beings are both producers and products of their historical situation. Sartre's golden path toward this reconciliation is to advocate for a dialectical reason that allows him to incorporate the individual within the dialectical consummation of history, and vice versa, based on the historical *praxis* of individuals.

To understand Sartre's approach, it is necessary to be familiar with some of the assumptions he develops in this introductory discussion to *Critique*. However, the broad scope of his argument means that only a few central thoughts can be briefly addressed here.[7]

Sartre's discussion in *Critique*'s introductory chapter revolves around the status, significance, and validity of Marxist dialectic as a scientific method for analyzing natural and historical processes. The discussion begins with general assumptions about the nature of the scientific method. About analytical science and the induction of scientific laws, Sartre claims that "[w]hatever the object of his research, whatever its orientation, the scientist, in his activity, assumes that reality will always manifest itself in such a way that a provisional and fluid rationality can be constituted in and through it" (Sartre 1978, 19). Sartre claims that scientific laws are not facts; they remain external to their research object and represent general assumptions that must be falsifiable. Sartre argues that the dialectic, on the contrary, is "both a method *and* a movement in the object. For the dialectician, it is grounded on a fundamental claim both about the structure of the real and about that of our *praxis*" (Sartre 1978, 20, emphasis in original).

According to Sartre, applying dialectical thinking to a research object allows one to demonstrate whether the object in question is dialectical or not by experiencing dialectical principles to be at work in the object. Therefore, the dialectic also represents the principle of its own intelligibility. Thus, for dialectical science to be valid, it must verify whether the *movement*, i.e. the behavior and internal processing, of its research object, is dialectical, and it must also substantiate its own methodological validity regarding the object in question. Based on these assumptions, Sartre discusses some Marxist paradigms of his time. He criticizes Engels' *Dialektik der Natur* in particular and accuses Engels' philosophical outlook on the dialectics of nature of ultimately failing in accounting for the research object in question. Engels intends to provide the most elementary dialectical laws of nature that govern not only natural but also historical and mental processes. He does so to ground dialectical materialism, i.e. a dialectic of matter, and to ultimately verify it as fundamental science (Engels 1975, 348–349; Remley 2012, 23–25). According to the conception of dialectical materialism, history, and human thought represent outcomes of nature, which is itself understood as the constant dialectical interpenetration of physicochemical processes and substances.

Sartre does not deny that natural processes can be conceived as dialectical. On the contrary, he agrees that given technological progress and the refinement of scientific methods and technologies, nature might indeed be proven dialectical (Sartre 1978, 33). Nevertheless, he insists that dialectical conceptions of nature do not necessarily confirm whether natural processes are in fact dialectical. Sartre claims that

---

7   For a nuanced analysis of the discussion and its historical background, see Remley (2012).

the experience of dialectical lawfulness in nature represents a specific point of view on nature. Such a dialectical experiencing is possible only because human reason itself conforms to dialectical principles. Sartre states that a dialectical notion of nature is itself a dialectical conception of nature by the human mind.[8] Given that the dialectic is not only a method but also the principle of its intelligibility, "the only dialectic one will find in Nature is a dialectic that one has put there oneself" (Sartre 1978, 31). Consequently, Sartre states:

> The procedure of *discovering* dialectical rationality in *praxis*, and then projecting it, as an unconditional law, on to the inorganic world, and then *returning* to the study of societies and claiming that this opaquely irrational law of nature conditions them, seems to us to be a complete aberration. (Sartre 1978, 33, emphasis in original)

Sartre argues that it would be fallacious to derive dialectical laws of nature from a dialectical understanding of natural processes and then use those dialectical laws for an understanding of human society and history. Sartre's rejection of Engel's theses culminates in his central point of criticism regarding the dialectic of nature. Sartre states that the only appropriate research objects for dialectical thinking are those that can be shown to process dialectically when these research objects are experienced as such from within their processing. Nature, however, cannot be experienced dialectically from the inside but only analyzed from the outside (Remley 2012, 36). Sartre claims that Engels fails to ground a dialectic of matter as a foundation for understanding history because he grounds it on an object toward which he must remain analytical and thus external. This means that he cannot substantiate the validity of his method regarding the research object in question.

Human Existence as Practical Mediation of Internal and External Dialectic

Rather than locating the dialectic of history in nature, Sartre thus locates it in human existence, which he understands as an ongoing mediation of individual action and experience. These two inherently interconnected processes represent practical ways of how humans relate to their physicochemical milieu. They are also fundamental for the constitution and intelligibility of human reality and history in the

---

8   In this regard, Sartre argues in similar ways to Kant in *Kritik der Urteilskraft*. Regarding the *technology of nature*, Kant states that a statement such as "nature processes purposively" must be distinguished from a statement such as "due to the purposive structure of human experience and reason, natural processes must be conceived to be purposive in order to be intelligible." For the formulation of scientific laws to be possible, nature itself must be conceived *as if* it was purposeful (Kant 1974, 349–350; also Hubig 2010). Sartre states that Engels' idea that nature is dialectical has similarities to a Kantian regulative idea that is "incapable of being corroborated by any particular experience" (Sartre 1978, 29).

first place (Remley 2012, 39). In dealing with material conditions, humans not only make history but can also understand history and thus themselves as being the results of their actions. Although this conception of the dialectic is also material, it must be understood as a dialectic *in* matter as opposed to Engels' dialectic *of* matter (Hartmann 1966, 71). For Sartre, the mediation of action and experience represents an expression of what he calls *dialectical reason*; a reason that constitutes "itself in and through the world, dissolving in itself all constituted Reasons in order to constitute new ones which it transcends and dissolves in turn" (Sartre 1978, 21). The entirety of *Critique* fundamentally rests on the premise that to understand the dialectic of history, history itself must be understood based on human existence; this happens by apprehending the dialectic that is at work in individual, world-directed actions, aimed at modifying physicochemical surroundings (Sartre 1978, 40–43). Only in this way can the dialectical method account for both the dialectical movement of its research object and its methodological validity.

With his strong emphasis on individual action and experience, Sartre stays true to his existentialist roots while also accounting for the constraints that material circumstances impose on the individual. Humans are organic entities that make history through free and active confrontation with material conditions. These conditions necessitate and enable their actions. In this regard, ontological freedom must be understood in its unfolding as the constant self-liberation from lacking states of things that are nevertheless rendered necessary as the milieus in which human beings realize themselves. According to Sartre, this dialectic of liberation and necessitation is the basic principle of understanding history. At the same time, history is the basic process through which the dialectic of liberation and necessitation can be understood.

To simplify this conjuncture, it is useful to analyze the basic dialectical principle that the later Sartre identifies to be at work in both action and experience: namely, the principle of totalization. This principle describes a "developing unification" (Sartre 1978, 46) of parts into a wholeness, which is called the totality. The principle of totalization represents a succession of the three dialectical moments: positing, negation, and negation of the negation, i.e. affirmation or sublation. Sartre uses the principle of totalization to explicate the dialectical process at play within the course of action and experience. Both represent complex interrelations between human and non-human things in which an initially meaningless, and contingent but objectively *given*, is negated in its positing through the transforming, identifying, concretizing, and qualifying practical relating of a human subject. Because totalization represents a synthetic activity, however, relation-specific objectivity and subjectivity are produced within the totalizing relation itself. This human negation of objective positing results in a contradiction that is fundamentally sublated in the form of a meaningful and practical relation in which both subject and object represent totalities. *Sublation* means that the initially separate aspects remain present as unified aspects of the totality in question. This relation comes about in this meaningful and practical way because of the structural dynamics of human action and experience on the one hand, and the structural characteristics and properties of objective reality on the other. For this reason, Sartre identifies action and experience as interplays of exteriorization and interiorization. More precisely, he identifies every totalization to be an exteriorization of interiority and an interiorization of exteriority. Through action and experience, humans transform interiority (a meaningful relation to the world, intended actions, subjective goals, etc.) into exteriority (the materiality of the world, realized actions, objective goals, etc., *as* totalities) and vice versa (by apprehending the givenness of being, identifying certain objects, and thus constituting meaningful relations with these objects *as* totalities). They do so by actively mediating between themselves and the world (Sartre 1978, 45–48). Sartre identifies individual action and experience at the heart of human existence to be totalizing processes that, to ultimately constitute human reality and history, dialectically unite interior and exterior aspects. He thus identifies human existence, as being-in-the-world, to be a lived contradiction with itself that continuously sublates itself to contradict itself anew.

Before the lived contradiction that is human existence can be explained in more detail, it is worthwhile examining the conceptual relation between Sartre's early and later works once more. It has been mentioned that Sartre emphasizes the internal dialectic of human existence in *Being and Nothingness*. The early Sartre focuses on the significance of human action as a self-projection and self-realization. Agents not only realize themselves through action but also modify the current state of things and even practically constitute an altered state through their actions. The later Sartre is mostly concerned with the relation between internal and external dialectic in *Critique*. He uses the concept of totalization to describe the relationship between human beings and their milieu as an inherently practical one. The concept of totalization incorporates the processes of human action and experience within an explicitly dialectical conception of the practical world-relatedness of individuals. Along these lines, Cannon (1991) identifies a conceptual similarity between an individual's world- and self-making action in *Being and Nothingness*, and totalization in *Critique*. She states that Sartre's earlier conception of action emphasizes the internal, mental processes of wanting, longing, and projecting, whereas Sartre's later conception of totalization emphasizes the external and more practical aspects of action (170–173). The current work agrees with Cannon's observation but argues for a conceptual *development* in Sartre's philosophy. Sartre retroactively explicates the internally dialectical processes underlying his earlier conception of human action and experience and then unites them with the externally dialectical processes that underlie the material embeddedness of human agents within societal constellations. In this regard, Sartre's early and later works are complementary. The processes outlined in *Being and Nothingness* are substantiated with dialectical principles and incorporated into a materialist conception of history—without losing the significance of Sartre's existentialist thoughts.

However, as a consequence of his later Marxism, the significance attributed to the materiality of human existence changes. In *Critique*, Sartre emphasizes the fact that human existence, although still understood as ontologically free, is strongly conditioned by its inert material conditions: the material requirements of one's physicality, one's education and upbringing, one's inborn or acquired features, abilities and capabilities, one's position within forms of societal constellation, and the concrete material circumstances of one's existence. According to Sartre, humans are materially inert organisms situated in equally inert socioculturally structured conditions that are characterized by scarcity. Most importantly, humans have concrete physical requirements, wants, and wishes that necessitate them to confront and modify their inert conditions to their satisfaction. Here, four interrelated concepts can be identified that are fundamental for understanding Sartre's later philosophical outlook, namely inertia (French *inertie*), scarcity (*rareté*), need (*besoin*), and *praxis*.

Inertia and Scarcity

Regarding the larger context of material conditions in which individuals find themselves, the concept of *inertia* refers to the pure givenness and recalcitrance of matter in the form of the human body and the material world on one hand, and the plasticity of both on the other (Hartmann 1966, 100). *Inertia* is closely connected to the concept of *scarcity*, which means the limited availability of commodities. Scarcity is understood as a "basic human relation, both to Nature and to men" (Sartre 1978, 123). It is inherent to the human condition to exist as an inert, organic entity that has certain material needs. Humans require certain forms of nutrition, access to water, protection from harsh weather conditions, and so on. To satisfy these needs, humans must work with and against inert matter. They must change themselves and the materiality around them to overcome the fact that their resources are scarce (see section 4.2).

From Desire to Need

Section 1.2 discussed how the early Sartre exemplifies and concretizes his idea of the *lack of being* in human existence through the fact that human beings have desires (French *désir*). Such desires bestow human existence with a certain directedness, practical intentionality, and finality toward the future. In desiring, human beings transcend the given toward the possible by projecting from the concrete facticity of their existence toward a potential future self. Despite his earlier reflections about the restraining factors of an agent's situation, and despite the significance he attributes to human desire as a specific mode of subjectively relating to the world in *Being and Nothingness*, Sartre does not reflect on how agents' individual histories fundamentally shape the ways those agents relate to the world by virtue of their desires. The early Sartre engages in intricate discussions about what it means to be moved and motivated by desires (Sartre 2021, 139–143) and to sexually desire the body of another human being in particular (Sartre 2021, 505, 511). He also analyzes the fundamental structures of desire alongside the existential dimensions of *doing*, *having*, and *possessing* (Sartre 2021, 746–777). However, by accepting the individualist nature of a person's structures of desire as a given fact, the early Sartre is ignorant of how these structures of desire are themselves shaped by an agent's lived experience. This experience necessarily takes place in a socioculturally structured and materially predisposed milieu. This milieu fundamentally affects an agent's upbringing, education, and experience. The desire of thirst, for instance, given as it may be, does not abstractly project toward water in general, but to a more or less concrete outline of action toward a familiar horizon of ends (Sartre 2021, 730, 747). Depending on how agents were socialized, how these agents have satiated their thirst in the past, and what their environments provide, different drinking actions will be projected. A person who grew up in an urban environment, for instance, initially projects toward different ends and thus, connectedly, to different courses of action than a person who grew up as a nomad in a desert area with no infrastructure. The urbanite may project towards taking a cup or a glass and filling it up at their faucet when at home. The desert dweller may have a completely different relationship with water because water is a rare resource in the desert. When thirsty, these people may project toward different ways of finding, preserving, and consuming water owing to their specific situation and experience. However, if both have a water bottle readily at hand or if there is the option to simply buy water, they may both do so.

In *Being and Nothingness*, Sartre does not reflect on the reason why desires express themselves differently based on a person's facticity. He simply accepts that human beings have desires as specific modes of subjectivity toward the world. However, the concrete outline of desires, and thus the ends toward which these desires project, as well as the actions that potentially ensue from them, must be understood as having been shaped by the agent's facticity, i.e. the whole of the material, social, and cultural conditions that gave rise to this specific form of human existence up to the point of the present action.

One can argue that Sartre must have recognized the fact that focusing on desires, without criticizing how the concrete outline of these desires is itself shaped by society, culture, matter, and the processing of history throughout a person's existence, does not provide a solid foundation for a critical theory of society. This is even more true because the dialectical interrelation between action and experience has to be considered as the very foundation of such a theory. To allow for structural analysis of the processing of history, the later Sartre thus introduces the concept of *need* (French *besoin*), stating:

> Everything is to be explained though *need* (*le besoin*); need is the first totalising relation between the material being, man, and the material ensemble of which he is part. This relation is *univocal*, and *of interiority*. Indeed, it is through need that the first negation of the negation and the first totalisation appear in matter. Need is a negation of the negation in so far as it expresses itself as a *lack* within the organism; and need is a positivity in so far as the organic totality tends to preserve itself *as such* through it. (Sartre 1978, 80, emphasis in original)

The lack of being that the early Sartre has located in human desire thus gains a much more prominent and much more fundamental significance in his later works. In *Critique*, need represents a fundamental affirmation of the synthetic, human being-in-the-world in its corporeality. Through their fundamental needfulness, humans necessarily engage in an interior relation to their exterior world. They lack whatever they manifest through their needs. Consequently, humans urge satisfaction in the future.

At first glance, Sartre's later conception of need as *besoin* is similar to his earlier conception of *desire* as *désir*. In her study of Sartre's philosophical works in the context of psychoanalysis, Cannon also remarks that Sartre's shift from structures of desire to structures of need might suggest that "the later Sartre has embraced some kind of instinctualism" (Cannon 1991, 172) and simply shifted his perspective from a person's internality to their externality. This, as Cannon rightly remarks, is not the case. Sartre's conception of need is not reduced to a mere physical drive toward the material world. It does not represent just a switch from the mental to the physical foundations of a human's world-relatedness. Rather, it remains a totalizing relation between a person and their surroundings. Furthermore, need is also not *some* totalizing relation, it is the *first* one. Given that human existence is a material endeavor, need, in its initially pure and simple form, is fundamental for human existence because it grounds the necessity for a person to practically relate with their surroundings to survive (Cannon 1991, 172–173). For Sartre, need, or, more precisely, the fact of *being needy*, grounds the possibility of a human being's continued existence, action, experience, and, most of all, freedom.[9] Need represents both the fundamental and abstract relation between a human being and that being's socioculturally structured material surroundings. Furthermore, this abstract relation of need is what instantiates concrete desires in the first place. Part of the current work is to further investigate how this instantiation takes place within forms of societal organization.

---

9   For a more prosaic approach to the relationship between needs and human freedom, see Sartre (2001).

The change in focus from desires in *Being and Nothingness* to needs in *Critique* fundamentally changes the conceptual grounding of Sartre's philosophical perspective, thereby opening up Sartre's philosophy toward those practical constraints, material potentials, and societal dynamics that condition human existence beyond the borders of the concrete action situation. Against the concept of *need* as the fundamental, abstract relation of a human's engagement with the world, Sartre can analyze how human desiring is shaped and thus potentially transformed in its concrete form by and through the larger form of societal organization in which individuals are situated. This allows him to reconstruct how forms of societal constellation, which began in the attempt to systematically provide for material requirements, wants, and wishes, transform in such a way that they change how individuals do so. Needs thus represent fundamental, abstract, and, most importantly, immediate ways of how people relate to their material surroundings for themselves. Without dismissing his earlier thoughts on desires, the later Sartre predominantly conceptualizes the lack of being as a lack of resources, commodities, skills, rights, knowledge, etc., that agents require to survive and persist in one way or another (Cannon 1992, 132). As a consequence, Sartre shifts his focus from the analysis of the internal structures of action to the concrete, historically situated *praxis* of individuals.

Cannon, referring to an unpublished manuscript by Sartre[10], claims that Sartre again developed his thoughts regarding the relation of needs and desires after *Critique*. According to Cannon, in this manuscript Sartre considers desires to be "socialized need" (Cannon 1992, 134), i.e. need that is transformed into desire "through relations with others in the socio-material world" (Cannon 1992, 135). According to this understanding, nutrition, for instance, as a person's physical requirement, which owes itself to the corporeality of human existence, is only ever a pure and simple need in the form of *besoin* in an infant state. Since this need can be satisfied through a number of different practical interrelations between the infant and whoever nourishes them, Sartre assumes that how this need is satisfied, socializes this need, and connects it to a larger societal form of organization. In this understanding, infants who lack nutrition cry initially because of an unpleasant physical symptom complex that is attributable to an abstract, undirected need in the form of *besoin*. However, as soon as this need has been taken care of a few times in a row, for instance through breastfeeding or a bottle, the abstract and undirected need is rendered into a concrete desire in the form of *désir*. These infants still cry because of the same unpleasant symptom complex resulting from a physical lack of nutrition. However, they no longer cry as a result of an abstract and undirected need but because of a concrete

---

10   Cannon refers to a manuscript of 589 pages of unorganized notes. According to Stone and Bowman (1986) this manuscript contains Sartre's unpublished notes for a lecture called *Morality and Society* (Bowman & Stone 1992; 2004) and other notes about ethics.

desire for their caregiver's breast or the bottle as a means to gain nutrition. In mutual interaction with their caregiver's action, these infants' need has been socialized so that it has become a structurally dependent desire relative to the form of societal organization in which both caregiver and infant are situated (Cannon 1992).

Throughout a person's life, abstract forms of initially undirected need may arise, for instance on account of changes in understanding or living conditions, or because of the larger dynamics of societal constellations themselves. Still, these forms of need will always be socialized and concretized into desires, because their satisfaction necessarily takes place within sociocultural surroundings that already scaffold a practical, instrumental horizon of possibilities. Most importantly, because human existence represents a constant struggle with scarcity, Sartre's conception of the dialectical relationship between needs and desires is constitutive for understanding the formation of societal constellations (see section 4.2).

Despite his thoughts on *socialized need* in his later manuscript, Cannon states that in *Critique* Sartre is already "careful to point out that need is always socialized" (Cannon 1992, 134), because how a person produces themselves "conditions not only the satisfaction of his need but also need itself" (Sartre 1978, 95). Throughout *Critique*, Sartre sporadically argues that how people suffer their need, become acquainted with and learn certain modes of behavior can itself become interiorized and habituated in the form of *hexis*, i.e. an acquired disposition that shapes a person's actions in relation to their position within forms of societal organization. In this context, Sartre discusses the intricacies of habit formation, the socialization of needs into desires, and the role of habits, or *hexeis* (which is the Greek plural of *hexis*), in the perpetuation of societal organization. However, because these discussions require an understanding of the course of human action, and because it is irrelevant for that course of action whether it takes place based on a need or a desire, the socialization of *need* into *desire* is discussed in more detail in section 4.5.

Based on these thoughts, a conceptual distinction between the notions of *need* and *desire* in Sartre's philosophy can be made. Desires, understood as *désirs*, represent concrete, directed, socioculturally shaped, and mediated as well as subjectively qualified modes in which human beings exteriorize themselves. They do so by relating to and engaging with their surroundings for themselves based on their requirements, wants, and wishes. Needs, understood as *besoins*, represent abstract and initially undirected modes in which these human beings relate to their surroundings. The way in which human beings practically do so is through *praxis*.

Praxis and History

Praxis is understood as "an organising project which transcends material conditions towards an end and inscribes itself, through labour, in inorganic matter as a rearrangement of the practical field and a reunification of means in the light of the end"

(Sartre 1978, 734). Sartre uses the notion of *praxis* to describe both individual actions in concrete situations, as well as the historically situated realization of human existence as a whole.[11] Sartre states that every *praxis* "presupposes a material agent (the organic individual) and the material organisation of an operation on and by matter" (Sartre 1978, 71). In this regard, *praxis* is the function of human existence, and human existence represents the form from which *praxis* is instantiated. As material entities, human beings are both agents and end. They are the ones who act for themselves within their material surroundings to satisfy themselves in and through their surrounding materiality. Accordingly, Sartre claims that human reality, as constituted by *praxis*, is fundamentally mediated by material reality. Furthermore, every *praxis* primarily is an "instrumentalisation of material reality" (Sartre 1978, 161). Breathing instrumentalizes air, walking instrumentalizes the soil, and so on, and owing to the materiality of human existence, action, and experience take place between material entities.

With the notion of *praxis*, Sartre emphasizes that humans must simultaneously be understood as the concrete quasi-product and the effective (re-)producer of their social and material situation and, concomitantly, their form of societal organization. Sartre claims that "[n]othing happens to men or to objects except in their material being and through the materiality of Being. But man is precisely the material reality from which matter gets its human functions" (Sartre 1978, 182). Through his conception of *praxis*, the interrelation between interiorization and exteriorization becomes clearer. As aspects of action and experience, interiorization and exteriorization represent two sides of the same coin. Sartre states that

> the human relation of exteriority is based on the direct bond of interiority as the basic type of human relation. Man lives in a universe where the future is a thing, where the idea is an object and where the violence of matter is the 'midwife of History'. But it is man who invests things with his own *praxis*, his own future and his own knowledge. (Sartre 1978, 181, emphasis in original)

In this context, the dialectic of liberation and necessitation becomes clearer. Human existence is a lived contradiction: it represents an irresolvable tension between the needs of an organic being that necessitate *praxis*, and the fact that this *praxis*, as a relation between human being and world, is based on ontological freedom through which the tension of liberation and necessitation becomes intelligible as unsolvable in the first place. Neither freedom nor necessity can be understood as *facts* that somehow condition human existence as a totality. Human existence is itself a totalizing activity in which human beings enact and promote their freedom in the pro-

---

11   By way of example, the individual *praxis* of writing this sentence takes place as a structural moment of the *praxis* of writing this section, this chapter, this work. All represent practical moments of the *praxis* or practical realization that is the author's existence.

cess of enacting and promoting their materiality and thus their structures of necessity (Sartre 1978, 70–71). By focusing on the concept of totalization, the later Sartre
places more emphasis on the synthetic process itself and less on its resulting totality. Thus, even if individuals appear to be somewhat determined by certain factors
such as material, social, or historical constellations and conditions, these factors
are themselves totalities that result from human action and experience in the first
place. This processual understanding allows Sartre to retrace the historicity of these
factors and to explain the entanglement of liberation and necessitation in practical
life. Furthermore, when human existence is understood as a totalizing process, the
significance of individual situations within the process changes. Rather than illus-
trating ontological freedom through individual choice and action within concrete
situations, every situation is itself a moment in a larger interlocking process that
proceeds from moment to moment and from situation to situation. A situation is
not something that individuals constitute anew each time they act by negating the
given and transcending it toward the possible. Rather, a situation is a concrete sublation of past situations that again represent concrete ways in which individuals have
(re-)produced themselves and the larger structures they are situated in through their
actions. Although situations are still understood to be transcended and surpassed,
the mode of how this happens is retained as well. Consequently, individual action
situations can only be entirely understood in relation to the historically produced
and history-producing process that is human existence.[12]

1.5 Concluding Remarks

The development of Sartre's philosophical thought throughout his works accounts
for the fundamental reality of human existence. All human beings find themselves
in relatively fixed sociocultural and material conditions and constellations, which
constrain their choices and influence their actions. Furthermore, to live their lives,
humans must act based on the conditions they find themselves in, which means that
these individuals must actively engage with the facticity of their lives. At first glance
human existence seems to be determined by a wide variety of factors that might inhibit or eliminate their agency, seemingly rendering them passive objects or cogs in
a machine, perhaps even to a point where there are zero choices and only one possible course of action. In the contemporary, highly technological world, this worry

---

12   Since this section is mainly intended as an introduction to certain fundamentals of Sartre's
philosophy, a deeper discussion about the concepts *totalization* and *totality* cannot be engaged here. Jay (1984) and Tomlinson (2014) give more theoretical insight into the significance of these concepts in Sartre's philosophy. However, a more technical analysis of these
concepts focusing on experience and action as totalizations can be found in section 2.2.

may be prevalent. However, the fact that action and experience represent relations with the world means that these relations ultimately express the ontological freedom of the human being. Human beings are not identical to being but exist as a relation to it. However slight it may be, there is always the chance for them to become aware of their situation. Given enough insight and self-reflection, they can analyze their constraints and possibilities so that they may take responsibility and understand the scope of their agency.

Sartre's way of further analyzing this scope leads to his theories on practical ensembles. Every instance of *praxis* necessarily takes place in connection to other material entities that support and/or challenge its outcome. By focusing on both *praxis* and context, Sartre can retrace, from a dialectical and praxeological point of view, the nature of predominant interrelations in certain constellations. According to Sartre, the dialectical progression of history mirrors the dialectical progression of individual human existence. Both progress as ongoing totalizations that are driven by lived contradictions. In the case of human existence, this contradiction is the oscillation of practical freedom and material necessity. However, in the case of history, it is the oscillation between *serial* and *communal* structures (see sections 4.3 and 4.4). Because human beings satisfy their needs and desires in different ways as situated in larger constellations, these constellations exhibit different forms of organization that are functionally differentiated and interrelated. Technology in the form of manufactured objects and structures, but also in the form of body techniques, plays an important part in the structuring of these constellations.

However, before these larger theoretical considerations can be engaged, it is necessary to analyze more thoroughly the concrete course of human action. Sartre claims that the processing totalization of practical ensembles is fundamentally driven by goal-directed human activities based on requirements, wants, and wishes. However, from the larger dialectical, materialist, and historical context of *Critique*, it does not become clear what this means on the exact level of action. If human action and experience are supposed to render the progression of history intelligible from the inside, the structural course of action and experience must be scrutinized first. This may require previously mentioned principles and dynamics to be analyzed again from an action-theoretical perspective, but the overall approach of this work benefits from a more thorough reconstruction and further development of Sartre's understanding of the course of action. This reconstruction is the subject of the next chapter.

2. Totalizing Action and Praxis-Process

2.1 Introduction

This chapter develops a unified account of human action and existence as a *praxis-process* in Sartre's philosophical works by combining action-theoretical thoughts from *Being and Nothingness*, *Search for a Method*, and *Critique*.[1]

Chapter 1 indicated the fundamental role of human action in the larger theoretical framework of Sartre's philosophy. Whereas Sartre's earlier philosophical focus mainly considers the internal dialectic of action, the later Sartre tries to account for the fact that human existence is a mediation of internal and external dialectics through action. This is due to a claim by Sartre that human existence becomes only truly intelligible based on how it dialectically processes through societal constellations based on its ontological freedom. Sartre refers to these constellations as practical ensembles. However, from these assumptions, it has not yet become clear how such a conception of action—as the practical mediation of internal and external dialectics—presents itself on the action level, i.e. in the concrete structural course of action.

The previous chapter introduced Sartre's early conception of free action and his later conception of *praxis*. Both, although initially similar, emphasize different aspects of human action. In *Being and Nothingness*, Sartre describes action as the ontologically free, intentional, material arrangement of means to ends. These ends arise in human desiring (*désir*) as a relation between human beings and the world. This perspective on action is predominantly focused on the internal dialectic of human action because it accounts for what it means to act, experience, and engage the world from a perspective on the synthetic relationship of being and consciousness. Based on this earlier conception of action, human existence appears to be fundamentally grounded in itself as a free project.

In *Critique*, in contrast, Sartre focuses on the historical *praxis* of individuals, which is best understood as an active, material modification of a state of the world

---

1   For a more condensed version of Sartre's dialectical conception of action as totalization, see Siegler (2022b).

that was deemed unsatisfactory into a potentially satisfying state of the world based on human needs (*besoin*). Although Sartre highlights the material aspects of human action and experience in his later work, his perspective on historical *praxis* captures human action as a mediation of the internal and external dialectics of human existence. It accounts for what it means to act as a goal-directed and intentional biological organism, necessarily confronted with and reliant on other such organisms and material entities, and for what it means to engage with often-times recalcitrant physicochemical surroundings in the long run. In contrast to his earlier conception of action, Sartre's later conception presents human existence as an inherently dependent, material, and, most importantly, socially determined process.

However, both the early and late perspectives highlight different yet inherently intertwined aspects of what it means to act, and these must be incorporated into a unified account of action in Sartre's philosophy. Among these aspects are the ontological freedom of human agents; the intentionality of their actions; the specific experience of the state of the physicochemical surroundings in the outset of action in relation to the motivational role of requirements, wants, and wishes; the relationship itself between needs as *besoins* and desires as *désirs*; the fact that human beings are biological organisms with an embodied consciousness; and the influence of sociocultural and material conditions on the course of actions. Notwithstanding the complex interrelations between these factors and the aforementioned mediation of internal and external perspectives on action, a unified account of human action in Sartre's philosophy is not only possible but also necessary for understanding human action as the foundation of his philosophical system in general, and for understanding his theories on the dialectics of technology and society in particular.

The key to developing such a unified account of action in Sartre is the functional principle of totalization. As mentioned in section 1.4, for Sartre totalization is the underlying dialectical principle of human action and experience. The later Sartre uses the principle of totalization to capture the internal dialectical dynamics of human existence that he mentioned in *Being and Nothingness*, while further developing those dynamics by adding a materially dialectical and external perspective. Through totalization as the underlying principle of human action and experience, human existence becomes intelligible throughout Sartre's works as a mediation of internal and external dialectics. In this regard, Sartre's philosophical works must be considered inherently complementary. By combining this unified account of action with Sartre's understanding of existence as a *praxis*-process, every situated action can be either understood on its own, as a material and totalizing process or as a structural moment in the larger totalization of human existence as a *praxis*-process.

To develop a unified account of action—as the ontologically free, intentional, sociomaterially dependent, material arrangement of means to ends based on *besoins* and *désirs*, through which human beings totalize themselves and their world—it must be shown to what extent human action and existence themselves represent totalizations. This means that the unified conception of action must not only account for the external synthetic relation between material agents and the world. It must also account for the internal synthetic relation between being-for-itself and being-in-itself. Consequently, the course of action must represent a mediation of action and experience that is entangled with the agent's corporeality and physico-chemical surroundings. In this way, the ontological freedom and intentionality of action, the motivational role of requirements, wants, and wishes, the materiality of these agents themselves, and the situatedness of these agents in sociocultural and material constellations can all be accounted for. However, this means that some of Sartre's more existentialist thoughts about the different modes of being of humans and non-human things must be taken into consideration as well. Also, it means that some of the concepts that were introduced in Chapter 1 must be brought up again and reinterpreted. This conception of action will be integrated into Sartre's understanding of existence as a *praxis*-process.

To lay the foundations for developing a unified conception of action, the chapter begins with a theoretical preface about Sartre's understanding of modes of being, and a focused reconstruction of the principles of *totalization* and *totality* in the context of human experience.

2.2 Modes of Being and their Synthesis

The overall aim of this section is to prepare the theoretical ground for the rest of the chapter. The section first introduces Sartre's thoughts on the different modes of being of humans and non-human things. Then, the section explicates Sartre's basic dialectical principle of totalization along with its implications by demonstrating how this principle plays out in the way humans experience the objective world.

Modes of Being

A fundamental point for understanding Sartre's philosophy is his basic differentiation between the modes of being for human beings and those for non-human things. The human mode of being is treated first. As discussed in section 1.2, human beings constitute meaningful relations with being *for* themselves, as ends in themselves, in virtue of their goal-directed relations with the world. For this reason, Sartre refers to the human mode of being as *being-for-itself* or *for-itself*. Sartre's phenomenological considerations are important for understanding this mode of being. Sartre claims that, unlike non-human things, humans are not only conscious of the world around them, but they also necessarily practically relate to and encounter it. For Sartre, consciousness is not a contemplative state of analyzing the world. Rather, consciousness has to be understood as an immediate connection between humans and other entities that are outside consciousness. This connection can be physical or mental.

Proponents of this view include Brentano and Husserl, the latter being the main representative of the phenomenological school. Husserl claims that consciousness is mainly characterized by its directedness toward something else. This directedness is referred to as *intentionality*. In Husserl's traditional transcendental phenomenology, the intentionality of consciousness is analyzed to draw conclusions about the conditions of the possibility of experience. Husserl's focus is on the structure of human experience as a result of perception and awareness. Hence he uses the terms *subject* and *object* as fixed points to describe how humans relate to things. Although a relation between subject and object—from active to passive—seems unidirectional at first, Husserl means quite the opposite. Within this conception of consciousness, subjectivity is possible only on the grounding of objectivity, and vice versa. There is no experiencing instance without an appearing one. Phenomenology derives its name from this appearing instance, the *phenomenon* (Greek *phainomenon*, a thing appearing to view). Sartre mostly follows this approach. However, he is less interested in the conditions of the possibility of experience. Combined with his ontological thinking, Sartre tries to uncover the conditions of the possibility of human existence (see section 1.2). With the introduction of his later concept of *totalization*, Sartre intends also to uncover the intricacies of how forms of human world-relatedness are constituted.

In Sartre's philosophy, every relation humans maintain to the world is itself a directed reference between subjective consciousness (for-itself) and the positive givenness of the objective phenomenal world (in-itself). Sartre does not proclaim a separation between body and mind. According to him, "[i]t is in its entirety that being-for-itself has to be body, and in its entirety that it has to be consciousness: it cannot be *joined* to a body" (Sartre 2021, 412, emphasis in original). Human existence is necessarily embodied and manifested in the materiality of being. Seeing, hearing, analyzing, categorizing, and acting, among others, are directed processes of human consciousness that produce subjective meaning by rendering meaningful the relations between subject and object. This directedness is not a choice; it is the structural characteristic of consciousness. To put it bluntly, human beings cannot decide not to see, hear, feel, or process information. They can merely decide to close their eyes and ears, to avoid tactile sensation, or to direct their awareness to something else. In this regard, the mode of being-for-itself is inherently characterized by transcendence. Human consciousness is "a project of itself beyond" (Sartre 2021, 53) as it reaches toward the world and envelops it in its spatiotemporal becoming. On the basis of materiality, consciousness represents a radical openness to the world. Furthermore, the structure of consciousness means that the for-itself also represents a relation to the world in a receptive, directed, and focused way. This will become clearer as it concerns human corporeality, as the focal point of human existence (see section 2.3).

Sartre's approach toward the phenomenal structure of human consciousness is innovative in that he differentiates between two modes of consciousness: the pre-reflective consciousness of something, and a second-order, reflective consciousness of one's consciousness of something. Intentional relations toward objects are constituted by pre-reflective consciousness. Depending on the level of technological mediation, these relations are relatively immediate. Touching, writing, and observing are typical pre-reflective relations of embodied consciousness. During writing, for instance, the act of writing itself is usually neither reflected upon nor said to be *performed*. One is simply writing (see section 3.2). Similarly, reflecting on a metaphysical concept means being pre-reflectively conscious of this concept. Reflective consciousness is pre-reflective consciousness of one's intentional processes. This means that human consciousness is always directed toward something, even if it does not reflect upon this directedness (Sartre 2021, 9–10).

Sartre argues that the processes of human consciousness have a double character. He states that "any positional consciousness of an object is at the same time a non-positional consciousness of itself" (Sartre 2021, 11). Among intentional relations, human consciousness pre-reflectively posits itself as the subject within its relation toward an object. Reflectively, consciousness is directed to its intentional directedness toward something. Although Sartre differentiates between pre-reflective and reflective consciousness, they together constitute a unity. The knowledge of pre-reflective relations is possible only on the grounding of reflective consciousness, and vice versa. As a consequence, Sartre concludes that human beings are self-conscious and that this self-consciousness is mediated as such through the interrelation between pre-reflective and reflective consciousness. Human beings relate to themselves by virtue of relating to their relating-to-the-world (Sartre 2021, 11–12). The *look* of others and the various ways in which human beings objectify themselves in the material world are significant for how humans may reflect their existence (see section 4.3).

Human existence structurally exists as both self-consciousness and embodied directedness. It is never contained in itself, but always outside itself, always engaging the material world. Due to the transcendent character of their existence, human beings are always in the process of existing. Even though they can be neither identical with nor completely free from being, they can modify their relation with being (Sartre 2021, 60–61). Sartre identifies this modifiability as ontological freedom—freedom of attitude, stance, or bearing. It is not a property of human consciousness, but a condition of human existence (Barata 2018, 125–126). By existing, human beings necessarily relate to being. Even though they are self-conscious, their self is defined as "a constantly unstable equilibrium between identity as a state of absolute cohesion without any trace of diversity, and unity as the synthesis of a multiplicity" (Sartre 2021, 126). In Sartre's existentialism, human existence must be understood as a temporal, future-oriented process comprising the various ways human beings exist in the world with and against the full givenness of being (see section 2.3). Within the process of existing, human beings realize themselves through their experiences and actions. However, they can never fully become the selves they strive to be. A fully synthesized being-in-and-for-itself would mean that directed consciousness for-itself ceases to exist (Sartre 2021, 143). Human existence must project toward itself over and over again. Human beings are, therefore, condemned to be free (Sartre 2021, 577). This *condemnation* is a constitutive aspect of the lived contradiction that human existence represents (see section 1.4).

In contrast to humans in the mode of being-for-itself, things are not self-conscious. Sartre mentions that "the constant reflection that constitutes any 'itself' merges into identity" (Sartre 2021, 27) in the case of things. Things thus exist in the mode of being-in-itself. In *Being and Nothingness*, Sartre identifies three distinct characteristics of being—*Being is, Being is in itself, Being is what it is.*

For human beings to relate to being, being itself must have a certain structure. Sartre then argues that being is neither active nor passive. According to him, because activity and passivity are human categories, being can appear only as active or passive within the scope of human experience or action. Being is also beyond affirmation, because *affirmation* would suggest an affirming act carried out by human consciousness. Yet Sartre claims that being *is*, even independent of human reality.

Because being cannot be the product of any activity, Sartre deduces the first characteristic: "*being is in itself*" (Sartre 2021, 27, emphasis in original). Since being neither self-reflects nor acts with intention, it cannot constitute a self in any meaningful way. It follows that its structural integrity is not a product of deliberation, but is given as it is. From this fact, Sartre derives the second characteristic: "*being is what it is*" (Sartre 2021, 27, emphasis in original), and nothing else. Because being is what it is, it "can neither be, nor be derived from, the possible, nor can it be equated with the necessary" (Sartre 2021, 28). It is given in pure contingent positivity, devoid of time or meaning. Sartre expresses this in the third characteristic: "*being-in-itself is*" (Sartre 2021, 28, emphasis in original).

Owing to these three characteristics, Sartre considers things in the mode of being-in-itself to be transcendent, much like being-for-itself (Sartre 2021, 21–22). It seems that Sartre's conception of the transcendent being of objective phenomena is deliberately ambivalent. Things must be what they are and must be how they appear. To conceptualize them as transcendent implies something toward which they transcend. But unlike the transcendent for-itself, being-in-itself can be understood as transcendent in that it appears the way it does due to the characteristics of being and not as a directed and focused consciousness. In Sartre's case, this means that things present themselves as they are. Sartre criticizes various epistemological approaches that propose a "dualism of being and appearing" (Sartre 2021, 2). Rather than assuming that a phenomenal thing "indicates behind its shoulder some true being" (Sartre 2021, 2) that is somehow concealed, such as Kant's *thing-in-itself*, Sartre concludes that how things appear discloses their being. He writes that the essence of the objective world is an "'appearing' that is no longer opposed to being but which is, on the contrary, its measure" (Sartre 2021, 2). This does not mean that things only exist insofar as they appear (Sartre 2021, 22), but that the objective world can be experienced in its phenomenality without missing any essential features. In the case of things, existence *is* essence. In the case of humans, existence *precedes* essence. In section 2.3, this is shown to be the most crucial difference between humans and things.

The ontological foundation of the materiality of being is omnipresent in Sartre's early philosophy and has been shown to carry over to his later philosophical works (see Chapter 1). Even in his later philosophy, Sartre implicitly incorporates the modes of being-in-itself and for-itself into his considerations. From Sartre's considerations about the different modes of being of humans and non-human things, his primacy of the human perspective, and his considerations about the significance of experience and action as the analytical ground for understanding history, it follows that humans typically are the active parts of human-world relations, whereas things represent the passive parts. However, under specific circumstances, the dynamics between humans and things can change (see section 4.3). As Sartre remarks, both modes of being may be analyzed on their own as *moments of a synthesis*. But a more complete comprehension of both is made possible only by analyzing how they interrelate.

The Basic Principle of Totalization

Distinguishing between the modes of being-for-itself and being-in-itself can be misleading, in that both modes of being seemingly refer to fixed and initially separated object areas in which human subjects remain on one side of the relationship and the objective world on the other. In the case of Sartre's philosophy, however, such a separation cannot easily be made. Being-for-itself and being-in-itself must not be considered as initially separated but instead as moments of a synthesis (Sartre 2021, 34), or, more precisely, as *relata* within an actively processing interrelation. In *Critique*, Sartre refers to this actively processing and synthetic interrelation as *totalization*, a process that produces totalities. With this view, Sartre stands in a thought tradition of philosophers concerned with the ideas and assumptions surrounding the concept of *totality*.

The concept of *totality* is one moment in a long history of assumptions, observations, and intuitions concerning the idea of a somewhat organized and self-contained whole: a *holon*, a *Ganzheit*, a composition larger than the sum of its parts, a system exhibiting more qualities than the mere sum of its elements would imply, etc. This concept has troubled thinkers throughout the entire history of philosophy.

In *Marxism and Totality*, Jay (1984) reconstructs the history of the concept of *totality* in Western thought, along with the never-ending struggle to formulate a coherent idea of what it means. In the aftermath of Hegel and Marx, the concept of *totality* rose to special prominence in Western Marxism. Among the most prominent thinkers who concerned themselves with totalities was Georg Lukács. For him, *totality* represents the "eigentliche Wirklichkeitskategorie" (Lukács 1923, 42)—the actual category of reality—through which a dialectical method can acquire an understanding of the complex interrelation between society and a capitalist mode of production. Following Marx, Lukács argues that the contradictions of capitalist societies can only be properly unveiled when society itself is understood through the category of *totality*. Processes of production, distribution, exchange, and consumption cannot be understood only as affecting each other. Rather, the fact that a process is understood as one of production or consumption is possible only when it is understood dialectically, as a moment in the processing of a capitalist society considered as an all-encompassing totality (Lukács 1923, 44; Burmann 2018, 22). The category of *totality* thus represents the condition of possibility for a dialectical understanding of society and history.

In *Search for a Method*, Sartre broadly criticizes the Western Marxist understanding of the concept of *totality* as a misattribution of cause and effect in historical processes. Rather than attempting to understand how totalities—such as individuals, specific societal constellations, or societal processes—come about through the actions of historically situated individuals, Sartre criticizes the Marxist understanding of totality as "heuristic; its principles and its prior knowledge appear as regulative in relation to its concrete research" (Sartre 1963, 26). Sartre's solution for this problem is his own modified version of Lefebvre's *regressive-progressive method* (see section 1.3). This methodology allows him to dialectically deconstruct and then reconstruct how specific totalities, like individuals, larger groupings of individuals, societal subsystems, and even society as a whole, have become what they are through the synthetic activities of human beings. These synthetic activities, such as experience and action, fundamentally follow the dialectical principle of *totalization*. To grasp this principle, Sartre employs a broader, more fluid, and most importantly, more open conception of totalities. He states:

> A totality is defined as a being which, while radically distinct from the sum of its parts, is present in its entirety, in one form or another, in each of these parts, and which relates to itself either through its relation to one or more of its parts or through its relation to the relations between all or some of them. If this reality is *created* (a painting or a symphony are examples, if one takes integration to an extreme), it can exist only in the imaginary (*l'imaginaire*) [...] Thus, as the active power of holding together its parts, the totality is only the correlative of an act of imagination [...] In the case of practical objects – machines, tools, consumer goods,

etc. – our present action makes them seem like totalities by resuscitating, in some way, the *praxis* which attempted to totalise their inertia [...] the *totality*, despite what one might think, is only a regulative principle of the totalisation (Sartre 1978, 45–46)

Things like a painting or a hammer can only be considered totalities through the synthetic act of experiencing, apprehending, or practically utilizing them. The meaning and practical significance of these things are not given per se but through the totalizing interrelation between humans and their material surroundings. According to Sartre, this totalizing interrelation fundamentally represents a synthesis of being-for-itself and being-in-itself. The synthesis plays out in the interlocking of human experience and action in relation to the corresponding socioculturally structured, material surroundings.

Unfortunately, Sartre does not provide a clear and all-encompassing definition of *totalization*. In *Critique II*, he states that a totalization is "simply a praxis achieving unity on the basis of specific circumstances, and in relation to a goal to be attained" (Sartre 1991, 3), which more or less equates totalization with a successful goal-directed activity. Throughout *Critique*, Sartre points out that totalizations, such as requiring something, experiencing specific environmental features, or realizing oneself through action, represent dialectical activities that play out as a succession of the three dialectical moments discussed previously (Sartre 1978, 47, 60, 80, 85, 89). Need, for instance, represents "the first totalizing relation between the material being, man, and the material ensemble from which he is part [...] it is through need that the first negation of the negation and the first totalisation appear in matter" (Sartre 1978, 80). In its abstractness, need projects toward a future state of the world in which an agent's requirements, wants, and wishes are satisfied. When an agent practically realizes this project by satisfying their need through action, this action fundamentally represents a sublation of this need for the acting subject. Also, totalizations proceed through an interlocking series of exteriorizations of interiority and interiorizations of exteriority between humans and their surrounding matter. To stay within the example of need and its projection toward an end, Sartre states:

The *project* [...] is merely the exteriorisation of immanence; transcendence itself is already present in the functional fact of nutrition and excretion, since what we find here is a relation of univocal interiority between two states of materiality. And, conversely, transcendence contains immanence within itself in that its link with its purpose and with the environment remains one of exteriorised interiority. (Sartre 1978, 83, emphasis in original)

Sartre's understanding of dialectical totalization can be illustrated by how he conceives the process of experience. Experience is inherent to all forms of human world-relations. It is a unifying and synthetic activity of embodied self-consciousness in which the meaning of an initially exterior phenomenal object is constituted for an experiencing subject based on a relationship that also constitutes object and subject in the first place. In this way, human beings constitute themselves as subjects within an objective world that corresponds to their horizon of reality and possibility. According to Sartre, the process of experiencing is dialectical. Subject, object, and meaning are outcomes of a synthesis of being and consciousness.

Structurally, the synthetic process of experiencing consists of directed human consciousness, i.e. being-for-itself, and phenomenon, i.e. being-in-itself with its aforementioned three characteristics. This being is transcendent in that it appears just as it is. It is given in the full positivity of its being. On its own, it is inert matter without any meaning whatsoever. From a phenomenological point of view, being cannot even be considered an object without a directed subject, and vice versa. This pure givenness of being-in-itself is a material presupposition for the experience. By virtue of its structure, being is posited as it is. It is present in its entirety as what it is. This positing is the first moment of dialectical totalization.[2]

---

2   In this regard, Sartre's understanding of being-in-itself differs from that of Hegel. For Sartre, being-in-itself represents a material positing for consciousness owing to the phenomenal structure of both matter and consciousness. For Hegel, being-in-itself is already a positing of consciousness. The difference here between Sartre's and Hegel's understanding of being-in-itself might be traced back to the slightly different intensions of Hegel's concept *An sich* and its French translation *en-soi*. In English, both concepts are simply translated as *in-itself*. The Hegelian concept *An sich* refers to an immediate and more general way in which an object is given so as to be potentially identified as something. The potential character is important here, as it represents the condition of possibility for any form of identification in the first place (Hubig 2016, 139). Sartre's understanding of *en-soi*, however, as proposed in *L'être et le néant*, does not refer to the potential character of an object but to the inner structure of the being of that object. It is more focused on what is *within* being that provides the condition of possibility for experience and action. The English translation of both concepts simply as *in-itself* obscures this difference in meaning. However, this difference has consequences for Hegel's and Sartre's philosophical outlook. Since *An sich* already represents a positing of consciousness, Hegel's dialectic takes place as a conceptual development within the human mind. In Sartre's case, being posits itself *en-soi*—within and through its material givenness—and is encountered by human consciousness. Consequently, Sartre's dialectic takes place as a synthetic process of being and consciousness within matter through experience and action. Therefore, Hegel can be called an idealist whereas Sartre must be called a materialist in this regard. Similarly, the translation of Hegel's German *Für sich* as *pour-soi* in French alters its Hegelian meaning and stresses a more proactive mode of being. In German, the term *Für sich* generally refers to something that is taken on its own. In Hegel's use, *Für sich* refers to the human mind which remains somewhat analytical as the instance that qualifies objects *An sich* through determination. Sartre's *pour-soi* is practical and engaged in the world *for* (French *pour*) its own sake. Again, the English translation of *Für sich* and *pour-soi* as *for-itself* obscures this slight yet crucial terminological difference. The author's appreciation goes to Christoph Hubig for these insights.

Embodied self-consciousness can encounter this positing of being-in-itself through its sensory organs. Initially, this encountering is an external relation. Within such a sensory relationship, consciousness can be regarded as subjective in relation to being-in-itself, which in this regard can now be called an object. Given that this object is transcendent and thus appears to a subject, the object can be considered a phenomenon in phenomenological terms. In this phenomenological relation, subjective consciousness both interiorizes and identifies certain characteristics that derive from how the phenomenal object appears based on its being. This object is not a sum of individual qualities. Rather, it is "simply experienced [...] as having a structure" (Føllesdal 2010, 10). This means that the object is an entity that nevertheless appears as having different interrelated characteristics. Depending on how consciousness relates to this object, some of these characteristics can be experienced and thus interiorized through its sensory organs. The embodied self-consciousness can see, feel, and hear among others. Its eyes are directed toward color and shape, its ears are directed toward sound, and so on. This leads to a series of concrete appearances of the object for the subject. After careful perceptive examination, for instance, the phenomenon may appear as colored, blue, far away, polished, with a handle, and cold. When the embodied self-consciousness interacts with the thing or reflects upon its practical use, practical implications of the thing in question can be found. It may turn out to be suitable for holding liquid, or that it breaks when it falls off the table. Moreover, because all these experiences take place in larger socioculturally structured material constellations, additional information can be gathered about the phenomenon. Depending on factors like culture, conventions of language, education, level of reflection about one's consciousness of the thing, and others, a common term can be derived that describes the phenomenon as a *cup* that is used for holding warm or even hot liquids. Sartre mentions that the being of this *cup* is transphenomenal. This means that it is present in relation to other phenomena, to which the *cup* refers: it is in the kitchen, next to the coffee maker, and so on (Sartre 2021, 23). In short, it has a specific location within *hodological space*, i.e. the space of relations in which a person finds the phenomenon in relation to themselves (Sartre 2021, 415, 432). The relations between objects constitute this person's *field of equipmentality* (see section 3.2). This Heideggerian concept describes the sum of a person's practical relations to the things that a person may use as means toward their ends.[3]

---

3   What is described here in terms of material objects works in similar ways for immaterial things. For instance, in their everyday lives humans may encounter the concept of *justice*. These humans may come to know that this concept describes certain ways of distributing wealth, social benefits, opportunities, possibilities, etc. This concept comprises a somewhat fixed object area, in that it describes a very special set of practices as well as the (moral) judgement regarding actions. Owing to how it presents itself in the corresponding actions, human consciousness can reflect on what the concept means for it by singling out what character-

This process of interiorizing and identifying individual aspects of the phenomenal object is rooted in the intentional structure of being-for-itself. Sartre claims that it is impossible for the full positivity of being to be present to consciousness (Sartre 2021, 20–23). According to him, human consciousness necessarily abstracts from the full positivity of objective being. Sartre identifies this relation between for-itself and in-itself to be a negation. Human consciousness introduces nothingness into being (Sartre 2021, 58–59). No single determination ever completely captures the full, positive givenness of being; within the intentional structure of human consciousness, any determination is perspectival and one-sided. Determinations as uttered in sentences like "This thing is blue," "This thing is polished," "This thing is a cup," or "The concept of X means..." might be appropriate for specific aspects of being, but they necessarily negate or stand against, other equally suitable determinations. None of these determinations, however, exhausts the full positivity of the thing in question. At this point of the totalizing process, experience is not yet a complete totalizing synthesis. Rather, it remains an opposition between two poles—so far, there is merely the givenness of being as a material positing and its pure negation carried out by consciousness without any refined representation of meaning. This is merely the second moment of experience as dialectical totalization.

It was mentioned before that in Sartre's philosophy, meaning is neither a quality of things nor a product of pure consciousness. Rather, how things appear as objective phenomena and how subjective consciousness is directed toward them constitutes meaningful relations as such. Meaning is the product of singling out aspects of the phenomenon and thus determining what the phenomenon as a determined one means for consciousness. From the visual perception of a polished, blue, far-away thing, to its practical implementation as a suitable container for holding liquids, and then to the name *cup*—the different ways of experiencing and handling this object represent possible determinations of being-in-itself. As such, these possible determinations abstract from and thus negate the full positive givenness of being. Such determinations become meaningful in that they may correspond to the object's essence or not. For Sartre, the essence of non-human things "understood as the principle of a series, is no more than the connection between the appearances—which means it is itself an appearance" (Sartre 2021, 3). This means that phenomena in the mode of being-in-itself can be determined from the outside. Their essence is their existence. How phenomena appear implies their essence as that which is meaningful for consciousness based on the being of these phenomena. Although Sartre is not a strict essentialist who considers things to have a human-independent essence, certain things still have intrinsic features or result from constitutive processes that give

---

izes a just act and what does not. Sartre exemplifies this with the color concept *red*, which can be experienced in the ways consciousness encounters things that reflect red light in the physicochemical world (Sartre 2021, 2–3).

the things shape. Sartre's concept of *essence* is linked to the conditions of the possibility of experience, which can be found in consciousness and the materiality of being. For him, essence is the sum of possible ways of conceiving and apprehending phenomenal objects.[4]

Yet, there are no ways of conceiving an object in such an essential way unless it is determined for consciousness within human reality. Every determination of being-in-itself is simultaneously a negation of positivity and a negation of that very negation. Determining thus means abstracting from—i.e. negation—the positivity of being-in-itself by affirming—i.e. negation of the negation—the phenomenon's being as that which manifests meaning in the form of an organized totality of qualities within human reality (Sartre 2021, 6–7). Regarding the title of Sartre's first major work, phenomena can be understood as the *nothingness* of positive being for human consciousness.

In this context, the inherent dialectic of experience becomes apparent. Rather than considering meaning to be *in* things or *in* consciousness, meaning must be understood in terms of a *meaningful relation* between things and consciousness, through which respective structures of subjectivity and objectivity become what they are in the first place. Human beings have meaningful mental conceptions of things because humans impart meaning both by how they relate to things and how things appear to them based on the things' material characteristics. Within these relations, action, and experience are closely linked. According to Sartre, there is no such thing as a purely contemplative consciousness. If there were, it would fail to reveal the practical implications of objects. Such a consciousness would not be able to make a practical connection between, for instance, hammers and nails, or between the physical symptoms of a lack of water in the organism and a glass of water (Sartre 2021, 432) (see Chapter 3).

Human beings affirm both the structure of their relatedness and the way this structure corresponds to the structure of being in every one of their relations to the phenomenal world. Within the lived experience of individual human beings, a phenomenal object is a cup because this object has a material structure that appears in a certain way, so that it may be used as the thing that is known and used as a cup. In dialectical terms, such a constituted meaningful relation is the ongoing sublation of the contingency of being and the negating determinations for human consciousness. Furthermore, this meaningful relation is either pre-reflectively or reflectively interiorized by human consciousness. In this third moment of dialectical experience, the negation of negations represents an affirmation of being as a manifested

---

4   This conception is somewhat reminiscent of a variant of Peirce's *pragmatic maxim*: "Consider what effects, which might conceivably have practical bearings, we conceive the object of our conception to have. Then, our conception of these effects is the whole of our conception of the object" (Peirce 1878, 293).

meaning for consciousness. Both subject and object, human and thing, exist relative to how they relate and transcend toward each other. With this affirmation, the process of experience as totalization has resulted in both a subject-totality, an *I*, and an object-totality, a *this*.

Object-Totality and World

The dialectical totalization of subject and object occurs in every relation between humans and things. It is at once a subjectification of for-itself and an objectification of in-itself. In the act of experience, the specific subjectivity of being-for-itself is constituted within its interrelation with specific phenomenal entities as objects. In this way, both subject and object are moments of a synthesis and both are constituted as totalities. To quote Sartre's definition of a totality again:

> A totality is defined as a being which, while radically distinct from the sum of its parts, is present in its entirety, in one form or another, in each of these parts, and which relates to itself either through its relation to one or more of its parts or through its relation to the relations between all or some of them. (Sartre 1978, 45)

The dialectic of totalization outlined above now allows slightly modifying Sartre's understanding of *totality* in comparison to that of Lukács. For Sartre, *totality* is a category describing entities understood as produced through a synthetic activity, or, more precisely, as results of a totalization. They are externally organized and have meaning only within human reality. *Totality* is thus a category that is onto-phenomenological, dialectical, and material. Sartre's example is electric current. He describes it as the "collection of physicochemical actions [...] that manifest it" (Sartre 2021, 2). Comprehending electric current as a totality means uniting various manifestations, effects, and other aspects and synthesizing them in the concept of *electric current*. This concept again instantiates its aspects.

The aforementioned cup can also be understood as a totality. It is the product of a totalization of relating human consciousness manifested in a material entity. The *parts* of the cup, i.e. its color, shape, weight, and utility, are manifested in the same being. The cup is more than the mere sum of its parts; it is not only blue, far away, with a handle, and so on. Each appearance of the objective phenomenon coincides with a subjective impression throughout consciousness from which information is deduced beyond what is presented. Within human reality, the cup is also *not* red, *not* coarse, *not* close, etc. Being thus does not include its negation within itself. Rather, this negation is an abstracting capacity of human consciousness. Within cup-being, each *part* relates to other parts. The *blue* of the cup has a specific extension, human beings have a specific distance to the cup's shape and weight, and so on. All of these appearances are manifested in the same being to which a meaningful relation is constituted.[5] However, this meaning does not change the cup's being—rather, it changes how human beings relate to it. In this regard, the object-totality *cup* exists as the correlative of an act of imagination within human reality. Its ontological status is that of being-in-itself (Sartre 1978, 45).

It Is important to note that Sartre's conception of *totality* must be understood as "only a regulative principle of the totalisation" (Sartre 1978, 46). Human beings refer to things as totalities *as if* these totalities were self-contained, completed, or completely independent of human activities or purposes. Once the totalizing subjects vanish, the interiorized meaning of the object vanishes as well. In this case the totality again is "reduced to itself, it reverts to the multiplicity of inertia" (Sartre 1978, 46).

Because object totalities are constituted through how human beings relate to them in their practical lives, object totalities represent totalized byproducts of human self-totalization. Object-totalities appear in spatiotemporal relation to each other. This adds an aspect of externality both to any object-totality within the ongoing totalization of consciousness and ultimately to the unification of external object-totalities into an organized whole. This organized whole can be referred to as *world*. As such, it is the synthetic unity of a subject-totality's meaningful relations to totalities that are experienced and thus totalized as in relation to each other.

Human beings are not outside a world that they examine from afar. Rather, human existence can be grasped only as an inherently dialectical totalization of a world comprising meaningful relations with constituted totalities. Humans engage with the world based on the meaning that they confer on it through their actions, whether these actions are perceptive, reflective, or practical. In this regard, human beings constitute their world as an organized totality to encounter. Human reality is thus a practically qualified reality (Sartre 2021, 127), a totality of human-world relations. It is the product of a dialectical synthesis between the full positivity of being and the negating structure of consciousness as that which determines this sheer positive givenness. In that regard, Sartre claims that "[m]an and the world *are* relative beings, and relation *is* the principle of their being" (Sartre 2021, 415, emphasis in original). To be in-the-world is to be an embodied self in confrontation with "things-which-exist-at-a-distance-from-me" (Sartre 2021, 415).

---

5   Sartre exemplifies this relation with the taste of a lemon and that of a cake: "[T]he lemon's yellow is not a subjective mode of apprehension of the lemon: it is the lemon. And nor is it true that the object-X appears as the empty form that holds the disparate qualities together. In fact, the lemon extends throughout its qualities, and each of these qualities extends throughout each of the others. It is the lemon's acidity that is yellow, and the lemon's yellowness that is acidic; we eat the color of a cake, and the taste of that cake is the instrument that discloses its form and its color to what we may call our 'alimentary intuition' (Sartre 2021, 263).

This confrontation between human beings and the objective world is the starting point for the next section. To identify human action both as a free and materially conditioned endeavor, the existential relation between facticity and freedom is analyzed.

2.3 Action as Totalization

This section unites Sartre's early understanding of action and his later understanding of *praxis* and develops a conception of *totalizing action* as a constant mediation of the internal and external dialectic of human existence. To do so, the section builds on the previous findings and reconstructs the consummation of action as a totalizing process in which human beings realize themselves by seeking to practically attain the ends that arise from their inherent needfulness.

Human beings realize themselves through their actions the ends of which arise from certain forms of need and desire (section 1.4). These actions follow the basic principle of totalization. Similar to how consciousness abstracts from the positivity of being, thus singles out certain concrete aspects of things, and imparts meaning to them as totalities, an action abstracts from the positivity of a person's facticity as situated in a socioculturally structured material milieu, strives toward an individual project as a certain concrete possibility of a person's future self, and modifies said person's material state of things to realize this individual project. The root for this totalizing process, that engages in the external dialectic of human existence, can be found in the internal dialectic of human existence.

Human Existence Between Facticity and Freedom

According to Sartre, human existence is a lived contradiction between being-for-itself and being-in-itself, and this contradiction is the first and most fundamental moment in the totalization of human existence. It is represented by the synthetic relation between the givenness of materiality as a material positing and a negating human consciousness.

Section 2.2 already mentioned that, structurally, the being of humans is the same being as that of things—it has the same tripartite structure. According to Sartre, this means that human existence is contingent to the extent that no human being can choose the conditions of their existence before actually existing. Human beings can neither choose their place of birth, nor whether they want to be born small or tall, with blond or black hair, in France or Germany, working- or upper-class. Despite the totalizing capacity of human consciousness, no change of relation or reflection toward their being can enable humans to fly by flapping their arms or to use their lungs for breathing under water. Because human consciousness is necessarily embodied, the human condition is ineluctable and at the same time without any necessity whatsoever, because it is founded in the contingency of being. The limitations that *a priori* define the situation of human beings consist of how the being of human existence is fundamentally structured (Sartre 2021, 133–134; Sartre 2005).

However, unlike things in the mode of being-in-itself, human consciousness is relational and can never exist in full identity with its contingent being (Sartre 2021, 61). Human beings always relate to themselves and their contingency in every single intentional relation, whether pre-reflective or reflective. Consequently, every relation of human consciousness is also a self-relation (see section 2.2).

Nevertheless, Sartre claims that this relation, although a presence to being, is an empty distance. The self is a constant, albeit at times pre-reflective, relation with, and therefore determination of, itself as *manifested* in its being. In Sartre's own words, "[t]he for-itself is the being that determines itself to exist, insofar as it is unable to coincide with itself" (Sartre 2021, 128). Embodied human consciousness thus exists as a still contingent and embodied self-relation without any necessity or meaning. Section 1.4 introduced this contingency of being-for-itself as *facticity* (Sartre 2021, 133).

Facticity not only includes the human condition and the bodily limitations of birth but also one's entire past. For Sartre, "'[f]acticity' and 'the past' are two words to refer to one and the same thing" (Sartre 2021, 178). By being an empty distance to themselves, human beings simultaneously exist and do not exist as their past. On the one hand, human beings represent the living embodiment of all their past decisions and actions. Everything they did comprises their past and has led to the way their existence is structured in the present. On the other hand, human beings can never fully *be* their past in the mode of being-in-itself. Owing to the temporal structure of embodied self-consciousness, human beings necessarily relate to their decisions and actions in retrospect. This means that they always relate to themselves as past selves.

Sartre admits that a human essence can be identified in retrospect. He accepts Hegel's statement: "*Wesen ist was gewesen ist*" (Sartre 2021, 180, emphasis in original), which translates to *essence is what has been*. In Sartre's interpretation of this statement, human essence can be conceived as the whole of actions and decisions according to which human existence was structured up until the present moment in which an action may take place. This givenness of being-in-itself as human facticity is the first moment of dialectical existence. It is the positing of human existence as a material fact, an "unjustifiable *presence to the world*" (Sartre 2021, 135), that already surpasses itself toward the future.

Inseparably rooted within this facticity is the seed of its constant transformation. As embodied self-consciousness and as empty distance, human beings can never exist in the factual state of being. They cannot be reduced to their physical and social origin, their sex or gender, the living limitations of their facticity. Rather, each human being exists as a self-relational attitude toward these factors. More precisely, contingent facticity appears only as a positing with regard to this self-relational attitude.

Sartre considers this self-relational attitude to be a negation of the givenness of being. Positing through facticity, and negating through consciousness, are simultaneously given. Human existence is constantly directed toward its being without the chance to fully identify with it. In referring to their past, human beings may only understand themselves as who they were and no longer are. Any attempt to identify with this past essence is a case of what Sartre calls *bad faith*. It is a vain attempt to stop existence in a fixed state of past identity and is a denial of ontological freedom. Claiming to *be* their facticity renders human beings entities in the mode of being-in-itself, i.e. a closed and timeless totality. Such claims are tantamount to a denial of the ontological freedom of human existence (Sartre 2021, 88–89).

However, according to Sartre, humans can never truly *be*. This is rendered impossible by the structure of their self-relational consciousness. Therefore, humans are condemned to actively *become* someone or something that they are not, solely by virtue of being. In this regard, any claim to unchangeably *be* someone or something is a false belief about human freedom. Nevertheless, this false belief is necessarily a human attitude toward being in that "consciousness is what it is not and is not what it is, in its being and simultaneously" (Sartre 2021, 117).

This internal contradiction of being and consciousness, of materiality and meaning, of facticity and freedom, manifests in human existence as a *lack of being*. It is a dynamic self-relation that results in an intricate interplay of requirements, wants, wishes, emotions, moods, possibilities, and their realizations in the world through goal-directed activity—that is, through the employment of available means to attain specific ends. This lack of being, a lived simultaneity as both lacking and lacked, transcends toward completion on account of the relationship of being and consciousness (Sartre 2021, 137).

The Lack of Being Toward Completion: Needs, Desires, and Ends

The most obvious way this lack of being manifests in human existence is in the form of certain material requirements, wants, and wishes that derive from human physicality, psychology, and sociality.

Chapter 1 has already mentioned that Sartre reconceptualizes the significance of these requirements, wants, and wishes between his earlier and later works. In *Being and Nothingness*, Sartre conceptualizes them as desires (*désir*) and reflects on what it means to act in concrete action situations based on these desires. He does so by accepting the facticity of certain structures of desire in human existence (Sartre 2021, 140–143) while granting that these structures themselves are understood as socially dependent. In *Critique*, Sartre reflects on the underlying structures of these desires themselves through the concept of need (*besoin*). He does so to reveal the conditions of possibility for human action, sociality, and historical transformation. In accordance with the materialistic and Marxist focus of his later works, the later Sartre attempts to analyze the most basic relations between human organisms and their material surroundings from the perspective of *need* to incorporate the common ground of all societal classes (Cannon 1992, 133).

Sartre states that "value arrives in the world" (Sartre 2021, 147) through human existence. Through the dialectic of need and desire, human beings are disclosed as incomplete totalities that should be brought into being (Anderson 2013, 198). The process for doing so is self-totalization through action. Action thus represents a (temporal) sublation of need or desire through the practical realization of the ends that are projected toward by certain requirements, wants, and wishes. Consequently, owing to their needs and desires, human beings are directed toward completion for their own sake (Sartre 2021, 140). In so doing, they pre-reflectively and/or reflectively recognize themselves as ends in themselves (Sartre 2021, 157–159). This means that human beings either non-consciously strive toward satisfaction or consciously reflect on how to act for themselves.

Whether needs are socialized into desires through engaging with the world, or whether needs are always socialized with regard to future needs and their surroundings, in Sartre's philosophy both perspectives represent two sides of the same coin. Both must be seen in a dynamic interrelation to an agent's socioculturally and materially structured societal constellations. In such constellations, new abstract needs arise while other already concretized desires are satisfied. Human beings can have undirected feelings of physical and mental lacks that can be redirected and overwritten with other, concrete plans for action.

Still, no matter how efficiently or enduringly human beings may satisfy their needs and desires through action, they exist as an imbalance that is impossible to smooth out. Lacks of being, such as the requirement for food and water or other practical wants arise again and again, in slight variations, because the human condition is ineluctable. Consequently, the inherent contradiction at the heart of human existence can never be fully resolved. Referring to section 2.2, humans can never sublate themselves so as to exist as being-in-and-for-itself. Human reality, according to Sartre, is thus "in its nature an unhappy consciousness, without any possibility of surpassing its state of unhappiness" (Sartre 2021, 143). With regard to Hegel's concept of the *unhappy consciousness* (Hegel 1986, 163–165), Sartre emphasizes that the only constant of human existence is a constant struggle, which facilitates an equally constant change. Structurally, this constant struggle derives from the lived contradiction at the heart of human existence and grounds its fundamental needfulness. It is due to this fundamental needfulness that human existence engages the world for itself.

In *Sein und Zeit*, Heidegger interprets the fact that being-in-the-world is always engaged in the world for itself as *care* (German *Sorge*, French *souci*). According to Heidegger, being-in-the-world is always in a *movement of concern* about itself (German *Besorgen*) and others (German *Fürsorge*). Heidegger's conception of *care* is ontological. He states that *care* represents the basic state of being-in-the-world which grounds all other human modes of being. Because *care* is the state of Being of *Dasein*, humans project toward the future and act for themselves (Heidegger 2006, 191–214; Merker 2015). Sartre, however, rejects Heidegger's ontological conception of *care*. He holds that "positive terms for *Dasein* [...] disguise implicit negations" (Sartre 2021, 53, emphasis in original) that take place in human existence. This means that a conception of being-in-the-world as *care* already ontologizes and thus synthesis the lived contradiction of positing being and negating consciousness at the heart of human existence. Sartre argues, that this contradiction is irresolvable. It is what grounds the ontological freedom of human existence as the condition of possibility for agents to commence actions for themselves. Sartre does not explicitly use Heidegger's conception of *care* in his works. However, the broader scope of Heidegger's thoughts concerning this concept is implicitly there, especially in *Being and Nothingness*. It can be argued that due to Sartre's focus on the lived contradiction at the heart of human existence and the negating character of human consciousness, he is more interested in the way human needfulness affects how human beings realize themselves than he is with *care* itself.

Human beings realize themselves by relating to the world through their actions. However, to satisfy their needs and desires, not just any random action will suffice. Thirst has to be satiated by seeking, finding, and drinking water; knowledge gaps have to be filled through reflection and communication. Even moods like boredom demand some sort of change in the way people encounter the world. Sartre remarks that "need [...] is in fact the lived revelation of a goal to aim at" (Sartre 1978, 90). This means that the modes of need and desire project toward certain goals or ends. Because they demand action, needs and desires thus have a specific existential urgency. Furthermore, they also provide an outline of the course of their associated actions. Because action is thus characterized by finality, which is "causality in reverse" (Sartre 2021, 187), it is first necessary to examine the existential urgency and motivational force of needs and desires.

The early and later Sartre differ in the nature of this existential urgency. In Sartre's early works, all ends as goals of action are relative to human beings as ends in themselves. In *Being and Nothingness*, human existence is considered as always striving for self-realization. What these human beings lack through their needs and desires is themselves as satisfied selves. In Sartre's later philosophy, the fact that human beings represent ends in themselves is less prominent. It is more important here that the needs of these human beings are ineluctable. Human beings thus always have specific ends that they attempt to attain through their actions.

Ends derive their urgency from how needs and desires both pre-reflectively and/or reflectively motivate human beings to attempt to attain those ends. Pre-reflectively, needs and desires may appear as *mobiles*, a French term.[6] These are subjective facts that consist of "the collection of desires, emotions, and passions that drive me to perform a certain act" (Sartre 2021, 586), and which urge human beings to perform actions. These subjective facts include physical feelings like thirst and hunger, but also other psychic phenomena (moods or emotions) like boredom. Human beings may *fear* starving, *yearn* for affection, be *ashamed* for not knowing something, *physically require* nutrition, or simply *want* to show off. In any of these cases, needs and desires manifest in these human beings in such a way that they pre-reflectively feel the urge to engage in goal-directed activities.

Reflectively, needs and desires may appear as *motifs*, a French term that can be translated as *reasons* for action. These *motifs* must be understood more objectively as "the set of rational considerations" (Sartre 2021, 585) that justify certain acts for agents themselves. Here, Sartre has in mind a more conscious way of tackling requirements, wants, and wishes. Whereas *mobiles* belong to human passions, *motifs* belong to human will, which Sartre understands as positing itself "as a reflective decision in relation to certain ends" (Sartre 2021, 582). By virtue of their will, human beings can reflect their needs and desires rather than just being affected by them. This is due to the relation of positing being and negating consciousness.

For Sartre, an *ideal rational action* would be one "whose motives are practically non-existent and whose sole inspiration is an objective assessment of the situation" (Sartre 2021, 586). However, similar to the relation between needs and desires, a clear distinction between *mobiles* and *motifs* can hardly be made. In the same way that ends are revealed through both needs and desires, concrete *mobiles* and *motifs* that eventually lead to action must be understood as correlative (Barata 2018, 128). According to Sartre, an affective act is a "purely unreflected [i.e. pre-reflective] consciousness of its reasons, through the pure and simple project of its act" (Sartre 2021, 591), whereas a voluntary act "requires the appearance of a reflective consciousness that grasps its motive as a quasi-object" (Sartre 2021, 591). As a consequence, there can be no *ideal rational act*. Every action is structured according to a dynamic hierarchy of personal preferences, emotions, and experience and the structure of ends. What is important to note, however, is that human beings can be understood as agents through

---

6   In Barnes' English translation of *L'être et le néant*, the French terms *mobile* and *motif* are translated as *motive* and *cause* (Sartre 2003, 467). In Richmond's translation, on which the current work mainly relies, these terms are translated as *motive* and *reason*. Richmond remarks that the French terms *mobile* and *motif* represent a pair of terms in French academic discourse where *mobile* refers to subjective motivational forces and *motif* to objective motivational forces (Sartre 2021, xlix). Owing to the action-theoretical implications of terms like *cause* and *reason*, and to keep the broader distinction between subjective and objective motivational forces in mind, the original French terms are used.

how their needs and desires mobilize or motivate them to attain certain ends based on being ends in themselves.

Needs and desires and the associated *mobiles* and *motifs* can have a rather spontaneous nature. Sartre exemplifies this with regard to sexual desire in *Being and Nothingness*. He writes that "[d]esire is a lived pro-ject that does not require any preliminary deliberation; rather it carries its meaning and its interpretation within itself" (Sartre 2021, 521). The structure of this desire determines how it must be satisfied. Because humans manifest this desire, they project toward specific ends in relation to it. With other structures of need and desire, these humans would project toward different ends. An example of a less spontaneous motivation would be the recognition of a knowledge-gap. Here, knowledge is not just missing in the structure of human consciousness. With the recognition of missing knowledge, the structure of consciousness is now shown to be incomplete with regard to a certain topic. It lacks itself as a more complete consciousness of the topic in question. A person may be ashamed about this, feel a sense of competition and eagerness to learn, experience a mixture of both, or react in some other way. Nevertheless, they must actively seek knowledge by interacting with the world and with other people. This example shows that the need to know something about the world can hardly be separated from the desire to know something. The motivation is itself a merger of *mobiles* and *motifs*.

Conceptions of Action

The structure of ends, and the way they pre-reflectively and/or reflectively mobilize and motivate human beings, give a sometimes clear and sometimes obscured outline of the course an action demands to attain these ends. It was mentioned before that action is the temporal sublation of needs and desires through the practical realization of the very ends these needs and desires project toward. In *Being and Nothingness*, Sartre describes this practical realization as follows:

> to act is to modify the way the world is *figured*, to arrange the means in view of an end; it is to produce an organized, instrumental structure such that, through a series of sequences and connections, the modification brought about in one of the links brings in its wake modifications in the entire series and, in the end, produces some foreseen result [...] The point we should note at the outset is that an action is, by definition, *intentional*. (Sartre 2021, 569, emphasis in original)

According to this definition, action is an intentional process in which an agent aims to modify and thus transform their exterior material world through the production of operational chains and the arrangement of instrumental means. These agents do so to attain certain previously set interior ends. Without needs and desires, there is no *foreseen result*, i.e. no end or goal, and thus no necessity for action nor an outline of how to act to attain the end. Given that, an agent's world is a totality comprising the material structure of being and the way agents relate to it, the action to modify it cannot only be understood as physical activity. It is also any mental modification of a world-relation through reflection, consideration, or any other activity of human consciousness.

However, owing to his conception of human existence as embodied self-consciousness, there is no clear distinction between physical and mental activities in Sartre's earlier conception of action. Physical and mental activities either happen within an agent's material relation to the world or they build on this relation. In Sartre's philosophy, there are no higher-tier immediate and reflective activities without a material base. Every action is a process in which physical and mental activities are performed in correspondence with the material, social, and cultural surroundings to transform them in accordance with certain ends projected by needs and desires. On account of human existence being a mediation of both internal and external dialectics, experience and action are inherently intertwined (Bonnemann 2009, 16–17). Every action is itself a complex process of sub-actions, in which embodied self-consciousness enacts the course of action in a *series of sequences and connections* toward a projected end (see section 2.4).

In this earlier definition of action, Sartre already briefly mentions both the *arrangement of means in view of an end* and the production of an *organized, instrumental structure* through which desired effects are caused. He states that "[w]e should understand *acts* as all of a person's synthetic activity, i.e. every ordering of means in view of ends" (Sartre 2021, 233, emphasis in original). In his earlier conception, Sartre observes that human action primarily instrumentalizes various things, which are practically located in an agent's field of equipmentality (section 3.2). In this regard, all human action is mediated through matter, either through the agent's own inert body or through the inertia of material objects. This emphasis on the exteriorities of a person's action becomes more evident in his later conception of action as *praxis*.

Section 1.4 mentioned that Sartre redefines his conception of action between *Being and Nothingness* and *Critique*. In his later works, action—now understood as historical *praxis*—is defined as "an organising project which transcends material conditions towards an end and inscribes itself, through labour, in inorganic matter as a rearrangement of the practical field and a reunification of means in the light of the end" (Sartre 1978, 734). Despite the later changes, all the necessary components of Sartre's earlier conception of action can be found in his definition of *praxis*. Action remains a transformative endeavor through which agents modify their material conditions, according to their ends, through a reorganization of their field of equipmentality. However, the later Sartre adds the fact that such an action leaves material traces both in an agent's material surroundings and in their bodily inertia.

Sartre's conception of *instrumentalization* can be derived from his earlier and later conceptions of action. As briefly mentioned in section 1.4, Sartre claims that every action is "primarily an instrumentalisation [French *instrumentalisation*] of material reality" (Sartre 1978, 161; Sartre 1960, 231). Given Sartre's materialist focus (see section 1.4), every action is understood as a relation between material agents and the material world. An agent's ends result from the intention to attain their needs and desires relative to themselves as ends in themselves. Consequently, agents use material things, such as their bodies or instrumental means, to act on matter. Accordingly, instrumentalization means the purposeful unification of matter by, through, and, most essentially, for the agents themselves. How actions are mediated through the body or instrumental means directs the somewhat abstract and theoretical course of action into concrete paths. It thus changes the way agents encounter the world. It also changes how needs and desires project toward certain ends, and how the world appears to these agents based on those ends.

From Sartre's action concepts, it follows that action is itself a complex totalizing endeavor. It is a complex existential engagement with the world that unites physical and mental aspects by causing certain effects through instrumental means to transform the world according to certain ends. This causation necessarily has a temporal course that can be understood as a practical transition from a present lacking to a future satisfied state of things, abstractly determined by an intended end.

Freedom

Disregarding whether needs and desires are more subjective, emotional, and affective *mobiles*, more objective, consciously reflected and volitional *motifs*, or something in between, they project toward ends. With this in mind, it could be argued that agents are materialistically determined by how forms of need and desire consciously or non-consciously cause these agents to attempt to perform goal-directed activities, according to Sartre. However, the opposite is true. Sartre is neither a determinist, a compatibilist, nor a libertarian with regard to the freedom of agents. Barata mentions that for Sartre "freedom as an ontological concept is rather removed from the idea of free will. Consciousness is free regardless of human will. Freedom is a transcendental condition for conscious being" (Barata 2018, 126) (see section 1.2). According to Sartre, this ontological *freedom of the acting being* represents the first express condition that must be given so that human behavior can be identified as an action (Sartre 2021, 570).

Even though human life is inevitably grounded in its past and its bodily and social limitations, it is a *relation to itself*. Agents only recognize themselves in this self-relation; if not as originators, then as authors of their existence. This is the source of the ontological freedom of human existence. Sartre himself emphasizes this by distinguishing his *technical and philosophical* concept of freedom from what he calls the *empirical and popular* concept of freedom. He says that "'to be free' does not mean 'to obtain what one wanted' but 'to be determined in one's wanting' (in the broad sense of 'choosing') by oneself" (Sartre 2021, 631). Sartre advocates for a freedom that is synonymous with the *autonomy of choice* regarding a resisting world (Sartre 2021, 631).

Existence is not a mechanical process. Needs and desires do not force agents to satisfy them, and they do not make agents behave like automatons. Rather, needs and desires have a revealing function in that they project toward what agents require, want, or wish for themselves. According to Sartre, whether agents act passionately or out of will is itself a matter of choice, which is taken through action based on ontologically free existence. Only after attempting to perform certain actions can agents know whether *mobiles* or *motifs* had more motivational force with regard to their ends. It is also only after action is taken that agents know whether they realized the intended ends or not. Nonetheless, whatever agents realized or did not realize, the product of their action belongs to their facticity. This is because agents already surpass the result of their actions toward themselves in the future. Nothing can mechanically determine them to act again in the same way because their negating consciousness is characterized by its *relation to* and not its *identity with* being. Human freedom is as such not the freedom of will, but the condition of possibility for agents to commence actions for themselves. Freedom is thus identical with existence, in that it is "the foundation of the ends that I will try to accomplish either through my will or through my impassioned efforts" (Sartre 2021, 583).

Intention

Regarding this first condition, every goal-directed activity, whether passionate or volitional, must be understood as intentional, because the agent's "intention, by choosing the end that announces it, makes itself be" (Sartre 2021, 623). In the very instant in which ends are given as goals for actions, the intention is also given to attain these ends against the backdrop of human existence. Sartre believes that ends are "state[s] *of* the world to be obtained, and not already in existence" (Sartre 2021, 624, emphasis in original). However, with regard to the intention of action, projected ends and intended actions have to be distinguished from ends realized through action.

The ends that agents initially strive toward, and the intention to perform these actions, do not depend on their actual realization. Sartre claims that "since any choice [to act emotionally or willingly] is identical to some *doing*, it presupposes, in order for it to be distinct from a dream or a wish, that its actualization has begun" (Sartre 2021, 631, emphasis in original). Intentions are thus relative to human existence as self-totalization, i.e. self-realization through action. Sartre exemplifies this with the relation between an *attempted* meal and *actually* eating the meal. He states:

my *end* may be a good meal, if I am hungry. But this meal, projected […] can only be grasped as the correlative of my […] project toward my own possibility of eating this meal. In this way, through its twofold but unitary arising, the intention lights up the world on the basis of an end that does not yet exist and which defines itself through the choice of its possible. My end is a specific objective state of the world, and my possible is a specific structure of my subjectivity. (Sartre 2021, 624, emphasis in original)

Both projected ends and realized ends are relative to their possible realization. Here, Sartre seems to borrow from Hegel's conception of action. *Subjective* or *abstract* ends and the associated *intended* actions must be distinguished from *objective* or *concrete* ends and the actual, *realized* actions themselves. This means that intended ends, as abstract ends, are relative to their possible attainability as concrete ends. Furthermore, intended actions are relative to their possible realizability as realized actions (Hubig 2006, 125–135).

Applied to Sartre's conception of intention, ends are the traces of an agent's intentions; this, in Sartre's case, means that both ends and intentions are correlative. This connection again illustrates Sartre's dialectical conception of human existence. The positing of contingent facticity is negated by consciousness. Agents thus exist as an ontologically free synthetic unity of being and nothingness. This unity manifests as a lack of being in the form of needs and desires, which again project toward ends and the associated actions to attain them. These ends exist based on agents who are both the ones needy and/or desiring and the ones intentionally striving toward satisfaction.

Sartre's second express condition for action—the *intention of action*—is seen here. Ends imply the intention to attempt to attain them (Sartre 2021, 573).

Sartre's conception of the dialectical interplay of needs, desires, requirements, wants, wishes, *mobiles*, *motifs*, actions, and ends, in connection to the *freedom of the acting being* and the *intention of action*, has enough explanatory strength to illuminate the whole spectrum of intriguing and contradictory aspects of human life. It allows one to conceive human existence as self-preservation because it illustrates how needs and desires motivate human beings to attempt to exteriorize their interior intentions by performing certain actions. It also explains instances in which agents can directly act against their self-preserving impulses. They can willingly stare into the sun, for instance, or sacrifice their lives for others. Sartre's thoughts also highlight indeterminate areas of human action and intention. Although agents want something and could possibly attain it, they can still reflect on their actions and decide not to. A problematic point here, though, is the fact that the ontological freedom of human existence is not always congruent with how agents experience and even recognize themselves as free. In more concrete terms, the problem boils down to the fact that agents sometimes feel forced to do something, or they believe they lack alternative options for action. This feeling relates to an agent's aware-ness regarding the situatedness of their actions and the nature of their situation. This conjunction—between what is objectively given and how this given is subjec-tively and socioculturally structured and interiorized—will be further investigated throughout this work.

Sartre's first express condition, *freedom of the acting being*, was shown to be the fundamental condition of the possibility of action. The second express condition, the *intention of acting*, is necessarily given as an outcome of his first condition. Action is not a determined or purely material process but an intentional and goal-oriented engagement with the world.

The Lacking State of Things

When agents intentionally attempt to attain the ends that their needs and desires project toward, they transform how they totalize themselves and the world. In this context, needs, desires, and the associated ends must not only be understood as pure self-relations; they must also be taken as totalizing relations between agents and the larger societal constellations they are situated in. Sartre states that

> need is a link of *univocal immanence* with surrounding materiality in so far as the or-ganism *tries to sustain itself* with it; it is already totalising [...] for it is nothing other than the living totality, manifesting itself as a totality and revealing the material environment [...] as the total field of possibilities of satisfaction. (Sartre 1978, 80, emphasis in original)

By intending to practically attain the ends toward which needs and desires project, agents mentally anticipate the world-directed action through which they may re-alize themselves as satisfied selves. In this regard, the intention itself already rep-resents a totalizing relation with the world. In the course of action, the agents' in-tention to act for themselves constitutes these agents as fixed entities in relation to their world as their objective counterpart. This relation subjectifies these agents as needy or desiring in a specific way, with the intention to satisfy their requirements, wants, and wishes in relation to the world. At the same time, the world as totality, i.e. as synthetic unity of an agent's subjective relations to object-totalities, is objec-tified and thus determined as a specific *lacking state of things*. In this way, agents dis-cover themselves to be in a state of *exigency*,[7] which requires action to be transformed

---

7   In *Critique*, Sartre uses the term *exigency* in two distinct ways. First, it can refer to entities and
     actions that are needed, desired, demanded, required, or must otherwise be taken care of
     as result of situational factors. When thirsty, for instance, water represents an exigency. In
     case of fire, both a fire extinguisher and the fire itself represent exigencies. Second, exigency
     can also refer to a certain needy, desiring, demanding, or requiring state in which human

(Sartre 1978, 165). This state of exigency represents the external correlate of the existential urgency of human existence that was mentioned above. For these agents, their world, as a meaningful totality of material things and subjective relations, represents a concrete lacking state of things regarding the satisfaction of their needs and desires (Sartre 1978, 90).

This *discovery of the world as a lacking state of things* represents the third express condition of action. However, neither agents nor the world alone constitute this state. Rather, the world's meaning is theoretically transformed through the agent's intention to attain their ends. This also means that needs and desires only generate their motivational force in relation to the agents' world.

The Practical Field of Possibilities

Correlatively, through the revelation of ends, the world as "surrounding matter is endowed with a passive unity" (Sartre 1978, 81) in which agents seek to find potential sources of satisfaction. Without any intention to attain ends, the world (as a totality of object-totalities and subjective relations) appears in-itself as structured by being. Agents impose meaning on it by how they practically relate to and thus totalize being (see section 2.2). However, the way this totalization occurs is transformed through ends. Depending on the concrete structures of need and desire, an artifact is totalized as a water fountain, which, for instance, may appear as a potential water source, a potential place to sit and rest, a potential landmark to use as orientation for a city trip, and so on.

Through needs and desires, agents interiorize their exterior surroundings as a practical field of possibilities for their attempted actions (Sartre 1978, 71). These surroundings become a "practical field with a quasi-synthetic unity" (Sartre 1978, 90) that serves as the foundation and mediating milieu of possible satisfaction. Although the water fountain or any other thing affords to be used in a certain way, the possibility of this specific use arises from how agents interiorize the exterior world through their needs, desires, and ends. Sartre explicates what this means in an analogy. He mentions that

> [t]he possibility of being stopped by a fold in the carpet belongs neither to the rolling marble nor to the carpet: it can arise only within a system in which the marble and the carpet are organized by a being who has an understanding of the possibles. But this understanding cannot come from *outside*, from the in-itself, and it cannot be limited to being only a thought, as a subjective mode of conscious-

---

beings and non-human entities find themselves. In both cases, exigencies point to the fact that urgent action is required to transform the situation in which they arise.

ness: it must coincide with the objective structure of the being who understands possibles. (Sartre 2021, 155, emphasis in original)

Agents intend to perform actions based on how their needs and desires project toward their ends; once again, this transforms their world so that they apprehend it as both exigency and as a practical field of possibility for their actions against the background of the world's materiality. Hence it becomes clear that agents are neither the sole originators of their actions nor are they the originators of the specific structure of their ends. Their mediating milieu and the things within it do not play this role alone either. Instead, both agent and milieu constitute and possibilize each other. They do so within the totalizing interrelation of projected, attainable ends, in relation to available means in the practical field of possibilities, based on surrounding materiality.

The ends that agents seek to attain, the needs and desires that project toward these ends, the course of associated actions to satisfy these needs and desires, the relation between agents and the world as an exigency, and the apprehension of the world as a practical field in which agents may realize themselves by realizing their actions, are all direct outcomes of human existence as an ongoing, materially dependent process of totalization. In the course of this totalization, agents unify vastly different yet interrelated material, social, and cultural factors for and through themselves. Through their interior physical and psychological urges, convictions, and expectations, agents are ready to act to tend to whatever they require, want, or wish for themselves. In getting or being ready, agents already totalize their world as a state of exigency, because it is the very world in which these agents manifest as requiring, wanting, or wishing.

Simultaneously, these agents interiorize the world as a practical field of possibilities to tend to their lacks of being. Although the agents may be the ones who initiate the associated actions to tend to these lacks, the lacks themselves, as well as their satisfaction and the specific structure of their ends, determine the course of actions in the form of practical constraints and physical or mental stimuli. As a consequence, action-specific possibilities become objective realities that affirm the agent's surroundings to be the whole of the conditions necessary for action. In this way, contingent being first becomes the agent's possibility, and then the necessary presupposition for their intended actions. Action is, therefore, an active, practical, and transformative engagement with the world, as well as the recognition of the world as the necessary horizon of action. The actual action, as the practical realization of the intended and anticipated result, is thus a totalization that then "*practically* makes the environment into a totality*" (Sartre 1978, 85, emphasis in original). Given that human beings exist as material entities within a physicochemical universe, this practical realization necessarily involves their bodily inertia as a material mediator.

Corporeal Inertia and Materiality

Sartre assigns a central position to the human body in action. According to Sartre, human existence is the practical, spatiotemporal perpetuation of a self-totalizing synthetic unity, i.e. a totality of body and consciousness. Human beings are not fleeting, abstract existences but material entities, *sectors of materiality* in an exterior relation to other material entities (Sartre 1978, 95). Self-totalization takes place in goal-directed and thus intentional engagement with the world based on bodily materiality.

Needs and desires manifest in human existence based on the human body and must be engaged through more or less intense interaction with the world's materiality. Basic physical requirements like hunger, thirst, or safety translate into abstract needs for food, water, or shelter, and then into concrete desires for a piece of bread, a glass of lemonade, or a warm room. How agents interiorize the world as a practical field of possibilities depends on how their physicochemical surroundings are equipped.

Especially in the case of physical requirements, the "living body [*corps vivant*] is [...] *in danger* in the universe, and the universe harbours the possibility of the *non-being* of the organism" (Sartre 1978, 81–82, emphasis in original; Sartre 1960, 167). As a consequence, agents always encounter nature in a humanized form as a *false organism* (Sartre 1978, 81), i.e. as synthetic world-totality, that is revealed as either abundant or scarce regarding certain needs and desires. The world is thus structured according to the agents' practical field of possibilities (see section 4.2). In this regard, material agents are subject to all the forces that govern the physicochemical universe.

Sartre believes that the human body is the very medium through which agents interface with their surrounding materiality. Through their bodily actions, agents totalize themselves in their interrelation with matter. They do so in virtue of their bodily inertia, which is *used* "to overcome the inertia of things" (Sartre 1978, 82), and to cause modifications so that desired effects (and, necessarily, side effects) may be caused. Agents thus actively mediate between the present exigent material state and the future satisfying one. Sartre argues that:

> The man of need is an organic totality [...] [that] acts on inert bodies through the medium of the inert body *which it is* and which it *makes itself*. It *is inert* in as much as it is already subjected to all the physical forces which reveal it to itself as pure passivity; it *makes itself* inert in its being in so far as it is only externally and through inertia itself that a body can act on another body in the milieu of exteriority. (Sartre 1978, 82, emphasis in original)

Their bodily inertia not only renders agents "visible, tangible and audible, such that we exist for others" (Crossley 2010, 215), but it also enables them to see, feel, hear, and communicate with others. In short, it allows them to *modify how the world is figured* based on situational factors, and thus mediate between present and future. Sartre mentions that human beings exteriorize their interiority into the materiality of the world in the course of their actions. Matter, in this regard, is ambivalent in this practical interrelation. It supports and necessarily constrains human action at the same time (Hartmann 1966, 98). Sartre states that

> [w]ithin praxis [...] there is a dialectical movement and dialectical relation between action as the negation of matter (in its present organisation and on the basis of a future re-organisation), and matter, as the real, *docile* support of the developing re-organisation, as the negation of action. (Sartre 1978, 159, emphasis in original)

Because they must abide by exterior forces, principles, and laws of nature, agents can be efficacious in acting through and for themselves as an inert medium. Their situated actions represent the intentional negation of their needs and desires, as well as the practical transcending of a present exigent state of the world toward a future satisfying state through material transformation and re-organization. The human body reflects light for others to see, and when agents see in return, reflected light enters their eyes. There it stimulates light-sensitive neurons in the retina, which then transmit the signals through the optic nerve and to the brain to be processed and interpreted. Because of this process, agents can see the phenomenal world and give meaning to it. They use their hands to grasp things, manipulate levers, push buttons, and work with tools. Agents sit in their cars and push the pedals with their feet while manipulating the steering wheel to keep the car on track. Other actions, such as drinking, are relations between agents as biological organisms and concrete organizations of matter in the form of water. Agents reach for a glass or form a bowl with their hands, bent toward the water source; they fill their vessel and guide it to their mouth to quench their thirst. In this way, agents use their inert bodies either to grasp a thing or to become a vessel themselves.

Bodily movement occurs through a combination of shifting one's weight, moving the legs, and creating friction between feet and ground. Another example is spoken language. Seen against the background of materiality, it is a direct and guided manipulation of air pressure as a result of a complex interplay between the lungs, diaphragm, vocal tract, and various parts of the brain to create specific sounds. These sounds are inert language, traveling in the medium of air through which they are received by the ears of other people before being transduced into electric signals. These are transmitted through nerves to the brain, then interpreted and comprehended as a means of communication. This engagement with materiality through the body also includes mental processes. Thinking, for instance, takes place within the central nervous system of a human being who interprets themselves and the world based on their embeddedness within larger societal constellations. In connection to Sartre's understanding of instrumentalization, the human body represents a *tool* (French *outil*) (Sartre 1943, 360; Sartre 1960, 167; Sartre 1978, 82; Sartre 2021, 434) that is instrumentalized as a means to certain ends based on an agent as an end in themselves (see section 3.2).

In the context of the human body, the term *inertia* suggests that the body does not change its inherent features when it interacts with matter through action. Although repeated interactions may leave hands callous or backs bent, the human body is fit with a relatively high structural integrity and plasticity to withstand intense forces. In this regard, inertia must be understood as positive passivity in terms of material stability, durability, and permanence when facing outside forces (Hartmann 1966, 100). A similar approach can be found in James' thoughts about the plasticity of inert material objects and the central nervous system in terms of habit formation. He states: "*Plasticity* [...] in the wide sense of the word, means the possession of a structure weak enough to yield to an influence, but strong enough not to yield all at once" (James 1890, 105, emphasis in original).

Human beings act on the inertia of their material surroundings inasmuch as this inertia works on them. In the course of their material lives, their material surroundings slowly but steadily take the shape of their practical effects and products and thus of themselves. This materiality bears a human mark because humans are the medium that modified it (Hubig 2006, 128). At the same time, these humans bear the mark of the world. They materially adapt to repeated interactions through growing muscles, muscle memory, and calloused hands. They also develop certain bodily skills and mental routines as action dispositions by interiorizing their use of certain objects in the form of *hexis* (see section 4.5). To frame this in more Sartrean terms, the human being-in-the-world is the product of its mutually consumptive, material interrelation with the material things it instrumentalizes and thus appropriates for itself within its bodily inertia.

The Dialectical Course of Action

To bring Sartre's thoughts on action into a unified form it can be exemplified and generalized how the motivational role of needs and desires, the ontological freedom and intentional goal-directedness of agents, their specific experience of the state of the physicochemical surroundings in the outset of action, and these agents' corporeality all interplay in the course of action.

Chapter 1 already introduced Sartre's example of how thirst arises within the human organism and the concomitant actions to satiate this thirst. This is a fitting example in that it allows one to very generally depict how a concrete need and a potential action to satisfy it arise in the totalizing mediation of the internal and external dialectic of human existence. A human organism's biological requirement for water makes itself known through a series of interior physical symptoms. These symptoms represent positings of being qua the human organism as a material entity. These positings are given owing to the interior processes of human physicality. Simultaneously, because these symptoms manifest within humans' physicality, these humans necessarily relate to their symptoms owing to the ontological freedom at the heart of human existence. Such a relating can take place either pre-reflectively—by recognizing unpleasant feelings or lust for water—or reflectively—by identifying their symptoms as a lack of water in their body. Either way, to a dialectical understanding, in striving toward satisfaction for themselves, a person negates the posited givenness of their lack of being by transcending the current state of their self toward a future self that is free of these physical symptoms. Their interior lack of being mobilizes or motivates these people to exteriorize themselves by engaging their material exteriority. In this way, requiring organisms totalize themselves as thirsty and potentially acting subjects. These subjects relate to their physicochemical surroundings with the intention to satiate their lack of water by exteriorizing their intention through realizing it in the course of action.

However, it is not only these agents that are in the process of totalization. In relating to their exterior milieu (Sartre 1978, 82), some of the material properties and characteristics of this milieu, including the material entities within it, are again dialectically interiorized. Similar to the interior physical symptoms of thirst, the physicochemical surroundings are posited as a materially exterior fact based on being for these potential agents. Upon interiorizing the properties of the physicochemical surroundings, the intention to satiate their thirst represents a negation of the positing of these properties and characteristics. Their material surroundings are thus also enveloped in a totalizing process. With the lack of water and the intention to attempt to satiate that lack of water, agents totalize themselves and their surroundings as an exigent, lacking state of things that already projects toward, and thus posits, a future state of things in which these agents are potentially satisfied. Their world is thus relative to the structure of those requirements, wants, and wishes in virtue of which agents have become engaged in it and in which they *seek their being* by acting with and through it (Sartre 1978, 81). Consequently, the lack of being that manifests itself in needs and desires is not just a mere negation of posited interiorities of being; rather, it represents a negation of the negation as it expresses itself as a commitment to dissolve itself (Sartre 1978, 83). It reveals an agent's surrounding as their practical field of possibilities that serves as a mediating milieu through which they can act for themselves as ends in themselves (Sartre 1978, 90).

Through this revelation, a water fountain or a glass of water become instrumental means because their material features enable them to be instrumentalized as potential sources of satisfaction. It must be noted that the concrete structures of subjectivity and objectivity of both agents and their surroundings are relative to each other through the concrete end of getting water, which itself arises in this concrete form within the interrelation between the two. Both their concrete subjectivity and objectivity would be structured differently if the lack of being were, for instance, a lack of food, information, or a place to sleep. Within each course of action, the concrete shape of subjectivity and objectivity depends both on the interplay between how needs and desires project agents toward ends and on what the surroundings offer those agents.

Thirst, in this regard, only ever arises as a need in the form of a *besoin* in an infant state (see section 1.4). An infant's need for nourishment is not essentially determined to be satiated by their mother's breastmilk alone. When the infant's mother's milk, for whatever reason, is not available, the infant can be nourished by other people who are capable of breastfeeding, by a bottle, or by other means. In this understanding, the infants' thirst expresses itself in an abstract and undirected mode of relating to their physicochemical surroundings. They cry and struggle because they feel thirsty. When their abstract thirst as *besoin* is repeatedly satiated in certain ways by a caregiver, infants become familiar with these strategies and cultivate certain individual preferences in interrelation with the forms of societal constellation they situate themselves in through their actions. After that, thirst arises as a desire in the form of a *désir* and this desire represents the synthesis of physical symptoms and a longing for something that satisfies them.

At this point, however, there is merely the intention to act and a fuzzy outline of a course of action, not the actual realization of an intention through concrete action itself. Consequently, to actually realize an intention to act, an agent must manipulate matter "through the medium of the inert body *which it is* and which it *makes itself*" (Sartre 1978, 82, emphasis in original).

By crying, asking for water, accessing a water fountain, throwing coins into a vending machine to buy a bottle of water, or turning faucets to fill glasses—and, finally, by drinking something—agents materially transform their exigent state of the world into a potentially satisfying state. In so doing, agents again exteriorize their formerly interiorized relation to the world as a transient state based on their needs and/or desires. They thus *practically make their surrounding materiality into a totality* (Sartre 1978, 85). Exteriorizing interiorities by realizing intended ends necessarily transforms the structure of those ends in relation to the material properties and characteristics of the physicochemical surroundings.

The transformed state of things in which agents find themselves represents a practical sublation in the dialectical course of action. This means that the antecedently posited state of things is simultaneously overcome and contained by being practically transcended and elevated in relation to the actually realized state of things. As such, it represents another positing qua being in matter for the agents to re-interiorize.

This re-interiorization is necessary for several reasons. It allows one to recognize whether an action was realized in the exterior world in the first place and whether this action has actually yielded intended or unintended results. Building on this, the assessment also allows for an identification of the degree to which the realized action corresponds to the agent's intentions, satisfies their requirements, wants, and wishes, and thus sublates their needs and desires. Furthermore, the assessment allows one to analyze how the practical realization of intended ends in the course of action was shaped by sociocultural and material factors, such as social norms or values, instrumental means, body techniques, or *hexeis* (see sections 3.2, 4.3, and 4.5). By re-interiorizing the material modifications they have caused, agents can reflectively or pre-reflectively compare their *outset* of action with their *endpoint* of action, so to speak. They may, for instance, still feel thirsty and desire more water or a different drink, or even learn that they have flooded their kitchen while drinking water, which affords them the opportunity to clean it up, and so on. In this regard, re-interiorizing the modifications they have caused in their surrounding socioculturally structured materiality represents another positing from which other actions may ensue. It must be noted that this practical sublation is only temporal. As *unhappy* and *embodied consciousness*, other requirements, wants, and wishes necessarily arise in the course of human existence.

2.4 Existence as Praxis-Process

From the unified account of action in Sartre's philosophy developed throughout this chapter, two findings can be derived. First, every action takes place as a practical interrelation between a human being and their socioculturally structured material surroundings as a mediating milieu. Second, every action follows its dialectical circularity, from positing through the course of realizing action and then again to another positing.

This section extends these two findings by outlining Sartre's thoughts about the duality of action and situation, as well as by representing individual action situations as moments within a larger conception of human existence as a *praxis*-process.

Action and Situation

According to Sartre, the practical totality of all meaningful factors that condition the entire course of action comprise the *situation* of this action. Although Sartre struggles to give a clear definition of the *situation*, he describes it rather poetically as follows:

> The situation is the subject in his entirety (it is *nothing* other than his situation) and it is also the 'thing' in its entirety (*there* is never anything more than the things). It is, if you like, the subject lighting things up through his very surpassing—or it is

things sending back to the subject his image. (Sartre 2021, 713, emphasis in original)

Every action situation consists of the givenness of being, certain entities with practical significance, the ontologically free agents themselves, their needs, desires, and intentions, realized objective ends, and the recognition of potential differences between subjective and objective ends—through which agents become aware of their actions' quality.

A situation is thus a totality of totalities (subject-totality, object-totality, world-totality) that is continuously constituted and theoretically synthesized by an agent's intentions. Furthermore, a situation is practically realized through actions in which agents simultaneously realize themselves as *in* and *beyond* the situation. The situation is neither purely subjective, as "the sum nor the unity of the *impressions* that things make on us" (Sartre 2021, 712, emphasis in original), nor is it purely objective "in the sense of a pure given which the subject could observe without being in any way committed within the system thereby constituted" (Sartre 2021, 712). The whole facticity of human existence, the place of birth, all actions taken so far, past decisions, the current position that agents adopt in societal constellations—all are contained in the situation that agents realize through their concrete totalizing actions. At the same time, the concrete meaning of the existence of these agents is derived from the constant confrontation between them and the conditions of their situation.

The dialectical constitutiveness of the action situation is at the same time a requirement and the product of human actions. Sartre mentions that

we are thrown into the world at every moment, and committed within it. We act, therefore, before we have posited our possibles, and these possibles—which are revealed as having been actualized, or as in the process of being actualized—direct us to meaning that can be called into question only by some special action. (Sartre 2021, 77)

The concrete action situation is dialectically posited by the action performed to surpass, modify, and thus negate the current situation itself (Bourdieu 1977, 74). Action and situation are mutually affirmed in the course of being realized.

Situated action is thus the goal-directed and intentional mediating activity of an ontologically free agent, in which the agent dialectically totalizes both themselves, as a practical totality in relation to the world, and the world, as a practical totality in relation to themselves. The agent does so by modifying the present, lacking state of the world through future-oriented use of means into a (temporarily) satisfying state that is roughly outlined according to certain ends. These ends arise by how the agent's needs and desires, in relation to the agent's material surroundings, affect how the agent interiorizes these surroundings as a world, as an exigency, and as a practical field. In short, situated action is the active, material negation of a materially posited and socioculturally structured state of the world, which is perceived as insufficient and exigent, toward a state of the world that was previously projected as satisfactory. Within this course of action, the agent as subject-totality, the utilized means as object-totalities, and the world as a totality are sublated in the totality of the situation. This means that all of these present totalities are simultaneously contained in the course of being transcended through the active, transformative engagement toward a different future state of materiality.

Situated action is a free engagement. Although ends are posited through needs and desires based on material or immaterial requirements, wants, and wishes, agents can neither be fully determined by these needs and desires nor by their material facticity. Human existence is a self-relational attitude toward these factors. It is only in the becoming of existence that these factors are qualified by how agents realize their possibilities. Sartre advocates that the freedom of human existence has to be understood not as a negative freedom *from* the limitations of being and materiality, but as an ontological freedom *despite, because, with*, and *against* these limitations and the self-relational structure of embodied self-consciousness.

Enacting Existence and World

Although Sartre uses the term *inertia* to refer to the human body as a material entity, it is not the case that actions have a straight trajectory and that agents *push*, so to say, their inert body so that it performs the act. The examples above show that, although only implicitly explained in Sartre's philosophy, what are considered to be singular actions must rather be considered more complex spatiotemporal relations of active totalizations within totalizations. Embodied consciousness, needs and desires, intention, ends, material entities, and the world as a totality do vaguely outline the course of action. However, at its most basic level, the exact course of action—the exact activity of an agent's muscles, the loudness of their voice, or how hard they have to push buttons, hit nails, and slam brake pedals—can only be known against the background of an agent's project. According to Sartre, "we cannot conceive of the for-itself possessing the slightest possibility of any thematic prediction [...] unless it is the being that, on the basis of its future, returns to itself, the being that makes itself exist as having its being outside itself, in the future" (Sartre 2021, 186).

Sartre's example involves actions during a tennis game. Here, each movement and position become meaningful in anticipation of the next one, all undertaken to hit a tennis ball with a racket. According to Sartre, there neither is a "clear representation" of each movement nor a "firm resolution" to exactly accomplish it. There is only the "future movement which, without even being thematically presented, turns backward to the positions I adopt, in order to illuminate, to connect and to modify them" (Sartre 2021, 186). An action situation like *playing tennis* is not posited in its entirety by reflective consciousness nor performed by pushing the inert body alongside a prefabricated course of action toward the desired end.

Rather, the course of actions and the concomitant totalization of the action situation must be understood as an active mediation that is enacted, each step of the way, by the constant adaptive, interactive, self-totalizing world-engagement of an inert material entity. In the tennis game example, this engagement involves the player, the tennis racket, the tennis ball, the court, the net, the competitor (and the player's relation to the competitor), whether the agents want to win or just have fun, the weather, the rules of the game, etc. Each positional change, as well as each exchange of the ball and each of the competitor's movements, alter the player's embodied relations to the material world, and thus the meaning each player gives to the overall situation.

Consequently, players adapt all further movements and positions according to what their finality roughly projects them toward—in this case, hitting the ball. In every action, "the meaning of my [acts of] consciousness is always at a distance, over there, outside" (Sartre 2021, 186).[8] Although what happens on the tennis court happens only as a result of the player's intentional directedness toward the world—maybe they play for fun or the win—the overall, concrete course of situated action first emerges from the player's mediating transformation.

In this regard, the course of situated action is the synthetic unity of various material entities that occupy a specific space in the player agent's organized practical field of possibilities; the unity also includes the meaning these agents give these entities, irrespective of a pre-reflective or reflective engagement. Against the background of an agent's embodied interrelation with the world, situated action must thus be understood as initiated—either through will or passion—by the agents' intention to attain their ends. These ends are a result of the agents themselves being needy/desiring in relation to the world. The exact course of action, although vaguely outlined by ends and the world as an exigent practical field of possibilities, is enacted by adapting each movement, position, and action in correspondence to the larger roughly outlined course of action, as well as to the feedback agents get through their intentional relation with the supporting and constraining entities in their practical field. Situated actions, like hitting a ball with a racket, drinking water, or telling a friend to reserve a table, comprise subactions in which agents make slight adaptations according to their altered situation. These subactions are again smaller-scale interrelations between themselves and the world, through which the whole action is enacted and possibilized.

Especially regarding situated action based on needs and desires, Ally connects Sartre's views on the body in action to biological theories of *autopoietic systems*. He

---

8   The square brackets are in the original source and were not added by the author.

quotes the following passage from Sartre's unfinished manuscript of part II of *Critique of Dialectical Reason*:

> For the organism, unity is actually the perpetual restoration of unity. From this viewpoint, there is no difference between its synthetic reality—as a consistency at the heart of temporalizations of envelopment—and the accomplishment of functions: eating to live, and living to eat, are one and the same thing. For unity manifests itself as the totalization of the functions that preserve it. These functions, moreover, ceaselessly turn back upon themselves in a circularity that is only the first temporalization of permanence, since their tasks are always similar and always conditioned by the same 'feedback'. (Sartre 1991, 344–345)

In this sense, embodied needs and desires, as well as an agent's ongoing adaptation to situational factors, reaffirm Sartre's theoretical considerations about the impossibility of fully being-in-and-for-itself (see section 2.3). By virtue of being a synthetic unity of self-consciousness and body, human existence necessarily is a totalization in progress, not a totality (Ally 2017, 445). In a human's corporeal existence, situated and goal-directed action is the active maintenance and preservation of itself as a physicochemical, organic, social, and cultural unity, through its inertial progression in a materially mediating milieu.

The constant and dynamic totalizing flow that is human existence necessarily becomes inert in the concrete course of situated actions to be efficacious. Agents are the adaptation to changing situational factors. They enact their possibilities through their very actions. In reciprocity with their milieu, agents *possibilize* their existence by realizing themselves. In doing so, agents disclose and thus synthesize their milieu as a practical field through their practical engagement (Sartre 2021, 158).

Sartre strikingly summarizes the dialectical interplay of needs, desires, and ends, as well as the existential urgency for action arising from human materiality within a mediating milieu, in the following passage:

> [M]an is a material being set in a material world; he wants to change the world which crushes him, that is, to act on the world of materiality through the mediation of matter and hence to change himself. His constant search is for a different *arrangement* of the universe, and a different statute for man; and in terms of this new order he is able to define himself as *the Other whom he will become*. Thus he constantly makes himself the instrument, the means, of this future statute which will realise him as other; and it is impossible for him to treat his own present as an end. In other words, man as the future of man is the regulative schema of every undertaking, but the end is always a remoulding of the material order which *by itself* will make man possible. (Sartre 1978, 112, emphasis in original)

The *regulative schema* of human existence, as a constant undertaking, is an agent's future self. Because human actions are mediated by socioculturally conditioned materiality, and because the effects of this mediation are "embodied and manifested in the *actual* and particular art" (Sartre 2021, 675, emphasis in original) of the situated selves of agents, the *practical* realization of this regulative schema is based on the constitutive principles of human becoming.

In this regard, human existence does not just become comprehensible as a constant totalization. Each situated action can also be understood as a singular, structural moment of this totalization. Consequently, human existence can itself be understood either in its processing as a whole or with regard to the situated actions that, as structural moments, represent totalizations themselves. Sartre states that

> we can understand any common *praxis* because we are always an organic individuality which realises a common individual: to exist, to act and to comprehend are one and the same. This reveals a schema of universality which we can call constituted dialectical Reason, because it governs the practical comprehension of a specific reality which I shall call *praxis*-process, in so far as it is the rule both of its construction and of my comprehension. (Sartre 1978, 558, emphasis in original)

Every situated action represents a structural moment in the temporal progression of individual human existence. Individual existence is itself a *praxis*-process that perpetuates itself through action (Flynn 2014, 345).

Fundamentally, the concrete subjectivity enacted throughout this process is continuously transformed through the interrelation between human beings and their surrounding materiality. From that materiality arise the situation-specific structures of needs, desires, ends, and intentions, as well as the structures of the practical field of possibility. Sartre's understanding of this practical relationship between human beings and objective materiality, and of how it constitutes both the concrete shape of their subjectivity and objectivity, can be analyzed in terms of an *intra-action*, i.e. an entangled interrelation between *relata* through which these *relata* are constituted in the first place (Barad 2007, 136–137).

In *Meeting the Universe Halfway*, Barad engages in a discussion with Nils Bohr's philosophical-physical considerations for a revised understanding of discursive practices. In such discursive practices, differences between phenomena are enacted first and foremost through their relation, or intra-action. Barad focuses on sociocultural factors that condition the discursive practice itself, which she refers to as *apparatus*. This allows her to consider not only phenomena as such, but the way they are perceived and the distinction that can potentially be made based on this perception itself of these phenomena. Barad argues for a reworking of the notion of *causality* so that it does not posit human beings front and center but also encompasses the supposed agency of materiality in the consummation of causal events. It is only within the larger perspective of the *apparatus*, i.e. "*the material conditions of possibility and impossibility of mattering*" (Barad 2007, 148, emphasis in original), that what matters is enacted and what does not matter is excluded. Against the background of Sartre's understanding of totalizing action developed throughout this chapter, and against his conception of human existence as a *praxis*-process, it becomes clear that there is a general and abstract form of human existence only in relation to how it concretizes itself through action. Understanding human existence as a *praxis*-process means understanding it as an intra-agential practice. Through this practice, the cut between the subjectivity of human beings and the objectivity of their surrounding materiality is enacted in the first place by their mutual becoming within their interrelation. Individual human existence thus represents the emergence of a situationally concretized, yet spatiotemporally coherent subjective entity that is practically entangled with a thusly situationally concretized and spatiotemporally coherent, objective materiality against the background of a larger socioculturally structured material occurrence.

2.5 Concluding Remarks

The analysis in this chapter has substantiated the fundamental role of human action in the course of human existence. The course of human existence is itself a complex mediation of internal and external factors. Meaning, practical relevance, needs, desires, and intentions interplay and together constitute a complex web of factors that condition how agents realize themselves through their actions. Simultaneously, each of these actions represents a structural moment in the overall totalizing processing of human existence as *praxis*-process. Human beings represent material entities that act for themselves, and thus they constitute their existential situation.

However, this situation is itself a constitutive factor for human existence. Depending on the larger societal constellation and the concrete material conditions in which actions take place, agents interiorize the world differently. They also subjectively relate to the world differently and thus act differently. The mutual influence of action and situation in Sartre's philosophy reflects the significance he attributes to both the individual and the societal context the individual is situated in.

Needs and desires are fundamental for the exact course of actions and even for how individuals apprehend themselves and the world. The agents' practical field is co-constituted by their needs and desires. Given that the structure of these needs and desires results from the agents' situation within a larger societal constellation, this constellation co-constitutes the agents' needs and desires and thus their situationally concretized subjectivity. Therefore, how needs and desires project toward certain ends is, to a degree, an outcome of the structure of societal constellations.

The conceptions of situated action and *praxis*-process further elucidate the relationship between individual and history addressed in section 1.4. The structural dynamic between situated action and existence as *praxis*-process instantiates and realizes the societal constellations that build the larger situational frame of individual action. Situated action on the micro-level is a structural moment of human existence as a *praxis*-process on the meso-level, which is a structural moment of the processing of larger societal constellations on the macro-level, which again affects the course of situated action on the micro-level. Because history dialectically progresses through material transformations of socioculturally and materially structured constellations, and because human actions represent the basic structural moments in these transformative processes, history itself becomes intelligible alongside the fundamental dialectic of human experience and action. With the conception of situated action and *praxis*-process, these transformative processes can now be represented by retracing their structural dynamics.

Despite the inherent situatedness of human existence, this analysis proves that action is ontologically free. Although practical freedom of choice might be limited by the position that agents adopt in their respective constellations, agents must be understood as remaining free to relate to themselves. This ontological freedom cannot be taken from human existence. However, the inherently material character of human existence already delimits an individual's practical field. Both the human body as well as the fact that actions must take place in the medium of matter affect human agency.

Now, with regard to the material realization of action, Sartre is not blind to the role of technology in human existence. In most of his works, Sartre illustrates certain ontological differences between human beings and things with examples of tools, instruments, and machines. He especially emphasizes the autotelic character of human existence—i.e. the fact that human beings engage in goal-directed actions by being ends in themselves—in contrast to the somewhat determined nature of technological artifacts. Technology plays a crucial role in Sartre's later works in particular. Practico-inert things and structures manifest the relations between individuals. These artifacts stabilize the structures of societal constellations and can even generate their complex demands and requirements.

However, *Critique* represents a culmination of some of Sartre's earlier thoughts. His reflections on human action are followed by further reflections on the nature of technical artifacts, their role as instrumental means, and the significance of these constructed things for human existence. Given that this current work intends to outline a theory of practical ensembles that can, with some modifications, be applied to urban mobility infrastructures, Sartre's philosophical thoughts on technology must be laid down first. This will be done in the next chapter.

3. Existence and Technology

3.1 Introduction

This chapter aims to explore Sartre's philosophical thoughts on technology. His theoretical considerations about practical ensembles in *Critique* rest on a specific understanding of the relationship between human agency and technology. This technology occurs in the form of artificial objects that, owing to the fundamentally instrumentalizing character of human action, serve not only as means to ends but also as a reification and material manifestation of this means-ends relation. Throughout his works, Sartre develops and refines his understanding of technological artifacts. These, as practico-inert residuals of former actions, serve as a counterpoint to the processual character of human existence within the scope of historical progression. The current work focuses on technology to provide a Sartrean framework for analyzing practical ensembles regarding human-technology relations.

Sartre's theories on practical ensembles are based on his philosophy of technology. He claims that social groups must be understood as practical interrelations between individuals, and these interrelations are mediated by socialized matter in the form of physical artifacts. These artifacts structure, scaffold, and manifest the practical interrelations these social groups consist of because the artifacts are themselves products of practical world interrelations with specific material properties.

Naturally, not all nuances of Sartre's view can be treated, although a general narrative is outlined according to which his philosophy of technology becomes understandable as a dialectical philosophy of technology.

Thinking of Sartre as a philosopher of technology may seem far-fetched at first, given that he does not explicitly engage in classical debates about technology. As is the case for most of his philosophical ideas, with regard to humans and technology, Sartre describes certain dynamics of their interrelation rather than providing clear definitions of what he understands as *technology*. Sartre's philosophy is neither specifically about technology nor about the objective world; it is mostly about human existence in relation to the world. In most of his works, however, Sartre discusses various characteristics of artifacts, objects of utility, certain commodities, and bodily techniques. On most occasions, these discussions serve to illustrate fundamental differences between humans and things on the one hand and the inherent connection between humans and objective reality on the other. When Sartre compares the autotelic nature of human existence with the seemingly predetermined nature of the objective world—especially that of manufactured objects such as tools and machines—he also makes a further observation: existence and objective reality necessarily interconnect in how practical significance, purposiveness, and equipmentality are constituted in a dialectical interrelation between humans and things. In this connection is found the root of Sartre's philosophy of technology.

However, it must be noted that Sartre's thought as presented in this chapter necessarily remains incomplete, especially regarding its implications for the forms of societal organization. This is because Sartre's thoughts presented here are constitutive for and thus, on their own, somewhat detached from the implications of technology's use in societal constellations. This chapter, therefore, builds on the last and focuses on the role of technological artifacts in the course of human action.

3.2 Dialectical Instrumentality

This section aims to reconstruct Sartre's conception of dialectical instrumentality. To do so, the section will introduce Sartre's engagement with philosophical questions surrounding the equipmentality of things and systems, their situation-specific utility and adversity, and their interrelation. The section will then embed these into the larger context of his dialectical philosophy.[1]

One of Sartre's more uninspired yet often cited engagements with technology can be found in his essay *Existentialism is a Humanism*. Here, Sartre uses a paper knife or letter opener (French *coupe-papier*) to illustrate the essential difference between human beings and technological artifacts. He claims that, because a paper knife is an instrument constructed for a specific purpose, it can be understood as having received its essence and *telos* from an external god-like artisan. In contrast, human beings constitute their essence as free, autotelic, and future-oriented beings that realize themselves through their actions (Sartre 2005, 148). This distinction is characteristic of Sartre's entire conception of technology. Human beings are active agents that make sense of the world for themselves through their actions, whereas non-human entities are passive things that are either completely devoid of meaning or receive their meaning and purpose from the outside through active human engagement. Although he revises this conception somewhat throughout his works, with regard to existence and technology, Sartre always locates true *praxis* in human exis-

---

1   For a more condensed account of Sartre's dialectical philosophy of technology, see Siegler (2022b).

tence; any activity that might be attributed to non-human entities remains a false *praxis*.

Primary Instrumentalization

However, in many ways, Sartre's engagement with technology from *Existentialism is a Humanism* takes a step backward in quality and nuance compared with his earlier thoughts in *Being and Nothingness* and, most of all, his later thoughts in *Critique*. The fundamental line of reasoning on which Sartre's philosophical thoughts on technology are grounded is his conception of human action as instrumentalization (French *instrumentalisation*) (Sartre 1960, 231). Section 2.3 showed that human existence is characterized by its autotelic and inherently practical orientation toward the material world. Every human being is an agent that acts for itself as an end in itself. Therefore, every action taking place in the course of human existence must be understood as a goal-directed activity that is relative to the agent as an end in itself. Because action necessarily takes place in relation to the material world, and because every action is an instrumentalization of matter, "[e]very *praxis* is primarily an instrumentalisation of material reality. It envelops the inanimate thing in a totalising project which gives it a pseudo-organic unity" (Sartre 1978, 161, emphasis in original). In this regard, every action must be understood as an implementation of means to ends. It must be noted that this conception of instrumentalization does not only refer to non-human entities but also, and most importantly, to the human body. Just like a non-human thing, the human body represents an inert sector of materiality that can be chained into "an organized, instrumental structure such that, through a series of sequences and connections, the modification brought about in one of the links brings in its wake modifications in the entire series and, in the end, produces some foreseen result" (Sartre 2021, 569). As biological organisms, human agents are material entities with complex needs and desires. As such, they rely on interacting with physicochemical reality to sustain themselves, communicate, and socialize. Regarding the human body within the course of action, Sartre states:

> The man of need is an organic totality perpetually making itself into its own tool [French *outil*] in the milieu of exteriority. The organic totality acts on inert bodies through the medium of the inert body *which it is* and which *it makes itself* [...] The action of a living body on the inert can be exercised either directly or through the mediation of another inert body, in which case we call the intermediary a tool [*outil*]. (Sartre 1978, 82, emphasis in original; Sartre 1960, 167)

In the course of action, human beings either make themselves into tools to act on matter or rely on tools to do so. Unfortunately, the English term *tool* obscures the wider intension of the original French term *outil*. With regard to certain non-human implements, such as hammers and knives or even machines and other more complex technical systems that can be used as means toward ends, the term *tool* rightly connotes a certain passivity and purposiveness. Regarding an agent's living body, the term *tool* is misleading. Section 2.4 showed that agents corporeally enact the course of action from situation to situation. In the course of action, an agent's body is not at all passive. Sartre's original use of the term *outil* both for the agent's living body in action and for non-human things used as intermediaries, i.e. means toward ends, suggests that the term must be interpreted with his conceptions of totalizing action and instrumentalization in mind. In the course of totalizing action, agents principally instrumentalize themselves as well as non-human things toward their ends. Both are thus totalized as *outils* because both are primarily posited into the functional position of instrumental means within the dialectical means-to-ends relation of totalizing action.

In accordance with his distinction between the modes of being for-itself and being in-itself, Sartre has different conceptions of how human agents and non-human things fulfill a functional role as means in the course of human existence. Whereas things are always disclosed as means to ends within a field of equipmentality, human agents exist as the individual center of this field to which practical references refer and from which they equally radiate.

The Field of Equipmentality

Given the fundamentally practical character of human existence, human reality is always "disclosed as haunted by absences to be actualized, and each *this* appears with a retinue of absences indicating and determining it" (Sartre 2021, 279, emphasis in original). This means that everything within individual human reality is always already in the process of being totalized as meaningful. The meaning comes about according to its practical and situation-specific relevance in dialectical relation to certain ends (French *fins*) for which these things may be instrumentalized as means (French *moyens*). In *Being and Nothingness*, Sartre states: "A thing is not first a thing, in order later to be an implement [French *ustensile*]; it is not first an implement, in order later to be disclosed as a thing: it is an implement-thing [French *chose-ustensile*]" (Sartre 2021, 280; Sartre 1943, 236).

In *Critique*, Sartre refers to these things as *practical objects* (French *objects pratiques*). This notion includes machines, tools, built structures, consumer goods, and any other objects of utility (Sartre 1978, 45–46; Sartre 1960, 138). Sartre claims that these things always appear as implement-things because they represent meaningful totalities resulting from the practical relationship between the agent and the world. Agents attribute meaning to objective reality by virtue of practically interrelating with it. Given that every action is an instrumentalization of material reality, every thing is totalized as an instrument by incorporating it into a potential course of action. Beyond this totalization, implement-things/practical objects rest "in the calm beatitude of indifference" (Sartre 2021, 280). In other words, without a practical interrelation, the totalizing activity that makes these entities instruments ceases; the instrument as a totality then disintegrates (Sartre 1978, 46). Their material being remains, but the attributed meaning vanishes with the attributing agent.

Human existence is inherently practical and oriented toward self-realization through action. Thus, implement-things always appear relative to individual agents. Implements constitute a *structure of equipment* that is organized by "axes whose reference is practical" (French *axes de référence pratiques*) (Sartre 2021, 431; Sartre 1943, 361). For this reason, Sartre refers to the original relation between instrumental-things within human reality as equipmentality (French *ustensilité*) (Sartre 2021, 280; Sartre 1943, 236) in the sense of Heidegger's *Zeughaftigkeit* of things (Heidegger 2006, 68). Implement-things are not isolated but comprise an equipment complex or field of equipmentality (French *champ d'ustensilité*) (Sartre 1943, 363). In this field of equipmentality, implement-things refer "to other implements: to the ones that are its *keys*, and to those of which it is the *key*" (Sartre 2021, 432, emphasis in original). Most importantly, regarding the practical reference for the user, implements refer to specific tasks that can be performed with them. According to Sartre, "these references would not be grasped by a purely contemplative consciousness" (Sartre 2021, 432), because that consciousness would fail to see the connection between means, other things, and ends.[2] In Heideggerian language, Sartre primarily conceives of instrumental-things as *equipment* (German *Zeug*), which is disclosed as always *in-order-to* (German *um-zu*) and which ultimately forms an *equipmental whole* (German *Zeugganzheit*) that is relative to a specific human world-relation (Heidegger 2005, 232–233; Heidegger 2006, 71–74).[3] An agent's pen, for instance, refers to paper, ink, or a table. By referring to the act of writing itself, a pen also refers back to the writer. Human reality, specifically understood as a world of tasks, is thus

---

2   Here, Sartre seems to suggest that either only a *practical consciousness*, which discloses the world as a field of instruments relative to itself as end in itself, or a not *purely* contemplative but also *practical* consciousness, is responsible for connecting means to ends. It can be suggested that an interrelated contemplative and practical consciousness corresponds to Sartre's conception of dialectical reason. However, the further investigation of this problem is reserved for future research.

3   Despite the terminological and conceptual similarities and the similar implications of Heidegger's and Sartre's thoughts on technology, however, Sartre's understanding of equipmentality implies a more engaged and proactive conception of a human's world relationality than the conceptual roots of his Heideggerian terminology initially convey. This is mostly attributable to the totalizing character of human existence, experience, and action. Whereas Heidegger's *Dasein* is somewhat inserted into an equipmental complex through which a person's world is disclosed, Sartre's being-for-itself more proactively constitutes and is constituted by what their surrounding matter provides them with. For Sartre's being-for-itself, their equipmental complex is the product of totalization. See Siegler (2022b).

objectively articulated. The world of tasks is represented in the means toward these tasks (Sartre 2021, 280, 432–433).

Consequently, because needs and desires project to individual ends based on how an individual's practical field of possibilities is equipped, an agent's inferential field of equipmentality correlates with their practical field of possibilities (Sartre 2021, 281, 432–433). An agent's totalizing action must not only be understood as a self-totalization and a totalization of the things around that agent and their world but also as a totalizing structuring of the field of equipmentality according to practical and situation-specific references toward certain ends (Sartre 2021, 431). Whenever a specific yet subjectively structured desire arises, for instance, it projects toward specific ends. Simultaneously, a vague outline of the course of action to attain these ends is given in relation to the availability of means in the field of equipmentality. When agents are thirsty, for instance, they practically structure their equipmental field through their actions in such a way as to look for and drink water. When there is no water available, however, these agents might structure their field so as to search for other water sources. In any case, the resulting structure of equipment represents the *organized, instrumental structure* that must be produced to eventually bring about intended modifications of the state of things in the course of action (Sartre 2021, 569).

Given that to be efficacious, agents must materially chain their corporeality into this organized instrumental structure, Sartre finds himself faced with what he calls a twofold contradictory necessity. On the one hand, human reality is a materially mediated world of tasks. This implies that agents must themselves be implements in order to act. On the other hand, a field of equipmentality, practically structured according to certain ends, must be structured and disclosed as such through a meaningful center from which these goal-directed structures of equipment arise in the first place. According to Sartre, the world "never refers to a creative subjectivity but to the infinite structures of equipment" (Sartre 2021, 433). The *key* to these complexes, i.e. the thing from which these complexes derive their meaning, is the human body in action. The human body in action represents the center of the individual's field of equipmentality:

> [T]his center is at the same time a tool [French *outil*] that is objectively defined by the instrumental field that refers to it, and the tool we are unable to *utilize* because we would be referred *ad infinitum*. We do not employ this instrument; we *are* it. It is not given to us in any way other than through the equipmental order of the world [...] through the univocal or reciprocal relations between machines, but it cannot be *given* to my action: I do not have to adapt to it, or to adapt some other tool to it; rather, it just is my adaptation to tools, the adaptation that I am. (Sartre 2021, 434–435, emphasis in original)

Sartre suggests that human beings exist as a tool to handle tools and that the action-signifying qualities of implements have ultimately arisen from the fact that agents make themselves into tools in order to act. In this quotation, Sartre's use of the French term *outil* becomes clearer. By occupying the position of means in the means-end relation, agents can take part in the inert causality of matter (see sections 2.3 and 2.4). As such, the body in "its *being-there* is justified in part by the situation that I create around me—as the presence of nails and the matting to be nailed to the wall justify the existence of the hammer" (Sartre 2021, 533, emphasis in original). The way humans *become* the tool to handle tools is thus an outcome of their free intention to act and their self-totalization. At the same time, it is a given that the only way to self-sustain is to act on the material world. In their totalizing world relation, human beings exist as "an instrument in the midst of other instruments [...] as *a tool for handling tools* [...] as a tool-machine [French *machine-outil*]" (Sartre 2021, 430, emphasis in original; Sartre 1943, 360). They exist as such at the center of a field of equipmentality that is structured in accordance with practical references in relation to certain tasks. It is the totalizing agent's ends through which implement-things refer to certain tasks within this field. These ends arise within practical human existence based on needs and/or desires.

Although implement-things refer to specific tasks, they do not prescribe actions. Sartre remains a vigorous defender of the fundamental significance of human freedom. Therefore, the factors that influence how and why certain implement-things are instrumentalized must be found within the course of totalizing action. Sartre thus advocates for a situation-specific instrumentalization of things based on their material properties.

The Coefficient of Utility and Adversity

As regards the integration of instrumental means in the course of actions, Sartre argues in favor of a relative and situation-specific spectrum of *utility* and *adversity* over which these instruments range. The same is true for the human body as a means to handle tools. Both the body and various material entities have specific material properties that enable certain actions when used, while simultaneously constraining others. A pencil, for instance, can be instrumentalized as a writing tool because it is thin, long, sharp, and pointed, with a pigment core that rubs on various materials and can also be erased. Furthermore, the pencil has an established meaning as a means for making erasable drafts. In the hands of a capable fighter or an angry person, a pencil can also be a stabbing weapon or a dart. This makes it different from other objects with similar properties. A bottle, for instance, is also long and thin and has a small opening. The material from which it is made usually depends on the kind of liquid it is meant to store. The bottle is thus built to store and pour liquids. However, its relatively hard bottom means that it can also be used as a hammer. A cup, in contrast, is made of porcelain and has a handle that allows the user to hold it while it carries a warm beverage without the user touching its warm surface. At the same time, a cup can be used to store other objects smaller than the cup itself. The same is true of more complex machines such as cars or trains. Both are highly specialized machines with specific material characteristics that render them useful for certain purposes and adverse for others. In postphenomenology, this is known as *multistability*, i.e. the potential of technological artifacts to support multiple practical relations.[4]

To account for the situation-specific utility and adversity of things in the course of action, Sartre borrows Bachelard's concept of the *coefficient of adversity* and further develops it into the so-called *objective coefficient of utility and adversity* (French *coefficient objectif d'utilité et d'adversité*) (Sartre, 2021, 435, 455; Sartre 1943, 380). This development stresses the fact that utility and adversity do not originate in things or the human body but in the user's specific status in relation to those things and the world. Sartre states:

> The screw is revealed as too big to be screwed into the nut, the support as too fragile to support the weight that I want to support, the stone as too heavy to be raised right up to the ridge of the wall, etc. Other objects appear as threatening for an equipment-structure that has already been established: the storm and hail for the harvest, phylloxera for the vine, the fire for the house. In this way, gradually and through the structures of equipment that are already established, their threat will extend right up to the center of reference that all these implements are indicating and it, in its turn, will indicate the threat through them. In this sense every *means* is at the same time favorable and adverse, but within the limits of the fundamental project that is actualized by the for-itself's arising in the world [French *tout moyen est à la fois favorable et adverse, mais dans les limites du projet fondamental réalisé par le surgissement du pour-soi dans le monde*]. (Sartre 2021, 436, emphasis in original; Sartre 1943, 364)

---

4   Postphenomenological approaches differ in their conception of *multistability*. Ihde (1990), for instance, deduces the multistability of technological artifacts from their initial ambiguity and from the fact that the "'same' technology in another cultural context becomes quite a 'different' technology" (144). Rosenberger (2014) extends the concept of multistability and supplements it with the conception of *symmetry* from Actor-Network-Theory, so that "it becomes possible to consider the roles of user experience, and the role of technological multistability, within the overall agency possessed by networks of actors" (381). In this context, Sartre's conception of instrumental things as ranging over a scale of utility and adversity represents a pre-postphenomenological conception of multistability. His view considers the material properties in relation to the situatedness of agents. A more detailed juxtaposition of Sartre's approach and postphenomenology can be found in Müller (2017).

It is in virtue of the principal goal-directedness at the heart of human existence that things reveal their dispositional properties of utility and adversity. Things are not useful or useless per se; their utility and adversity arise in concrete action situations. When a person wants to commute between two distant places, for instance, a car's specific properties in connection to the properties of road infrastructure render it more useful than the human legs, given that both places are sufficiently connected. Of course, one's legs can be used to walk the distance but the outcome and side-effects of this action would be different if the same action were performed with a car. Section 2.3 showed that Sartre's theory of action takes the whole range of human possibilities into account. Action situations are imaginable in which the agent's very intention is to show the possibility of walking said distance, for instance. In this regard, the legs as means would have a higher utility than the car. Of course, in their everyday life, a person's intentions are more complex and interrelated. If the person intends to commute while also using the travel time to work, or when the person intends to commute more sustainably, a train may have a higher utility than a car.

In the context of using implements, Sartre plays on Heidegger's concepts of *ready-to-hand* (German *Zuhandenheit)* and *present-to-hand* (German *Vorhandenheit*). In Heidegger's philosophy of technology, these concepts refer to two modes in which equipmental things are given to the being-in-the-world. An equipmental thing is ready-to-hand when it is integrated into a person's practical dealings. In this mode, being-in-the-world does not reflect on the nature of the equipmental thing. When the equipmental thing, for whatever reason, causes disturbances in a person's practical dealings, it becomes present-at-hand. Now, the equipmental thing is reflected upon and disclosed as what it is, how it appears, etc. (Heidegger 2006, 66–76).

Sartre claims that the agent's body is not usually present in certain actions. According to him, in the act of writing, for instance, agents do not conceive themselves as holding a pen. Rather, they conceive themselves as using the pen to write or even as writing. This is because "[t]he consciousness of a man *in action* is unreflected consciousness" (Sartre 2021, 75). Consequently, instrumental action must not be understood as the mere use of an instrumental means with a fixed purpose. Rather, instrumental action is an enaction of the utility and/or adversity that is rooted in the materiality of the instrument as an inert medium in relation to an agent's needs and desires. Sartre states that "it is the chop of the axe that reveals the axe, the hammering of the hammer that reveals the hammer" (Sartre 2021, 674–675). The tool-being of the human body and instrumental things consists in the goal-directed and situated implementation of things, whose utility and adversity are enacted through processual, kinesthetic adaptation (see section 2.4). Hence, retracing and reversing instrumental reference always leads to the user as an end in itself (Sartre 2021, 436–437).

Sartre's understanding of how equipmentality and purposiveness are attributed to instrumental means culminates in a conception of the world as an exact correlate of individual possibilities that every agent actively enacts, in the course of practical existence (Sartre 2021, 436) (see section 2.4). The individual field of instruments correlates with the individual field of possibilities. Given that each human being is the center of an individual field of equipmentality that comprises instrumental-things/practical objects, and because this field is relative to the practical attribution of meaning through action in relation to the agent as an end in itself, the equipmentality of objects cannot be conceived as a solely objective property, nor can individual possibilities be conceived as solely subjective structures. Action possibilities are not something agents have, but rather something they enact by unifying their instrumental field toward their ends. The instrumental field of possibilities is not provided by the material world alone, nor is it constituted by the agent alone; it arises from the practical projection of ends in relation to given means (see section 2.3). Sartre states that:

> In the organism, bonds of interiority overlay those of exteriority; in the instrumental field, it is the other way round: a bond of internal unification underlies the multiplicity of exteriority, and it is *praxis* which, in the light of the end, constantly reshapes the order of exteriority on the basis of a deeper unity. (Sartre 1978, 87, emphasis in original)

Individual action projects toward intended ends according to which available things become instrumental means with situation-specific coefficients of adversity and utility. At the same time, the ends that individual action projects toward derive their attainability from the fact that there are instrumental means available through which these ends can be attained. Accordingly, the field of instruments corresponds to the field of possibilities, because the field of instruments as the unity of available means is always transcended toward attainable ends. Instruments are material potentials that require human action to be realized as such. Human action as a goal-directed activity must simultaneously rely on potentials that both exist and are available in order to be realized. Equipmentality is thus a result of dialectical human existence. Ends are apprehended as such when they are conceived as attainable through available means. Means in return are apprehended as available in relation to attainable ends (Hubig 2006, 127, 173). Implement-things thus shape how agents actually realize their intended ends in the course of action (see section 2.3). They do so by enabling the practical realization of certain ends based on the relationship between intended ends and their suitability and availability for practically attaining these ends.

Owing to the principally practical character of human existence, agents instrumentalize their surrounding materiality based on its situation-specific properties. Therefore, Sartre states that human beings exist "in the form of being-an-instrument-in-the-midst-of-the-world" (Sartre 2021, 436), which, in the original French, reads "d'être-instrument-au-milieu-du-monde" (Sartre 1943, 365). Following this understanding, human existence represents an instrumental mode of being according to which surrounding things are principally structured along "axes whose reference is practical" (French *axes de référence pratiques*) (Sartre 2021, 431; Sartre 1943, 361). The world that is totalized in the course of action thus has an instrumental character to it. It arises in relation to the intentional means-ends structures of individuals.

3.3 The Social Side of Things

This section focuses on Sartre's thoughts about the relationship between implements, body techniques, and the social milieu in which these come to use. Although Sartre advocates for the fact that equipmentality is dialectically attributed to things in virtue of individual, practical world-directedness, he is not blind to the fact that human beings necessarily find themselves engaged in a world of subject-independent meaning—meaning which they have not put there themselves, but which nevertheless influences their mode of self-realization (Bonnemann 2009, 14). Sartre states that things have a fundamentally signifying character because meaning is inscribed into them through human action. For him, human beings relate to a larger social structure through the use of both technological artifacts and body techniques.

Inscription

Sartre's thoughts on inscription can be illustrated by how he distinguishes between the experience of objects that have not been *worked on*, and the experience of objects that have been *worked on*, i.e. manufactured objects. Again, the distinction Sartre has in mind does not concern the ontological status of these objects in particular but the nature of the relations that humans engage in by virtue of the objects' features. It is not a distinction between *artificial* and somewhat *naturally occurring* objects. He states:

> Faced with an inanimate and uncrafted object, whose operation I myself determine, and to which I myself assign a new use (if, for example, I use a stone as a hammer), I have [an immediate] consciousness of my *person* [...] of my own ends and my free inventiveness. (Sartre 2021, 561, emphasis in original)

Objects that have not been worked on initially refer to the agent who discovers them and to whom these objects signify an individual possibility for action. The experience of these objects is characterized by individuality (especially in terms of the agent's ends), inventiveness, and spontaneity. The meaning of these objects derives from how they are incorporated into the agent's project. Various meanings might be, for instance, attributed to a rock. When the rock is discovered while strolling or hiking on a path, it may be an obstacle to be circumvented or a landmark to be contemplated; when discovered in an urgent situation where something has to be shattered, the rock may be a hammer or a weapon, and so on. The rock is not an obstacle or an object of contemplation by virtue of being but becomes those things in relation to the agent's course of action (Sartre 2021, 665). As such, this object influences the course of action. However, the exact scope of this influence depends on the agent's apprehension of means and ends in relation to their self-realizing project.

The experience of manufactured objects is different from that of objects that have not been worked on. According to Sartre,

> any manufactured object must—in order to qualify as such—invoke the producers who made it and the rules for using it which other people have determined [...] As a matter of their essential structure, the rules for use, the 'instructions' for manufactured objects—which in their simultaneous rigidity and ideality, resemble *taboos*—place me in the other's presence. (Sartre 2021, 561, emphasis in original)

In contrast to objects that have not been worked on, manufactured objects do not initially refer to the agent but to the larger social milieu, the agent is part of. Although the notion of *manufactured* implies *artificial* as an ontological quality of these objects, Sartre emphasizes the fact that manufactured objects first and foremost express a certain supraindividual purposiveness. This purposiveness precedes individual action and manifests in these objects. Rather than signifying individual *possibility* based on the agent as a free project, manufactured objects signify an *opportunity* as a fixed and socially predetermined way of doing things. This can be understood as an *affordance*, i.e. a material cue that solicits agents to interact with it in certain ways (Gibson 1966; Rietveld & Kiverstein 2014; Dings 2018). In *The Design of Everyday Things*, Norman states the following about affordances:

> The term *affordance* refers to the relationship between a physical object and a person (or for that matter, any interacting agent, whether animal or human, or even machines and robots). An affordance is a relationship between the properties of an object and the capabilities of the agent that determine just how the object could possibly be used. A chair affords ('is for') support and, therefore, affords sitting. Most chairs can also be carried by a single person (they afford lifting), but some can only be lifted by a strong person or by a team of people. If young or relatively weak people cannot lift a chair, then for these people, the chair does not have that affordance, it does not afford lifting. The presence of an affordance is jointly determined by the qualities of the object and the abilities of the agent that is interacting. This relational definition of affordance gives considerable difficulty to many people. We are used to thinking that properties are associated with objects. But affordance is not a property. An affordance is a relationship. Whether an

affordance exists depends upon the properties of both the object and the agent. (Norman 2013, 11, emphasis in original)

This passage brings the concept of affordance close to Sartre's thoughts about the coefficient of utility and adversity of things. In Sartre's case, affordance must be extended to the socioculturally established and accepted meaning and purpose of objects. The shape of a handle or a button, for instance, affords it to be pushed because, on the one hand, it is built so as to be pushed, and, on the other, it has an established meaning as a thing that is to be pushed in an agent's sociocultural milieu. The difference here between possibility and opportunity is marginal only with regard to the actual course of individual action, but the difference directly expresses a variability in how the individual agent relates to the world and to the sociocultural milieu it is part of by virtue of using manufactured objects. The use of manufactured objects according to relatively fixed methods not only represents an individual action in the sense of a means-end relation. It also represents a social relation to a larger societal constellation already in place. The individual experience of manufactured objects is thus characterized by (relative) uniformity and anonymity. Sartre claims that manufactured objects address themselves to everyone in their field of equipmentality and that "a human transcendence, guiding my transcendence, has already slipped in between the object and myself; the object is already *humanized*, and signifies 'the human kingdom'" (Sartre 2021, 561, emphasis in original).

Sartre illustrates the fact that manufactured objects signify subject-independent human ends by the various meanings discovered to have preceded individual choice when walking through a lively city:

Consider, for example, the countless meanings, independent of *my* choice, that I encounter if I live in a town: streets, shops, trams and buses, signposts, the sounds of car horns, wireless music, etc [...] When I encounter a house at a bend in the road I do not reveal only a brute existent within the world; I do not make it the case only that *there* is a 'this,' characterized in such and such a way. Rather, the meaning of the object revealed to me here resists and remains independent of me: I discover that the building is an apartment building if the offices of the Compagnie du Gaz, or a prison, etc. Here the meaning is contingent, and independent of my choice, and it is presented with the same indifference as the in-itself's reality: it has become a *thing* and cannot be distinguished from the in-itself's *quality*. In the same way, I encounter things' coefficient of adversity before I experience it; a host of notices warn me: 'Slow down, dangerous bend,' 'Attention! School,' 'Danger of Death,' '100m to Cassis,' etc. But the fact that these meanings are deeply inscribed in things and share their indifferent externality—at least in appearance—does not make them any less indicative of a mode of behavior to be adopted that concerns me directly [...] Do I not discover here some narrow limits to my freedom? [...] I submit to these directions: to the coefficient of adversity in things that is engendered by me, they add a coefficient of adversity that is strictly human. In addition, if I submit to this structure, I depend on it. (Sartre 2021, 664–665, emphasis in original)

Street signs, traffic lights, and buildings are not *brute existents* to which meaning is conferred through individual action in the first place. These things already constitute a world, a meaningful totality that informs, supports, and directs individual action. Of course, the practical meaning, utility, and adversity of these things still arise within the agent's project, but this project itself must be understood less as a practically free invention of the world and more as an ontologically free self-embedding. The embedding happens into an already social, cultural, material, and thus historically structured wholeness that is shared with others. This wholeness of things and social expectations, norms, values, and opportunities scaffolds the agent a certain socially formed way of practical interrelating and thus a certain way of existing.

Body Techniques

The same is true for the implementation of several body, social, and intellectual techniques.[5] The employment of these techniques, such as "to know how to walk, to know how to pick something up, how to judge the relief and the relative size of perceived objects, how to talk, how to distinguish, in general, between the true and the false, etc." (Sartre 2021, 667) further delimits and focuses actions. Such techniques as *knowing how to speak* are not "an abstract and pure knowledge of the language, as it is defined by dictionaries and academic grammars" (Sartre 2021, 667), but are the execution of practical language competency with which agents both situate themselves in a societal constellation and apprehend the world according to this constellation. This can be applied to other techniques. In that people, for instance, ski like a Savoy, talk like a German, work like a proletarian or an academic, and so on, they accordingly disclose their world as Savoyens, Germans, proletarians, or academics. Furthermore, they situate and embed themselves in these respective social milieus by implementing the techniques that refer to these milieus. According to Sartre,

> [t]hese techniques will determine my membership of communities: of the *human species*, the national community, the professional and familial group [...] the only positive way in which I can *exist my de facto membership* of these communities is the use that I constantly make of the techniques associated with them. (Sartre 2021, 666–667, emphasis in original)

---

5   Sartre's thoughts on body techniques resemble those of Mauss' *Les techniques du corps* (1934, transl. 1973).

The way agents give meaning to the world through their actions is thus also conditioned by the culture-specific techniques by which they embed themselves in it (Bonnemann 2009, 16). This means not only that the nature of the agents' meaningful relations to the world depends on the way they interiorize the world as a practical field of possibility, but also that this interiorization is itself technically mediated by culture-specific bodily, social, and cultural techniques (Sartre 2021, 668). People neither fully constitute these techniques nor can it be said that these techniques constitute people. Sartre mentions that just as agents enact their existence in the course of action by adapting their embodied self to their situation (see section 2.4), and just as they enact the equipmentality of things (see section 3.2), these agents also enact the effects of techniques—the existence of words, for instance, by speaking, or the revelation of instruments through their practical use (Sartre 2021, 672–675).

In other words, agents realize the facticity of techniques and thus of the societal milieu, these techniques arise from. Although belonging to such constellations is contingent, agents enact this belonging through their actions. In this regard, these agents establish the necessity of the technical connections between themselves and their world in the self-totalizing course of their goal-directed actions. Through these techniques, the supraindividual structure these agents are situated in conditions the course of actions in fundamental ways. Through their situated actions, agents are not only "thrown into a world that is working-class, French, with the character of Lorraine or of the South, and which offers me its meanings when I have done nothing to reveal them" (Sartre 2021, 668)—they also realize themselves as situated in this world.

By employing such techniques, agents not only embed themselves in larger societal constellations but also recognize the significance of these constellations as action-guiding by acting according to the constellations' structures (Sartre 2021, 665–668) (see section 2.4). The later Sartre refers to language and similar body techniques as belonging to the practico-inert field; this is discussed in section 4.5. Although manufactured objects and certain body techniques seem to impose structured and predisposed activities on the individual, instead of allowing it to freely organize their situation according to its mediating milieu (Sartre 2021, 666), Sartre makes clear that these activities and the dialectical instrumentality of manufactured objects nevertheless have to be enacted through individual action to exist. According to him, instrumental means and techniques have no validity outside human reality (Sartre 2021, 674–675) (see section 2.4).[6]

---

6   In this context, Sartre offers an interesting argument on the nature and application of techniques. He mentions that techniques do not apply themselves according to a fixed inner logic. This means that techniques, as means, do not automatically provide the agents that employ them with fixed ends. If it were so, these agents would resemble pilots who make "use of the determined forces of the wind, the waves, the tides, in order to steer a ship" (Sartre 2021, 672).

3.4 The Practical Inertia of Technological Objects

The goal of this section is to examine how some of Sartre's thoughts on technology, such as dialectical instrumentality and the social side of things, find their conclusion in his conception of the practico-inert for technological artifacts. The practico-inert complements Sartre's earlier thoughts about both the significance of instrumental means in the course of action and the way these means propose certain action potentials to their users. It plays a significant role in Sartre's later philosophy as it allows one to make more general assumptions about the role of technology in human history. Therefore, it relates to the view that this work outlines for practical ensembles.

The Practico-Inert

The practico-inert is a complex concept in Sartre's philosophy. It combines assumptions about the dynamics of human action, the relation between humans, materiality in general, technology in the form of technological artifacts and body techniques in particular, as well as the processual nature of history. According to Flynn, "'[p]ractico-inert' denotes that realm of worked matter, sedimented praxis, passivity, and counterfinality—matter as the negation of action" (Flynn 1997, 121). Although this description represents the practico-inert in a seemingly negative light, all the factors Flynn mentions ultimately illustrate why this concept is so significant for both Sartre's understanding of history and his theories on practical ensembles.

In its more general meaning, the practico-inert denotes a certain way in which the meaning of an active practical world-relation is reified as a materially inert, passive fact in the world. This fact, through its materiality, remains a material fact and both faces and potentially outlasts human existence and action. In the context of Sartre's theory of history, the practico-inert enables historical transformation and the stabilization of order in any regard. Despite the emphasis on inert matter, the practico-inert is not limited to non-human entities such as technology in the form of instrumental means or artificial objects. K. S. Engels (2018) identifies five layers of the practico-inert in Sartre's philosophy: physical artifacts, language, deeply ingrained ideas or attitudes, social objects such as social formations and categories that are stabilized by matter, and *class-being*, or collectively shared life conditions

---

This would require a *technique of techniques* which, if also applying itself, would end in a vicious circle where "any possibility of meeting the technician" (Sartre 2021, 672) would be lost forever. Consequently, it must be the agents themselves who enact these techniques and their practical effects. This line of thought, as well as the example of a pilot steering a ship through the use of techniques, resembles the art of steersmanship known as cybernetics (Ashby 1957, 1).

that predispose the actions of individuals belonging to the collective. All these layers have certain practico-inert characteristics. However, fundamentally these layers can be traced back to practical human interrelations with other material entities. These interrelations are mediated by worked matter, either in the form of material objects and structures that coerce humans to modify their actions under certain conditions or in the form of the *hexis* of the human body itself, through which routinized actions and societal norms are enacted (see section 4.5). For this reason, this analysis puts less emphasis on all possible layers of the practico-inert as such and more on the practico-inert as it is found in the practical inertia of technological artifacts as well as on the way agents interrelate with these artifacts.

From a philosophical perspective toward technology, the appeal of Sartre's conception of the practical inertia of physical artifacts lies in how it allows one to more generally reflect on the role of technology in human history. Practico-inert artifacts are seen to interfere with the course of individual action in intricate ways. Sartre's entire theory of history is built on these slight interferences of action, and on the fact that human beings necessarily have to come to terms with the interferences. Despite the focus on technology, some of Sartre's thoughts about history and society must therefore be treated here to understand the full spectrum of the practical inertia of physical artifacts.

With the practico-inert, Sartre underpins this fundamentally signifying character of technological objects with a materialist and historical basis and explores how history itself is manifested in the tools and machines humans use to tackle their needs and desires.

Exteriorized Function

In his introductory passages on the concepts of *totality* and *totalization* in *Critique*, Sartre claims that a material thing to which meaning has been fixed through totalization is not entirely reduced to nothing when the totalization ceases—for instance when it is no longer used, when the function for which it is supposed to be used is forgotten, or when its usual use context has become obsolete. This thing remains a material entity with specific built-in material properties. As such, it still lays claim to the ontological status of the in-itself (Sartre 1978, 45). It still has a situation-specific utility and adversity attributable to it based on its material properties and in relation to the agent's situation.

In the case of non-manufactured objects, the properties that render them useful and adverse result from physicochemical processes of growth, decay, climate, tectonics, etc.—a branch has grown in a specific way so as to be used as a pointer or a weapon, yeast ferments complex carbohydrates into more digestible ones which makes yeast useful for food processing, penicillium molds produce antibiotic substances that can be used in medical production. Even chance plays an important role in resulting in the properties that make non-manufactured things useful. A stone, for instance, can roll off a hill, hit another rock, split, and thus have sharp edges which makes the stone useful for cutting, stabbing, etc.

In the specific case of technological artifacts, such as tools, machines, and certain built structures, the manufacturing process itself is responsible for the properties that make them useful for aiding in certain tasks and for performing or enabling certain actions. When it comes to tool construction, Sartre states that in human existence, *praxis* "is function exteriorised" (Sartre 1978, 83) (see section 2.3). According to Sartre, tools, machines, and other manufactured objects of utility serve three purposes. First, they are the means by which human beings put their inertia into practice to realize themselves in relation to their material surroundings. Second, tools and machines support the inertia of the human body in performing specific tasks. Third, tools and machines are materialized options for action and forms of conduct. They represent the "passive unity of the practical relation between an undertaking and its result" (Sartre 1978, 165).

According to Sartre, "[a] tool is in fact a *praxis* which has been crystallised and inverted by the inertia which sustains it, and this *praxis* addresses itself in the tool to anyone" (Sartre 1978, 186, emphasis in original). In Sartre's understanding, the same is true for any other practical object of utility. Through their practical interrelations, both in terms of totalizing action and experience, human beings not only inscribe their projects into matter through utilization and social significance. They also form said matter so that it can be used as a means toward an end. Things are constructed blunt, sharp, pointy, heavy, shining bright, with specific forms and shapes, with drives, rotators, wheels, wings, analog and digital functions, and so on. As such, they afford one the opportunity to smash, cut, sting, weigh down, illuminate, hold, accelerate, drill, carry, lift off, calculate, and connect. All of these things represent materially inert facts that are residuals of the prior exteriorizing and totalizing practical interrelations between human beings and their surroundings.

According to Sartre, the fact that human action is materialized in inert matter changes the character of the thusly engraved project:

> In losing their human properties, human projects are engraved in Being, their translucidity becomes opacity, their tenuousness thickness, their volatile lightness permanence. They *become Being* by losing their quality as lived events; and in so far as they are Being they cannot be dissolved into knowledge even if they are deciphered and known. (Sartre 1978, 178, emphasis in original)

In becoming materialized, practical relations lose their human characteristics. Fluid activity becomes a passive being (Sartre 1978, 161). Human action/*praxis*, as an inventive and goal-directed process toward the future, becomes a materially manifested entity. As it unfolds the action-signifying qualities that were discussed in section 3.3., the tool, the sign, and the machine "proposes itself to men and imposes itself on them; it defines them and indicates to them how it is to be used [...] the tool is a *signifier* [...] man *here* is *signified*" (Sartre 1978, 161, emphasis in original).

However, in becoming material facts, practical interrelations between humans and their surroundings escape their control. Sartre states:

> But precisely because signification takes on the character of materiality, it enters into relation with the entire Universe. This means that infinitely many unforesee-able relations are established, through the mediation of social practice, between the matter which absorbs *praxis* and other materialised significations. (Sartre 1978, 161, emphasis in original)

Although technological artifacts imply their equipmentality and the social conditions of their production, they are material facts detached from a factual course of action. As such, they represent materialized action potentials that must be awakened by an individual agent:

> A project *awakens* significations; it momentarily restores their vigour and true unity in the transcendence which finally engraves this totality in some completely inert but already signifying material, which might be iron, marble or language, and which others animate with their movement from beneath, like stage-hands creating waves by crawling around under a piece of canvas. (Sartre 1987, 182, emphasis in original)

Tools and machines are inert material entities that are open to being used as means by whoever intends and can do so. They exist as such only at the outskirts of a person's concrete practical field of possibility and equipmentality: as an abstract, not yet concretized and actualized potential for certain courses of action.

Sartre contrasts human tool construction with how, according to him, other species "make tools of themselves" (Sartre 1978, 83). He mentions that certain species of animals "make themselves permanently inert in order to protect their lives [...] instead of using their inertia they hide it behind a created inertia" (Sartre 1978, 83). With this statement, Sartre seems to suggest that, owing to their organic functioning, certain animals are restricted to specific ways of life. They must satisfy their organic requirements within specific habitats and ecological niches because their particular bodily inertia (organs like lungs and gills; appendages like wings, claws, beaks, trunks, etc.) has become adapted to this ecological niche. In contrast, human beings do not make their inertia permanently inert. What becomes permanently inert is their action, their *praxis*, as a function of human existence, when it is reified and manifested in matter through the construction of tools, machines, and other structures. In Sartre's understanding, a tool, a machine, or any built structure or practical object, for that matter, thus represents an exteriorized function of a concrete human existence situated within a socioculturally structured mediating milieu. In reverting to the strategy of situation-specific tool construction and use, humans do not directly restrict themselves to specific ways of life. They can adapt to given conditions as a result of their dialectical relation to a scarce environment in the course of history. Human beings thus not only exist as the adaptation to tools in the mode of being-an-instrument-in-the-midst-of-the-world (see section 3.2). They also adapt themselves to the exigencies of their environment that result from their inherent needfulness (see section 2.3).

Sartre's reasoning about human tool construction and use allows for two anthropological statements about human nature. Both are prominent in the philosophy of technology. The first is that humans essentially are *beings of excess*, and the second is that humans essentially are *beings of deficiency*. The idea that humans are excessive beings can be found in Kapp's *Grundlinien einer Philosophie der Technik*. The main thesis of this book is that tools and machines must be understood as projections of human organs and of the human body as such. Accordingly, a hammer, for instance, is understood as a reinforced and exteriorized projection of the human hand (Kapp 2015, 52); optical and acoustic technologies represent projections of eyes and ears (Kapp 2015, 84), and so on. Kapp claims that the whole of technological culture represents a continuation of human evolution ultimately driven by the fact that human beings have the urge to exceed the limitations of their milieu (Huning 2013, 216; Hubig 2006, 85). In this regard, technology has to be comprehended as an exteriorization of human nature. In tools and machines, humanity faces itself as *Deus ex Machina*, an ever-creative being that emerges from its built environment (Kapp 2015, 311). In opposition to such rather optimistic and appreciative thoughts about humans and technology, Gehlen's *Die Seele im technischen Zeitalter* goes in a different direction. Here, technology is considered a supplement for human deficiency. According to Gehlen, humans are senseless, weaponless, and naked, and thus dependent on action and technology (Gehlen 2007, 6). Eventually, technological development leads to the application of technological principles to social processes, which ultimately causes a general loss of meaning regarding the way humans relate to the world in industrialized society (Hubig 2013a, 152).

Sartre does not endorse such general statements about human essence, however. Despite the anthropological agenda of his philosophical writings, Sartre rejects general assumptions about human essence. Rather than conceiving tools, machines, and other structures to be a necessity of human existence, either as a result of excess or deficiency, Sartre considers these entities to simply be outcomes of the dialectical character of human existence, human needfulness, and the plasticity of the physicochemical universe in the process of history. Although smartphones, spaceships, or the internet, for instance, are highly technological achievements, Sartre would refrain from tracing them back to some essential human deficiency or ingenuity. According to his understanding, humankind did not fly to the moon out of a supposedly insatiable and general curiosity inherent to human beings. They did so to demonstrate power and technological prowess in a given historical situation, or to close gaps in their respective knowledge of the universe.

Technology and History

In every practical interrelation with surrounding, inert materiality, human actions are exteriorized and translated into matter and thus inverted into a passivized form. This passivized form represents a synthetic unity of its materiality, potential purposiveness and equipmentality, and sociocultural history. In a rather dense passage from *Critique*, Sartre brings these ideas together. He states:

> Every *praxis* [...] envelops the inanimate things in a totalising project which gives it a pseudo-organic unity. By this I mean that this unity is indeed that of a whole, but that it remains social and human; *in itself* it does not achieve the structures of exteriority which constitute the molecular world. However, if the unity persists, it does so through material *inertia*. But this unity is nothing other than the passive reflection of *praxis*, that is to say, of a human enterprise undertaken in particular circumstances, with well defined tools and in a historical society at a certain point in its development, and therefore the object produced reflects the whole collectivity. But it reflects it in the dimension of passivity. (Sartre 1978, 161, emphasis in original)

In Sartre's understanding, tools, machines, and practical objects, and any residuals of human action, must not merely be understood as material objects plain and simple. These residuals bear witness to the never-ending struggle against scarcity that is human history. Like a wax seal, humans imprint their actions into the material world, which then *"returns (retourne)* the act [...] [and] reflects the *doing* as pure *being-there"* (Sartre 1978, 161, emphasis in original). A trampled path, fingerprints, chipped corners on a table, dog-eared pages and stains in much-read books, and callous hands are only minor instances in which human actions resist these humans by being passivized, factual, and material effects of past actions. Every tool and machine, each part of the built environment, roads, and houses, straightened rivers, domesticated animals, deforested and reforested woods, the organization of societies around material symbols or their function carriers, the way institutions exert their power as real relations between things, individuals, and collectives—all of these represent human causality, cultural history, and finality in the form of passive, material entities and their interrelations.

With this conception of the practico-inert, Sartre's thoughts about the dialectic of action and technology come full circle. They link a person's individual and goal-directed use of technology to the entire history of their becoming as well as to their existential struggle with their surroundings. An implement-thing is always disclosed as such owing to the practical character and finality of human existence. Through these factors the material properties of the implement-thing have come to be produced in a certain way, within a given historical situation; this again connects the implement-thing as a potential implement to a certain course of action that can be actualized with it.

These artifacts, in the wide sense of that term, reflect the actions, strategies, and struggles through which individuals tackle their needs and desires. The inertia of these artifacts has been constructed in correlation with these actions and strategies and it is ongoing *praxis* that keeps these artifacts in the constant process of totalization. Sartre states:

> In the case of practical objects—machines, tools, consumer goods, etc.—our present action makes them seem like totalities by resuscitating, in some way, the *praxis* which attempted to totalise their inertia [...] these inert totalities are of crucial importance [...] they create the kind of relation between men which we will refer to, later, as the practico-inert. These *human* objects are worthy of attention in the human world, for it is there that they attain their practico-inert statute; that is to say, they lie heavy on our destiny because of the contradiction which opposes *praxis* (the labour which made them and the labour which utilises them) and inertia within them. But, as these remarks show, they are products. (Sartre 1978, 45–46, emphasis in original)

The practical inertia of tools, machines, and practical objects reflects their artifactuality and thus the societal conditions and constellations in which these artifacts were produced. In the case of technological artifacts, the term *practico-inert*, therefore, denotes the tension of their general becoming through human action and their specific historical-practical becoming under certain sociocultural conditions. This is because these artifacts are passive traces of past actions. In this regard, the practico-inert is history's counterpart to the essence of human existence. It is "the *essence* of man in the sense that essence, as transcended past, is inert and becomes the transcended objectification of the practical agent" (Sartre 1978, 72, emphasis in original) (see section 2.3). It is factually given and retroactively relates the current course of history, based on totalizing action through the instrumental means used, with the way the course of history has unfolded up until a certain point in time. The practico-inert is thus a dialectical and historical category rather than a material or ontological one. As a discursive phenomenon, it expresses the fundamental contradiction of human history—it represents humanity's ongoing struggle against scarcity through the oscillation of liberation and necessitation, based on totalizing action, in a more or less self-contained, passive material totality.

Human activity inscribed into matter in the form of the practico-inert is neither a social construction nor a mental addendum to lifeless materiality. Sartre writes, in discussion with Hegel and Marx, that the *idea* of things that confront agents in their practical existence is in these things themselves. Sartre agrees with Marx's materialistic reinterpretation of Hegel's conception of thought or *idea* as the *demiurge* of the world. According to Marx, the real world is not thought but the interiorized relation to the material world (Marx & Engels 1962, 27). To this, Sartre adds that the interiorized world is not a clear mirror image but rather a distorted picture of the material world, because human beings apprehend the world through their practical existence as a practico-inert residual of past actions. The material world is as much an enabling as a constraining factor that transforms and translates *praxis* into inertia, and because of this human beings recognize themselves and reflect their actions as mediated by *worked* matter. Sartre claims that his *idea of matter* is thus both naturalistic, because the natural properties of things are the source of their utility, and materialistic because these things appear just how they are by virtue of being—but "above all, it is *praxis* [and thus history] reverberating through a thing" (Sartre 1978, 171, emphasis in original).

Concretized Need

Technological artifacts are materialized, passive, and unrealized potentials for action within a given form of societal organization at a certain time in history. These artifacts are readily available, concrete means that enable the realization of concrete ends. It is not the case that humans must always look for or even construct the material means to attain the ends deriving from a person's abstract structures of need over and over. Technological artifacts simultaneously propose the already practically concretized efficient and effective satisfaction of socioculturally accepted structures of desire. Consequently, technological artifacts, in Sartre's understanding, manifest abstract structures of need in a concrete form. They thus scaffold the necessary conditions for the possibility of satisfying human requirements, wants, and wishes by opening up certain practical fields of equipmentality and possibility. By entering their practical field of equipmentality and possibility through their totalizing action, human beings thus leave their abstract structures of need for the sake of the materially mediated and technologically manifested structures of desire that are prevalent in their form of societal organization. They thus delimit their practical freedom in a way that also includes the risk of total obliteration for the strategies that are proven to be efficient, effective, socioculturally accepted, and, most importantly, ready at hand.

Sartre thus mentions the practical inertia of technological artifacts in the context of what he refers to as the field of *passive activity*. Although he does not give a clear definition of what he means by this term, it seems to denote roughly the conditions of possibility for potential courses of action, scaffolded and disposed by the socioculturally structured arrangement of concrete materiality in historical situations (Sartre 1978, 189, 199, 365). This passive sociomaterial disposition of the practico-inert is specified and realized in the course of individual action in virtue of a person's *active passivity*, which occurs in the form of an action disposition within that person's corporeality. Sartre argues that this action disposition can be found in the habituated routines of tool use known as *hexis* (see section 4.5).[7]

3.5 Technologically Mediated Existence

This section builds on the previous findings and explores how Sartre frames the way human existence is inherently mediated by technology. This conception of a technologically mediated existence is foundational for his theory of practical ensembles.

The close conjunction of self-realization and materiality shining through Sartre's thoughts on technology and the practico-inert illustrates the dialectical interrelation between liberation and necessitation that characterizes human existence. Ontologically free expression and self-realization through action afford a somewhat pre-structured whole of instruments and sociocultural norms that delimit options for action and thus enable action in the first place by providing a manageable field of possibilities. As a consequence, Sartre claims that the relation to the self and the relation to the world is ultimately modified by the objective world in general, and by practico-inert instrumental means and body techniques in particular. He states that every human being *is* the ends they have chosen to realize, on the one hand, and the means that realize these ends through the implementation of other means on the other. If both instrumental-things and body techniques play a role in how individual ends are chosen and realized, then the self, as the lived unity of realized ends, must be understood as objectively articulated and thus mediated through sociocultural and material settings that scaffold, predispose,

---

7   Against this background, the creation of practico-inert objects represents a technological *path creation* or *path constitution* in the sense of a *path dependence*. A *path* can be understood as the result of a process in which multiple options for action are narrowed down to a fixed set of options in the course of multiple interrelated events (Sydow et al. 2012). In Sartre's case, this means that the material properties put into these objects in the process of their creation affect the potential context of their future use. Processes of path creation involve processes of self-reinforcement (Garud et al. 2010). For Sartre this can be illustrated through the self-reinforcing role of *hexis* as active passivity, in combination with the passively active practical inertia of artificial objects. This is explained in more detail in section 4.5. Simultaneously, the creation of practico-inert objects is path dependent itself, as it is based on the needs and desires of their creators. When future agents use these objects as instrumental means, they enact and perpetuate the same structures of need, desire, and satisfaction. Through the practical inertia of material artifacts, the past works its way into the future in the form of materialized strategies of satisfying needs and desires. This wider sense of path dependence can be specified by analyzing concrete cases in which specific properties of objects, resulting from how past agents responded to their needs and desires, affect future courses of action (Mayntz 2002). This is shown in section 4.3.

and hence enable and modify its realization (Sartre 2021, 665). The same is true for the relationship between human beings and the world, as Sartre expresses in the following quotation: "the world only ever appears to me through the techniques that I use [...] This world, seen through the use that I make of the bicycle, the car, or the train to travel through it, shows me a face that is strictly correlative to the means I am using" (Sartre 2021, 666).

Here, Sartre advocates for an understanding of self and world where these entities are fundamentally mediated by the means employed to totalize and thus realize both in the course of individual action.[8]

In *Critique*, Sartre states that "all matter conditions human *praxis* through the passive unity of prefabricated meanings. There are no material objects which do not communicate among themselves through the mediation of men, and there is no man who is not born into a world of humanised materialities and materialised institutions" (Sartre 1978, 169, emphasis in original). Since all *praxis* is conditioned by prefabricated meanings of the practico-inert and since existence represents a *praxis*-process, existence itself is technologically mediated. Human action/*praxis* is thus more than a self-realizing activity. It is a process deeply grounded in materially and socioculturally structured constellations from which practical opportunities are derived in the first place. However, owing to the fact that human existence, as a lived reality, still rests on the foundation of ontological freedom, the system of meanings into which human beings are thrown represents merely an abstract structure that finds its concretization in individual self-realization (Sartre 2021, 677). By enacting the equipmentality of objects and the reality of body techniques, human beings appropriate and thus fix and reinforce the meaning of objects and techniques for themselves and others. Through goal-directed use, objects and techniques are transcended toward individual ends. The experience of attaining (or not attaining) individual ends through objects and techniques (as means) represents an interiorization of exteriority through which certain means are inherently associated with certain

---

8   Earlier, it was already mentioned that Sartre precedes the postphenomenological conception of *multistability*. With his thoughts on a technologically mediated existence, he also precedes one major postphenomenological conception, namely that of *technological mediation*. Postphenomenologists claim that human experience and therefore human reality is fundamentally mediated by technology in the form of material technology. By carefully retracing human-technology-world relations, postphenomenology seeks a better understanding of both human reality and technology (Ihde 1990; Rosenberger & Verbeek 2015). However, Sartre does not limit himself to material technologies. He also incorporates how social, cultural, and intellectual techniques mediate individual action and experience, and how these techniques mediate the relation between an individual and the societal constellation from which these techniques originate. His analysis therefore transcends the levels of experience and action. For a juxtaposition of Sartre's thoughts on mediation with those of Latour and postphenomenology, see Siegler (2022b).

ends (Sartre 2021, 680). The same is true for the simple fact that human beings learn from others which means to use for which ends. Either way, concrete actions and thus social concepts are conceived to be inscribed into material entities or forms of conduct. A guitar, for instance, represents the act of playing chords and music, a car the act of driving, a road the act of walking or driving on, walking and talking in a certain way represents a certain attitude or social membership, and so on.

Sartre develops this topic in his later works, claiming in *Search for a Method* that things signify actions and thus guide behavior as a mediating milieu in concrete situations. These mediated action situations represent *abstract schemata* that are *insufficiently determined* without an action that unifies them toward the future (Sartre 1963, 153). However, owing to the fact that human existence is inherently practical, human beings transcend every such abstract schema and relate it to themselves as concrete, self-totalizing existents that do not exist yet. Hence, the entities comprising these abstract action schemata represent *signs* that, as available means, indicate attainable ends and thus action situations that can be realized by the individual. Because this system of means and techniques is not a purely objective set of entities but a constituted wholeness structured according to sociocultural factors, the system not only signifies concrete actions but also reveals "men and relations among men across the structures of our society" (Sartre 1963, 156). The manifold relations between human beings and their technological means reveal the functional interrelations of their form of societal organization.

3.6 Concluding Remarks

The exploration has shown the connections between Sartre's action theory and his philosophical thoughts on technology. Technology represents a fundamental aspect of human reality. It must be understood against the background of human existence, experience, and action. These processes represent ongoing and spatiotemporal syntheses through which a human being enacts their existence (see Chapter 2). Tools and machines are enveloped in these processes and it is this envelopment from which these things derive their situation-specific meaning and equipmentality.

Sartre applies the same dialectical thinking to the material and artificial as he does to human existence. Human existence is not first a mere occurrence of being that is fused with consciousness. It is a synthetic process of the two and cannot be reduced to either the realm of being and matter, or the realm of consciousness and the mental. Tools, machines, and other practical objects also represent syntheses of being and consciousness. They are material entities to which meaning and practical relevance are ascribed in the course of human existence. These things are always disclosed as implement-things, due to the fundamentally instrumentalizing character of human action. Humans engage the material world in a practical and goal-directed manner and totalize it as their practical field of equipmentality and pos-sibility. Within this field, all things are already either bestowed with or questioned about their practical relevance for the totalizing individual. In this regard, things are always engaged against the background of the dialectic of means and ends.

The material properties of things and the social context in which these things are instrumentalized are important. Tools, machines, and other practical objects are constructed with specific material properties that render them useful for some and adverse for other use contexts. The socioculturally established and accepted mean-ing and purpose of these things also plays a role in how they are instrumentalized. By using such things and by employing certain body techniques, agents enact their equipmentality and effects. In doing so, agents also realize a social relation through which they situate themselves in a certain form of social organization. Furthermore, since technological objects result from goal-directed human actions in a specific his-torical situation, these objects are the practico-inert residuals of the strategies that human beings implemented to satisfy their needs and desires in the course of his-tory.

When it comes to the role of implement-things in the course of action, Sartre is careful not to grant too much power to the things themselves. On the one hand, he argues that agents instrumentalize things based on their material properties and so-ciocultural meaning, that things shape the course of human action, and that things signify which use contexts they afford. Things thus not only directly influence how agents realize their ends, but they can also alter an agent's intended ends or enable certain ends to arise in the first place simply by providing the opportunity to attain them. On the other hand, he advocates that all of these effects of implement-things are possibilized based on an agent's ontological freedom and the practical directed-ness of human existence. In accepting both the determinative character of imple-ment-things in a person's practical interrelation with the world and the condition of possibility for this determinative character in human freedom, Sartre points out that the relationship between humans, technology, and the physicochemical envi-ronment has a certain contradictory quality.

This tension between the somewhat determinative and action-shaping charac-ter of things and the ontological freedom and self-realization of human beings must be seen in the larger context of Sartre's philosophy. Chapter 1 already explored how Sartre's works focus on two interconnected planes of the existential reality of human beings: the internal perspective *of* an ontologically free agent in *Being and Nothing-ness* and the external perspective *on* this agent as a needful material being in *Search for a Method* and *Critique*. These two planes are dialectically mediated in the totalizing character of human action as outlined in Chapter 2. Sartre's philosophical thoughts on technology further explore how these planes intertwine, without necessarily try-ing to give a definitive answer to the contradictions of human action and technology.

In this regard, Sartre's philosophy can be called a dialectical philosophy of technology.[9] It is situated between the dialectical accounts of technology that lean toward a more Hegelian and a more Marxist dialectical school of thought. More Hegelian accounts of technology reflect on the dialectic of means and ends. Rooted in the Greek concept of *techne*—Greek for art, skill, but also a set of rules and the right knowledge of how to make or produce something (Aristotle trans. 2015, 198; LSJ n.d b)—such accounts expand the instrumental character of things toward the realm of knowledge and explore how to practically orient oneself in the world by reflecting on various aspects of technology. More Marxist accounts of technology reflect and criticize the societal implications of technological artifacts and systems. These accounts typically scrutinize the dynamics of power, society, and history with regard to technology.

Whereas Marxist accounts of technology dialectically scrutinize the relationship between society and technology, Hegelian accounts apply a dialectical thinking to reflect on the conditions of possibility that allow for something to be understood as *technological*. However, both accounts seek to do justice to the potentials and contingencies between human action and technology, both in the form of technological artifacts, processes, and rationales.

Based on his conception of totalizing action and dialectical instrumentality, Sartre advocates for a specific understanding of how the dialectical interrelation between human existence and physicochemical reality gives rise to its own possibilities and practical constraints. His understanding of technology is not specifically about technology in the sense of technological artifacts, structures, or systems. Rather, it is about the principally instrumental mode of being of the human condition.

Sartre uses the implications of his thoughts on technology to deconstruct and criticize how the forms of societal organization predispose the basic existential conditions of individuals throughout individual and collective history. The specific way in which such forms of societal organization form, transform, persist, and eventually disrupt, is fundamentally shaped by and manifested in the practico-inert technological objects that human beings use to satisfy their requirements, wants, and wishes. Also, *la force des choses* that was discussed in section 1.3 as the power of things and circumstances arises, when individuals within such forms of organization are coerced to satisfy their needs and desires and thus realize their concrete existence in socioculturally pre-determined ways.

Part 1 of this work has explored and systematized the theoretical foundations of practical ensembles. It provided an overview of Sartre's philosophical themes, outlined his change in perspective on the role of needs and desires throughout his

9   The following is condensed version of a discussion on Sartre's dialectical philosophy of technology that can be found in Siegler 2022b.

works, developed a unified account of totalizing action and existence as *praxis-process*, and explored Sartre's dialectical philosophy of technology. Part 2 builds on these foundations, outlines Sartre's theory of practical ensembles, and applies it to sociotechnical systems of urban mobility.

II The Dialectic of Practical Ensembles

4. Theory of Practical Ensembles: Structures in Action

4.1 Introduction

The purpose of this chapter is to develop the theoretical framework of practical ensembles based on some of Sartre's central lines of thought regarding human agency, technology, and the dialectical progression of history. The main difficulty with this undertaking lies in grasping both the fundamentals of practical ensembles and their inner workings, while not drifting too far into the details of Sartre's thoughts on society and history.

As mentioned in Chapter 1, Sartre's *Critique* takes a dialectical and praxeological perspective to reveal how human history, driven by free *praxis*, dialectically progresses through material transformations of socioculturally and materially structured constellations of human and non-human elements in a scarce milieu. With this perspective, Sartre can unveil the mechanisms by which these constellations form, the nature of practical interrelations the constellations consist of, and how these interrelations are supported, mediated, and catalyzed by the practico-inert in the form of artificial objects and the human body.

Sartre's method to analyze the inner workings of these constellations is an interlocking set of assumptions and considerations that together comprise a theoretical framework for describing and analyzing practical ensembles. Any constellation in which humans practically interrelate with other humans and/or non-human elements in a scarce milieu can be understood as a practical ensemble. This includes, for instance, traffic, the government, a family, or people at a train station. In understanding any such constellation as a practical ensemble, its larger mode of organization is seen to be the result of human action. By referring to these constellations as ensembles, Sartre emphasizes the fact that the elements comprising them practically interrelate but do not meld into a supposedly higher form of an organic entity. Rather, they remain individual. This view does not just allow him to examine the significance of individual action in the formation of these ensembles. It also enables him to analyze how the ensembles' larger form of organization affects and conditions human action. Practical ensembles are constituted through the employment of techniques and things. They are held together by the practico-inert. In this regard, they are *made* rather than *grown*, which means that their mode of structuring is not necessary but contingent; it could be otherwise.

According to Sartre, human beings enter "into ensembles of very different kinds, for instance, into what are called *groups* and what I shall call *series*" (Sartre 1978, 65, emphasis in original). This is due to the lived contradiction at the heart of human existence (see section 1.4). Groups and series represent two essentially different modes in which the practical interrelations of human and non-human elements in practical ensembles can be structured. A seemingly contingent gathering of people waiting for a bus, a societal class, or people sharing a road on their way to work, for instance, can be shown to exhibit predominantly serial structures when understood as practical ensembles. These constellations represent passive gatherings of individuals who face the same contingent action conditions that are scaffolded by practico-inert objects or structures. In practical ensembles with a serial structure, the satisfaction of need is concretized in specific fixed means and forms of conduct. Practical freedom of choice and self-realization is limited to a narrowed field of possibilities.

On the other hand, compare a political party or a task force, for instance. These can be shown to exhibit predominantly communal or group structures when understood as practical ensembles. These constellations consist of individuals who actively form and organize themselves to overcome seemingly contingent action conditions by transforming the scaffolding through practico-inert objects or structures. Such constellations are, for instance, political parties, interest groups, or larger social movements like Fridays for Future. Also, smaller constellations of people, who, for instance, organize to grass or plant public spaces in cities represent communal ensembles. However, according to Sartre, groups may become institutions in the course of their undertaking. If this is the case, institutions then develop predominantly serial structures through which the practical freedom of an individual is again limited to certain options for action, while at the same time creating more opportunities for those actions to be realized. It must be noted that in most practical ensembles, serial and communal structures interplay.

Despite the examples Sartre uses to examine the structures of series and groups, and despite the Marxist focus of *Critique*, Sartre's thoughts must be understood to be less specifically about the social interrelations of these ensembles, and more about the way these social interrelations can be dialectically and praxeologically examined to elucidate the historical action conditions of human beings. Sartre's analysis of how groups transform into institutions, for instance, can be applied to mass movements during the French Revolution. These eventually turn into revolutionary tribunals that reign with terror. The same analysis can be applied to the organization and concomitant institutionalization of public traffic regulations governing road traffic. This is because, for Sartre, historical processes in any form represent constant oscillations between practical freedom and material necessity. As such, they motivate and actively further transitions from series to groups and back. Practical freedom exists in the process of transforming structures of seriality into structures of communality, by negating given limiting conditions in accordance with the mode of how individuals satisfy their needs and desires. This negating, however, entails another transformational process in which groups organize and eventually ossify into the very structures established to transform seriality into communality. Therefore, history, much like human existence, must be understood as a lived contradiction too. Its very processing consists of a never-ending oscillation between liberation and necessitation (Sartre 1978, 72–74).

The potential of Sartre's practical ensemble framework lies in its deconstructive and reconstructive power toward the dynamics of complex constellations. When applied to such constellations, the principles and processes of Sartre's framework allow one to disclose the various modes in which practical interrelations are structured in them. This disclosure may reveal more fundamental interrelations and the modes of their structuring, as well as the ways these structures again mediate, enable, and constrain each other. Based on these interplays, the complexity of the constellations in question can be reconstructed as functionally interdependent networks of structured interrelations between humans and other material entities.

From a philosophical perspective on technology, Sartre's theoretical view on such constellations as practical ensembles offers the possibility to investigate how technology, in the form of artificial objects and bodily techniques, affects human action in various ways. According to Sartre, *la force des choses* arises as a consequence of specific forms of supraindividual organization that determine how individuals enter into certain constellations, reproduce themselves with limited practico-inert means at their disposal within these constellations, adapt to the inner structure of these constellations by cultivating *hexeis*—which represent a form of the practico-inert (see section 4.5)—and potentially initiate transformations that further affect these constellations. Despite the various connotations of the notion of *force* or the phrasing of *power of circumstances*, it must be noted that this force or power does not necessarily imply only negative consequences. Sartre points out numerous ways in which individuals are coerced to modify their actions, owing, for instance, to the position these individuals adopt within practical ensembles, or to the necessity that these individuals feel to reproduce themselves with certain available instrumental means. However, he also acknowledges that the same instrumental means that individuals are somehow coerced to use also enable them to effectively satisfy their needs and desires in some way. Furthermore, Sartre's theory not only allows one to focus on the immediate field of equipmentality but to reveal more profound ways in which technological settings interconnect and mediate each other so as to enable the realization of human action.

For Sartre, individual and supraindividual requirements, wants, and wishes in the dialectic of need and desire provide the starting point and the basis for investigation. Needs and desires render human actions intelligible as situated in relation to a socioculturally and materially structured surrounding as a mediating milieu. To outline a general theory of practical ensembles that can be modified and applied to analyze the possibilities and constraints of human agency as situated in large technological systems, the general relation of scarcity and human agency must be analyzed first.

4.2 Scarcity and Society

In this section, Sartre's view on the human struggle against scarcity is examined. This struggle represents the fundamental condition for the formation, reinforcement, transformation, persistence, crisis, and potential disruption of practical ensembles.

The Struggle against Scarcity

On account of the specific understanding of the relationship between human existence and history that is prominent in Sartre's *Critique*, historically situated individuals must first and foremost be understood as needful beings. Their requirements, wants, and wishes derive from their socioculturally and materially mediated relation to the material complex (or ensemble) they are situated in. According to Sartre, every human being always exists in a state of exigency in relation to a world characterized by scarcity (French *rareté*) (Sartre 1960, 200; Sartre 1978, 123). This exigent state requires material modification to be transformed (see Chapter 2). Despite the fundamental significance Sartre attributes to scarcity, he does not want it to be understood as a statement about human nature or human essence. Rather, it is a conclusion derived from the fact that every human being must necessarily sustain itself by interacting with the material world. Scarcity is both a contingent fact of human life and the sufficient cause of historical development (Monahan 2008, 50–51). Emphasizing its significance for human existence illustrates the fundamental structures of historical development as a "real and constant tension both between man and his environment and between man and man" (Sartre 1978, 127). Based on this tension, Sartre claims the "fundamental structures (techniques and institutions)" can be explained not as immediate results of scarcity but because they were "produced in the *milieu of scarcity*" (Sartre 1978, 127, emphasis in original).

Despite the focus on materiality, scarcity does not solely refer to a lack of material goods, but also to any state in which individuals lack something they require, want, and wish (Monahan 2008, 52). This could be any type of good or service, rights, political representation, etc., as long as the lack represents an incentive for action. The reason for Sartre's focus on material action comes from the material character of human existence (see section 1.4). The nature of scarcity is not only determined by the requirements, wants, and wishes of individuals and supraindividual groupings (see section 2.3), but also mediated by how technology in the form of practico-inert means concretizes abstract structures of need into concrete structures of desire (see section 3.4). When the abstract need for mobility in the form of the requirement to be able to move, for instance, is partly satisfied by the concrete existence of some modes of transportation, the requirement for other modes of transportation is itself mediated by the relationship between supply and demand prevalent in the mediating milieu. According to Monahan's interpretation, scarcity so fundamentally structures human existence that it represents the background condition of all human action, not only for the present but also for future action. Because totalizing human action is a materially transcending projection toward the future, and because the relation between human beings and the material world is characterized by scarcity, everything that presents itself as a possible option for action is seen as a good that might be scarce in the future—and so it is to be secured and preserved. Monahan phrases it like this: "If I think I have enough water for the present, but I believe I *could* need more tomorrow, or next week, then it turns out that I really do not have *enough* water—I have a scarcity of water despite the fact that I have ample supply for my immediate needs" (Monahan 2008, 58, emphasis in original).

Sartre himself states that "[a]s soon as need appears, surrounding matter is endowed with a passive unity, in that a developing totalisation is reflected in it as a totality: matter revealed as passive totality by an organic being seeking its being in it—this is Nature in its initial form" (Sartre 1978, 81). Ally (2012) points out that Sartre's use of the term *nature* is somewhat ambiguous throughout his philosophical works. In the early Sartre, Nature—capitalized to highlight it as an abstract nominative, according to Ally—is used to refer to passive being and exteriority in relation to the interiority of human existence. The later Sartre sees *nature* as an inert and somewhat opaque physicochemical complex surrounding human beings and governed by its own dynamics and laws. This complex can never be fully understood in a dialectical way from the inside but is subject only to analytical science (see section 1.4). The reason is that the whole of nature, as physicochemical reality, becomes a synthetic totality only as a result of the fact that human beings appropriate it by relating to it in a dialectically practical way. Here is seen one instantiation of a three-step dialectical relation. The givenness of physicochemical reality represents a positing that is negated through need and thus disclosed and affirmed as a scarce source of sustenance for human beings (see section 2.3).

However, this human-nature relation should not be seen as a purely rationalized, unidirectional, or exploitative reduction of *nature*, in the sense of Heidegger's notion of *Bestand* (Heidegger 2000). Rather, Sartre's conception of the human-nature relation must be seen as a result of his focus on the dialectical and material fundamentals of human existence. Sartre notes that, as biological organisms, humans must necessarily practically engage with physicochemical reality and instrumentalize it to provide for themselves. In this context, Ally defends Sartre's conception of instrumentalization, as it seems to be true for all self-sustaining organisms. Ally states that in Sartre's understanding of instrumentalization, "[b]eavers fell trees to make their dams and they swim with the fishes who gather in the place. We mix gravel and sand to make our dams, and we fell trees to make space and lumber and pulp" (Ally 2017, 376).

Systematic Provision of Goods and Services

Sartre has a nuanced understanding of how individuals organize themselves in historical situations and how they preserve these forms of organization with the help of the practico-inert. His understanding goes beyond both general statements about humanity's instrumentalization of physicochemical reality and mere presumptions about a supposed original relationship between humans and nature. Some of Sartre's main interests in *Critique* are the multiplicity of forms of organization in human societies, and the many ways people have instrumentalized their material surroundings in their struggle against scarcity throughout human history. Sartre believes that although scarcity necessitates the instrumentalization of physicochemical reality, and although individual action has a certain rationality, the specific form of an organization through which this instrumentalization is realized and preserved seems to be contingent. Forms of societal organization do not result from an underlying rationality that is present before the dialectical rationality of human action and experience (Sartre 1978, 124). This does not mean, however, that the formation processes themselves are contingent as well. Sartre shows that humanity's relation to *nature*—in all the meanings of the term—takes place in a sociocultural milieu that is enacted through individual and supraindividual action as an ontologically free endeavor on the one hand and necessarily manifested in a practico-inert way on the other. Organizational variation arises when human freedom and creativity clash with material inertia. However, scarcity must always be considered as the medium in which this clash takes place.

The fact that people must satisfy their needs and desires, in confrontation with scarce material conditions, also puts these people in fundamental confrontation with others. Scarcity means that "[t]*here is not enough for everybody*" (Sartre 1978, 128, emphasis in original). In this context, Sartre shows one application of his understanding of practical ensembles. Regarding the way human beings relate to the world, he states that "need is the first totalising relation between the material being, man, and the material ensemble of which he is part" (Sartre 1978, 80). Furthermore, "the world (the ensemble) exists for anyone insofar as the consumption of such and such a product elsewhere, by others, deprives him *here* of the opportunity of getting and consuming something of the same kind" (Sartre 1978, 128, emphasis in original). Here, Sartre illustrates one of the advantages of conceiving certain constellations between human and non-human entities as practical ensembles. By referring to the world as a material ensemble in the context of individual action and scarcity as well as in relation to others, Sartre illustrates that the world as a totality can be deconstructed into the elements that totalize it. When reconstructed, it can be understood as a wholeness that is continuously totalized by the functional inter-relations of self-reproducing individuals in a scarce milieu. In this regard, scarcity is not only conceived as a material relation between individuals and surrounding materiality; it is also disclosed as a social relation to others.

The social relation of scarcity is not necessarily characterized by hostility. People are usually situated in larger, potentially overlapping, social constellations, such as families, groupings, gatherings, political parties, corporations, institutions, societal classes, and ultimately society as a whole. Conceiving these constellations as practical ensembles deconstructs their alleged status as totalities, and reveals the dialectical and praxeological conditions of their totalizing formation, the functional inter-relationship of their elements, the specific way this interrelationship is structured, and the functional requirement this structured interrelation fulfills. Sartre refers to these social constellations as social ensembles. Through the conceptual lens of practical ensembles, the reasons for these constellations to form appear to be manifold, but the reasons are all grounded in people's needs and desires and in their inability to satisfy them on their own in relation to their common sociocultural and material conditions.

Sartre states that people (re-)produce themselves amid others who do the same. As a consequence, they form larger constellations to systematically provide for their needs and desires. These constellations "constitute and institutionalise themselves not because scarcity appears to everyone in need through the need of Others, but because it is negated, in the unified field, by *praxis, by labour*" (Sartre 1978, 136, emphasis in original). Individual action represents the active attempt to negate scarcity by affirming the individual as an end in itself. However, this action is not individual action pure and simple. It is conditioned, in its entire course, by the structure of the practical ensembles in which the action is situated. At the same time, this structure is itself defined, manifested, and reinforced by the functional requirements of its elements to satisfy their exigencies. This satisfaction takes place through actions undertaken to transform these exigencies and by the practico-inert means that come to use in this transformation.

A family with children, for instance, can, very generally, be understood as a practical (social) ensemble structured to fulfill the functional requirement of raising children and supporting each other. The structured interrelations of this ensemble consist of an unequal spread of giving and demanding from its members in relation to a sociocultural and material surrounding milieu. In terms of the material requirements of the members of the family, parents contribute more, while children contribute less. In terms of the wants and wishes of its members, all members—parents and children—invest love, emotional support, and energy. The inner structure and logic of such ensembles are conditioned by the concrete social interrelations of all members, their individual needs and desires, and their capacities.

This family, as a social ensemble, might live in a city, for instance. This city can itself be understood as a practical ensemble. It consists of human and non-human elements such as citizens, commuters, city government, buses, cars, roads, housing, shopping malls, and so on. The actions of the human elements to satisfy their requirements and wants are interrelated with other human and non-human elements. This inner structure is again conditioned by sociocultural factors.

Both ensembles are in the constant process of totalization, as driven by the actions of their human elements and their interrelations with the practico-inert. In this way, the exigencies of individuals, their concomitant options for action, and their practical constraints present themselves differently. If the family ensemble is situated in the city ensemble—an ensemble of ensembles—the actions of this specific family as a whole and its members individually can be understood in relation to what possibilities and constraints their situation in the city provide them with.

Since practico-inert objects and structures mediate the functional interrelations of their elements in relation to prevailing material conditions, these objects not only represent exteriorized action potentials (see section 3.4) but also material manners through which potentially scarce goods and services are secured and provisioned in individual and supraindividual ways. However, these practico-inert objects are not just advantageous. They also have certain demands and requirements themselves, which can eventually invert the relationship between the user and the used (see 4.3).

The understanding of functionally interrelated constellations of human and non-human elements, through the conceptual lens of practical ensembles, has similarities to an understanding of such constellations as sociotechnical systems. Both models reveal that the larger mode of interrelations between their elements is structured according to the functional requirements of their human elements on the one hand, and according to their mediation through non-human elements on the other.[1]

Practical ensembles may indeed be understood as sociotechnical systems with a fixed system status, an organizational structure, and forms of behavior that illustrate their inner workings and portray their overall function. In this regard, the structures of practical ensembles are seen to provide for the ends of their human elements—such as the satisfaction of requirements, wants, and wishes—while also preserving the mode in which this provision takes place as a strategic implementation of technological means.

---

1   A short overview of the concept of *sociotechnical system* can be found in Karafyllis (2019). For a more thorough analysis of the concept, see Ropohl (2009).

Although a system understanding of practical ensembles like this one thus seems to fit, it neglects the inherent dialectical historicity of practical ensembles. The theory of sociotechnical systems presupposes that the rationality of the system corresponds to the rational structure of human action, especially in terms of instrumental action. In most theoretical conceptions of sociotechnical systems, system constraints result from conflicts of interest that can be transformed through communication, technological development, and general optimization of the ensemble as a sociotechnical system (Hubig 2007, 31).

Therefore, while it may account for functional interrelations of human and nonhuman elements or even for the way their larger form of organization conditions and constrains their respective operations, a system understanding remains ahistorical with respect to Sartre's theory of history. According to Sartre's regressive-progressive method (see section 1.3), how historical situations both constitute and are constituted by individuals can only be fully understood through the dialectical conditions of their becoming through action. In this regard, Sartre's theory of practical ensembles represents a deconstructive and reconstructive understanding of the becoming of any form of societal constellation. According to him, this understanding ultimately accounts for the significance of human action in the progression of history, for the role of action in the formation of societal constellations, and for the conditions in which this action eventually acts back on itself (see sections 1.4 and 3.4). Furthermore, this strong focus on the role of action in the becoming of larger constellations illustrates the inherent historicity of the dialectical interrelation between action, scarcity, and the practico-inert.

Against this historical background, the entire collection of practico-inert objects that can be found in a societal constellation at any given time represents the material culture of this society at a certain stage. More precisely, practico-inert objects represent the material side of strategies employed by individuals and larger constellations to tackle needs and desires. They face these as a result of their specific socioculturally structured relation to a scarce material environment. Ancient roads and artifacts, stone tools and weapons, burial grounds, and grave goods, physical remains of past civilizations—any form of material settings—represent ways that past and present societies organize the provision of goods and the concomitant satisfaction of individual and collective needs.

In this respect, Sartre's understanding of practical ensembles shows thematic similarities to Heidegger's *Ge-Stell*. This is evident in the way in which, at different stages of technological development, practico-inert objects condition how individuals in practical ensembles disclose some goods to be scarce whereas the provision of other goods can be effectively preserved with technological means. This point is further developed in section 4.3.

Structural Features of Practical Ensembles

According to the deconstructive and reconstructive agenda of Sartre's theory of practical ensembles, the structural features of historical constellations are understood to result from how individuals practically respond to and satisfy their needs and desires in combination with practico-inert instrumental means. Such interrelations are future-oriented and thus path dependent. Eventually, these interrelations lead to multiple complex forms of organization. The exact constitution of these forms of organization is contingent.

This work has discussed how Sartre conceives human action to be a practical engagement with *socioculturally structured* materiality. Concerning the features of practical ensembles, it becomes more clear, what it means for materiality to be *socioculturally structured* in a certain way. The later Sartre somewhat develops his conception of *structure* in response to Lévi-Strauss' *The Elementary Structures of Kinship*. *Structures* represent the material, social, cultural, and ideological foundations that give rise to and shape the free actions of individuals. After discussing the genesis of groups, Sartre recognizes Lévi-Strauss' contribution to the analysis of structures and states: "Function as lived *praxis* appears in the study of the group as objectivity in the *objectified* form of structure. And we shall not understand anything of the intelligibility of organised *praxis* as long as we do not raise the question of the intelligibility of structures" (Sartre 1978, 480, emphasis in original). Sartre agrees with Lévi-Strauss in that individuals shape their sociocultural and material milieu through action inasmuch as they are shaped by it. The *structures* of this milieu, i.e. the situational factors that scaffold, shape, and give rise to individuals' practical fields (see section 2.4), represent these individuals' *necessity of freedom* to totalize themselves (Sartre 1978, 489). In contrast to Lévi-Strauss, however, Sartre stresses the fact that "what we are dealing with here is not a totality but a totalization [...] a multiplicity which totalises itself in order to totalise the practical field from a certain perspective" (Sartre 1978, 492). Sartre's most basic conclusion is that the existence of structures is not a presupposition of action. Rather, structures emerge through the totalizing activity of historically situated agents and further affect how these agents form practical relations.

In historical situations, individuals dialectically depend on and totalize their available practico-inert practical field of equipmentality through their actions. These totalizing actions are goal-oriented on the basis that these individuals are ends in themselves. Needs and desires, as well as the respective ends of action, arise in the interplay of individual requirements, wants, and wishes and what the practical field of equipmentality provides as instrumental means. Sometimes these individuals repeat the way they practically respond to and satisfy their inherent needfulness because they repeatedly re-interiorize their specific practical field of equipmentality and possibility. When this enables a practical response to be somewhat successful, it can be said that the individuals' actions are *structured* according to their practical interrelation with their surrounding materiality. This means that the abstract course of the totalizing actions of these individuals is scaffolded and shaped by the fact that these individuals, as ends in themselves, must rely on the practical field of equipmentality and possibility materially available to them—in the relatively limited ways it is available to them—if they want to practically respond to and satisfy their needs and desires. These individuals always enact the already socially meaningful equipmentality of things and the effects of techniques in a social milieu. Given that this social milieu consists of the practical interrelations of other individuals and their surrounding materiality, the actions of individuals thus take place in relation to their socioculturally *structured* materiality. *Structure*, in this regard, represents an abstract, practically instantiated and thus concretized set of rules, regulations, and expectations of practical fields of equipmentality and possibility that normalize, mediate and thus shape how individuals realize their intended ends (Hubig 2015, 74).[2]

According to Sartre, two ideal modes can be identified in which the practical responses of individuals are structured: *seriality* and *communality*. Sartre also refers to these modes of structuring as two *types of human mediation* (Sartre 1978, 170–171). A practical ensemble can form based on how human beings respond to their needs and desires individually in interrelation with a prefabricated field of equipmentality. Such ensembles exhibit predominantly serial structures. A communally structured ensemble forms when human beings unite to actively overcome how such a prefabricated field of equipmentality is given to them.

Consequently, to examine the general conditions, possibilities, and practical constraints of individual action, the structural features of constellations in which this action is situated must be scrutinized through the conceptual lens of practical ensembles. In the next section, this is done by examining some ways in which historical constellations form and reinforce through technologically mediated action.

---

2   In this regard, Sartre's thoughts on action and structure resemble Giddens' thoughts on the *duality of structure* in *The Constitution of Society*. Giddens states: "Structure, as recursively organized sets of rules and resources, is out of time and space, save in its instantiations and co-ordination as memory traces, and is marked by an 'absence of the subject'. The social systems in which structure is recursively implicated, on the contrary, comprise the situated activities of human agents, reproduced across time and space. Analysing the structuration of social systems means studying the modes in which such systems, grounded in the knowledgeable activities of situated actors who draw upon rules and resources in the diversity of action contexts, are produced and reproduced in interaction" (Giddens 1986, 25).

4.3 Formation, Reinforcement, and Stabilization

In this section, some ways in which practical ensembles form and some ways in which their inner structures are reinforced will be exemplified through constellations that predominantly exhibit serial structures. Following this, the transformation of practical ensembles is exemplified through the transition from ensembles with predominantly serial structures to ensembles with predominantly communal structures and back.

The Formation of Serial Structures

When a practical ensemble is united by isolated practical relations of human elements to non-human, practico-inert objects and structures in dependence on prevalent material conditions, and when this practical ensemble furthermore remains defined by this conjunction, it is called a *collective* (Sartre 1978, 255). In collectives, each member's belonging to the ensemble is not a result of a conscious choice but comes from their isolated practical relation based on their functional requirements/exigencies. As a consequence of this mode of structuring, the human elements in these ensembles remain in a pure exterior relation to each other without interior cohesion (Blättler 2012, 71). Hence, not individuality but interchangeability and even competition lie at the heart of these practical ensembles (Rae 2011, 191). For this reason, Sartre refers to this mode of structuring as seriality. Because structures of seriality result from an individual's practical relations to given practico-inert objects and structures, the unity of collectives is scaffolded and prefabricated. For this reason, Sartre refrains from referring to practical ensembles with serial structures as *organizations* or as being *organized*. In his understanding, *organization* implies that a practical ensemble has interior cohesion as a result of an active synthesis through its human elements (see section 4.4). By contrast, practical ensembles with a serial structure result from passive synthesis. Nevertheless, because the practical ensemble is united, it constitutes what Sartre calls a *partial totality*, which defines itself from the inside through the specific mode that distinguishes it from its outside. In this regard, any serially structured ensemble may represent a moment in the larger totalization of another ensemble (Sartre 1978, 88).[3]

Sartre uses people waiting for the bus to exemplify serial structuring. Initially, these people do not appear to be a structured totality. They look like a general gathering consisting of a random number of individuals. However, when this gathering is conceived in a dialectical and praxeological way, their "generality [...] is just an abstract appearance, for it is actually constituted in its very multiplicity by its transcendent unity as a structured multiplicity" (Sartre 1978, 262). Although the gathering ap-

---

3   This is more thoroughly discussed in sections 4.4 and 4.6.

pears like a random number of people, the people are structured. What unites these people is that they all gather at the bus stop in pursuit of getting a seat on the bus. Through Sartre's conceptual lens, this multiplicity can be reconstructed according to the goal-oriented actions of its human elements. This means that the general gathering of the multiplicity of individuals at the bus stop is indeed a structured gathering that is united by the common individual goals of these people. In this regard, the multiplicity of people presents itself as a practical ensemble with serially structured functional interrelations between its human and non-human elements. The individuals at the bus stop indeed represent a fixed constellation, because the human elements of the ensemble are unified as isolated individuals whose *praxis* (waiting) is equally conditioned by the same non-human, practico-inert element (bus). The non-human element thus fulfills two functions. First, it functions as a common and available means (of transportation) by which the human elements must satisfy their needs and desires (for mobility in general or for reaching their workplace in particular, etc.). Second, the means also functions as a concrete way in which the provision of a required good or service is reliably preserved for future use. In that these individuals have to rely on the repeated use of the same means of subsistence—understood abstractly—they are subject to a passive synthesis. Although such a passive synthesis is still enacted by individual *praxis*, the unity it represents must be dialectically understood as the affirmation of a pre-established positing through sociocultural and material conditions, instead of being an active engagement with these conditions in the sense of dialectical negation. Passive synthesis is characterized by the fact that it takes place in a historical context in which individuals necessarily have to sustain themselves with prefabricated, fixed, and limited means and that these individuals acquiesce to this fact. This means not only that individuals in serial structures are not organized; they are also separated and atomized, and thus represent competitors for the means at their disposal—in this case, a seat in the bus (Sartre 1978, 130, 259). The competition between these individuals represents a contradiction that is sublated insofar as the bus provides everyone with a seat.

The serial gathering of people at the bus station is thus revealed to be structured by how exigencies gather individuals around a practico-inert object because all individuals relate to this object in the same way while not questioning this relating. The structure of the gathering fulfills the functional requirements of its elements in a specific way. According to Kleinherenbrink and Gusman (2018), the bus represents a social object, as it mediates the concrete relations of individuals.

The serial gathering of people at the bus station exemplifies what Sartre refers to as a *direct* gathering, in which people are immediately present on-site. He distinguishes different kinds of *presence* in predominantly serially structured ensembles and links them to the possible kinds of interrelations between individuals. He defines gatherings by the co-presence of their members in the sense that the possibility of reciprocity and thus transformation is immediately given. In *direct* gatherings, like at a bus stop or in front of a bakery, these people have the possibility to unite and diffuse their serial structuring because they are directly present to each other on-site (see section 4.4).

In contrast to such direct gatherings, technological artifacts and structures can also condition the actions of individuals in such a way as to induce the constitution of *indirect gatherings*. These are characterized by *absence*. In such gatherings, people gather around a practico-inert object or structure serially while also being separated from each other through their specific way of practical interrelating. Sartre's example is a radio broadcast in which each listener remains passive and singular with regard to the broadcaster on the radio. Although the whole of listeners is a structured ensemble that forms by people gathering around the radio in the act of listening, their listening itself is what separates these listeners from one another (Sartre 1978, 270–271). More modern examples of such indirect gatherings are social networks. Platforms like Facebook or Twitter claim to engender social exchange between individuals. By design, however, such platforms must rather be seen to mediate such an exchange. Platform users who *like* another user's post or tweet interact with the platform which then interacts with the other user. The instantaneous nature of this mediation obscures the fact that users on social networks are situated in a serially structured practical ensemble.

In both examples, one effect of technology via artificial objects or structures in the formation of practical ensembles is revealed in how practico-inert instrumental means passively gathering human beings around them. They do so by enabling these individuals to repeatedly satisfy certain needs and desires within larger functionally interrelated constellations.

Interest and the Demands of Things

This effect of technology can be further scrutinized regarding the material properties of the practico-inert object. Insofar as the people in the serial gathering at the bus stop depend on the bus to satisfy their need for mobility, the bus represents what Sartre calls their *interest* to which he also refers their *being-wholly-outside-oneself-in-a-thing* (Sartre 1978, 259). According to Sartre, interest is a "relation between man and thing in a social field [...] it exists in a more or less developed form wherever men live in the midst of a material set of tools which impose their techniques on them" (Sartre 1978, 197). In that these people require the service provided by the bus, they have to abide by the rules of the practico-inert object they use as means. Owing to this predicament, the relation between agent and means is inverted. It is no longer according to the needs and desires of individuals that actions are performed, but according to the demands of the instrumental means that are supposed to support these actions. In this way, the demands and requirements as well as the structural integrity of practico-inert objects become associated and even equated with the concrete possibility of these individuals to sustain themselves as organic entities through these objects as means. The effect is that certain instrumental means become critical for the individuals who must rely on them when these means are associated as *interests*.[4] This inverts the relation of equipmentality between the user and means. Sartre mentions that for a house, for instance, to "preserve its reality as a *dwelling* a house must be *inhabited*, that is to say, looked after, heated, swept, re-painted, etc.; otherwise it deteriorates. This vampire object constantly absorbs human action, lives on blood taken from man and finally lives in symbiosis with him" (Sartre 1978, 169, emphasis in original).

Sartre points out that this reversed designation, from means to user, can be more abstract or concrete depending on the exact nature of the position individuals adopt in specific practical ensembles with a serial structure. Reflecting on his position in French society in the 1950s and 1960s, Sartre states the following:

> a brace and bit and a monkey-wrench designate me as much as my neighbour. But when these designations are addressed to me, they generally remain abstract and purely logical, because I am a petty-bourgeois intellectual, or rather, because I am designated as a petty bourgeois intellectual by the very fact that these relations remain pure, dead possibilities. However, in the practical field of actual common labour, the skilled worker is really and directly designated by the tool or the machine to which he is assigned. (Sartre 1978, 186)

The structural integrity of practico-inert objects along with their strong association as means of subsistence not only renders them critical for an individual's mode of reproduction—it also results in certain forms of coercion and necessitation. This can be extrapolated to the practico-inert setting at the bus stop.

The bus, as a practico-inert object, is built to have certain material properties, such as a limited seating capacity, among others. These properties represent materialized ways in which past designers and creators responded to the needs and desires of their historical situation. These needs and desires work their way into the future in the form of the bus as practico-inert object (see section 3.4). The properties of the bus refer to specific forms of conduct through which needs and desires can be satisfied using the bus. In this example, the bus is useful for satisfying a set number of people's needs or desires for mobility. Through the conceptual lens of practical ensembles, the operations revolving around the constellation of bus, bus driver, and passengers can be further scrutinized regarding certain factors that enable them. This scrutiny reveals that the bus itself requires another larger infrastructure, such as a road and a system of traffic regulations, to fulfill its purpose. The road infrastructure must be maintained by people, who require this form of labor to earn money

---

4   In section 4.6, it is argued that the association of instrumental means as *interest* generates vulnerabilities in the case of crises and disruptions.

to satisfy their needs and desires. Thus, right away, layered forms of structured interrelations are revealed, and they all interplay to enable the passive gathering at the bus stop.

Not only the seating capacity but also the condition of the road infrastructure, the distribution of stops, and other factors delimit both the number of people who can take the bus and the route this bus can potentially take. This implies that practico-inert objects and structures themselves not only passively gather a series of needy/desiring people around them, whose social interrelations are arranged by these very objects and structures. The way these objects and structures mediate the social relations between individual human beings is also based on the ends that were manifested in the material properties of these objects and structures. Furthermore, besides the needs and desires of its human elements, the demands and requirements of practico-inert objects and structures, as well as the way these demands and requirements must be taken care of, affect how practical ensembles are structured. Given those human and non-human elements contribute to the overall *praxis* of the ensemble, either by adopting a functional role themselves or by attributing a functional role to other elements, Sartre considers practical ensembles to be functionally interrelated and mutually mediated. He states:

> [P]*raxis* as the unification of inorganic plurality becomes the *practical* unity of matter. Material forces gathered together in the passive unity of tools and machines *perform actions* [French *font des actes*]: they *unify* other inorganic dispersals and thereby impose a material unification on the plurality of men. The movement of materiality, in fact, derives from men. But the *praxis* inscribed in the instrument by past labour defines behaviour *a priori* [French *définit apriori les conduites*] by sketching in its passive rigidity the outline of a sort of mechanical alterity which culminates in a division of labour. Precisely because matter mediates between men, men mediate between materialised *praxes*, and dispersal orders itself into a sort of quasi-synthetic hierarchy reproducing the particular ordering imposed on materiality by past labour in the form of a human order. (Sartre 1978, 184, emphasis in original; Sartre 1960, 250–251)

How serial structures in practical ensembles are particularly ordered reflects the mode in which the functional requirements or exigencies of their elements—in the form of human needs and desires, as well as practico-inert demands and requirements—are taken care of. Through the material properties established by others in the practico-inert objects and systems that people rely on in serial gatherings, materialized meaning intrudes on individual forms of conduct. As a result, the actions of the human elements are transformed by the fact that an object or structure is used as a means that has been constructed for a specific purpose. Although the means itself does not strictly alter an action, the use of practico-inert objects still coerces the human elements to deviate from their initially intended course of action (Sartre 1978,

223). Though individuals may realize their ends, this realization must be understood as a transformation of subjective ends into objective ends through the means (Hubig 2006, 129).

For Sartre's earlier theoretical conception of ontological freedom and human existence (see section 2.3), this form of coercion initially poses no problem. If an ontologically free and informed agent is assumed, whose choice of means is rational, transparent, and directed toward the attainment of clearly defined individual ends, this type of coercion through instrumental means is only hypothetical. Agents remain ontologically free in the ends they choose by pursuing them, and in the means they seek to employ toward these ends. Only when they wish to attain certain ends must they adjust their actions and abide by the pre-established ways of performing actions that others have manifested in the means at hand (Sartre 2021, 557). However, in any given historical situation the attainment of ends is not a free choice but a practical necessity. Consequently, these individuals face categorical coercions to modify their actions.

Exigency, Necessitation of Action, and Structural Reinforcement

This becomes clearer through Sartre's conception of how historical situations necessitate individuals to rely on a limited instrumental field of possibilities. Sartre illustrates this with class-being, in particular that of the working class. As is the case with his entire later philosophy, Sartre's view on societal classes is shaped by a Marxist understanding of the social developments of the 1950s and 1960s. He claims that the working class, when conceived as a practical ensemble, is revealed to be constituted by the social stratification of capitalist societies, as it manifests in the shared exigencies of individuals and the way these individuals must sustain themselves under common sociocultural and material conditions.

Despite Sartre's Marxist understanding, his assumptions prove to be adequate beyond a Marxist class analysis. He summarizes his understanding of class-being in a rather conclusive passage, stating that at the origin of class-membership, there are

> passive syntheses of materiality [...] these syntheses represent both the general conditions of social activity and our most immediate, crudest objective reality [...] they are simply the *crystallized practice* of previous generations [French *pratique cristallisée des générations précédentes*]: individuals find an existence already sketched out [French *préesquissée*] for them at birth [...] What is 'assigned' to them is a type of work, and a material condition and a standard of living tied to this activity; it is a fundamental *attitude* [French *attitude fondamentale*], as well as a determinative provision of material and intellectual tools; it is a strictly limited

field of possibilities [*un champ de possibilités rigoureusement limité*]. (Sartre 1978, 232, emphasis in original; Sartre 1960, 289)

According to this understanding, a societal class can be conceived as a practical ensemble with certain structures of seriality. The same applies to basically any constellation in which individuals share similar life conditions. The human elements in these ensembles are usually united not by a common, interior cause and undertaking, but by their prefabricated means of subsistence on the one hand, and by the *attitude* they adopt as a result of their shared material conditions on the other. This section focuses on the interplay between practico-inert means and individual action treated, especially regarding the inner structure of practical ensembles. How attitude is formed and how it affects the inner structure of practical ensembles will be analyzed in section 4.5.

According to Sartre, through membership in serial constellations, individual freedom is mostly limited to the means provided by the general conditions and possibilities predominant in those constellations. The layers of the practico-inert that K. S. Engels (2018) identifies (see section 3.4) can all be found in class-being. A certain group of physical artifacts represents the means of subsistence for every class. Language as a body technique is enacted through various dialects and sociolects that mark class-membership. This membership also comes with deeply ingrained ideas or attitudes about the self and others in society. Here other body techniques can also be found, such as specific modes of recreation or consumption. These attitudes again represent social objects, or, more precisely, social modes of interaction manifested in individuals.

Human beings are necessarily situated in socioculturally and materially structured constellations that scaffold a field of possibilities for them; these individuals must also practically satisfy their needs and desires with certain limited practico-inert means available to them. From these facts, it follows that these individuals do not face a hypothetical but rather what Sartre refers to as *categorical* coercion to modify their course of action to reproduce themselves. This coercion is categorical because it corresponds to the necessity of self-reproduction (Sartre 1978, 190). Given that instrumental means represent practico-inert objects and structures, the meaning and purpose of which have been established by others in the form of material properties (see section 3.4), individuals who must rely on these means must necessarily acquiesce to the fact that extrasubjective meaning intrudes into their practical interrelation with their surroundings. Despite their ontological freedom, historically situated individuals do not remain practically free to choose the ways they realize themselves through their actions. Their course of action must necessarily be performed with the means prescribed by the position that these individuals adopt within their respective practical ensembles (Sartre 1978, 190). In this context, Sartre states:

Exigency, in fact, whether in the form of an order or a categorical imperative, constitutes itself in everyone as other than him. (He cannot modify it, but simply has to conform to it; it is beyond his control, and he may change entirely without changing it; in short, it does not enter into the dialectical movement of behaviour.) In this way, exigency constitutes him as other than himself, In so far as he is characterised by *praxis*, his *praxis* does not originate in need or in desire [French *celle-ci ne prend pas sa source dans le besoin ou dans le désir*]; it is not the process of realizing his project, but in so far as it is constituted so as to achieve an alien object, it is, in the agent himself, the *praxis* of another; and it is another who objectifies himself in the result. (Sartre 1978, 187–188, emphasis in original; Sartre 1960, 253)

Through exigencies, or the material claims prevalent in practical ensembles, individuals exhibit certain forms of behavior. These forms no longer originate in their free and self-totalizing interrelation with their sociocultural and material mediating milieu, based on their needs and desires. Rather, these forms of behavior come from the material necessity of another sector of materiality. In that the historical situation of individuals, i.e. their position within practical ensembles, necessitates their reliance on certain means of subsistence, their totalizing action no longer derives directly from their exigencies. It comes instead from how the means at their disposal are structured, and from how the utility of these means creates a new practical setting that not only yields intended effects but also side effects (Sartre 1978, 183–186). This interplay—between the necessity for human beings to sustain themselves within a strictly limited practical field of equipmentality, and the possibility ascribed to them in virtue of their position in forms of societal organization—is the root of *la force des choses*.

In the case of the working class, understood as a practical ensemble, their means of subsistence are structured so as to produce laborers, products, and profit in a capitalist mode of production. This mode of production can itself be understood as a practical ensemble consisting of human and non-human elements, or even as an ensemble of ensembles.[5] These individuals persistently rely on a prefabricated

---

5   In this regard Sartre's theories are somewhat limited. Although he acknowledges that groups form sub-groups with differentiated functions (Sartre 1978, 417), he does not provide the terminology to clearly differentiate between micro-, meso-, and macro-ensembles. The point of Sartre's practical ensembles is not primarily to illustrate the complexity of systems, but to examine the possibilities and practical constraints individuals face in practical constellations. For this reason, every larger functionally interrelated constellation of human and non-human elements represents a practical ensemble; the analysis of its structures reveals the historical situation of individuals. In section 4.6, it is shown that Sartre's conception of counter-finalities allows one to conceive of structures of coupled ensembles.

instrumental field of possibilities through which their needs and desires are effectively taken care of, and the inner structure of practical ensembles is consolidated, reinforced, and perpetuated based on the pre-established forms of conduct associated with and affected by technology in the form of artificial objects and body techniques. In Sartrean terms, individuals totalize the inner structure of their practical ensembles and thus reinforce these ensembles as totalities. They do so based on the practical interrelations between the elements of these ensembles. Sartre's example involves the processes in a factory:

> [I]ndividuals in an organisation interiorise the exigency of matter and re-exteriorise it as the exigency of man. Through supervisors and inspectors, machines demand a particular rhythm of the worker: and it makes no difference whether the producers are supervised by particular *men* or whether, when the equipment allows it, the supervisors are replaced by a more or less automatic system of checks. In either case, material exigency, whether it is expressed through a machine-man or a human machine, comes to the machine through man to precisely the extent that it comes to man through the machines. Whether *in the machine*, as imperative expectation and as power, or *in man*, as mimicry (imitating the inert in giving orders), as action and coercive power, exigency is *always* both man as a practical agent and matter as worked product in an indivisible symbiosis. (Sartre 1978, 190–191, emphasis in original)

As a result, the totalizing activity of individuals or groups "ceases to be the free organisation of the practical field and becomes the re-organisation of one sector of materiality in accordance with the exigencies of another sector of materiality" (Sartre 1978, 191). This furthers the divide between the concrete form of subjectivity and objectivity realized through historically situated totalizing actions, as mentioned in section 2.4. Furthermore, through this form of reinforcement, practical ensembles actively resist change, and individuals associate the structure of these ensembles with their interests. In this regard, practical ensembles generate a certain functional criticality for the individuals situated in them.

Objectification and Alienation

Although what was described above is reminiscent of a Marxist understanding of alienation, Sartre hesitates to recognize it as such. He states that in a classical Marxist understanding, alienation comes with exploitation in capitalist societies. However, the specific practical constraints he reveals to affect individuals in practical ensembles go beyond capitalist exploitation. In all practical ensembles, practical constraints arise as a result of the lived contradiction that is human existence. As such, these constraints represent constitutive aspects of human existence, irrespective of the overall societal mode of production. Sartre also struggles to recognize this circumstance as alienation in a Hegelian sense, according to which all forms of human objectification, through labor or otherwise, essentially represent forms of alienation. Rather, Sartre reevaluates the relationship between objectification and alienation in human existence.

According to Sartre, objectification must not be understood merely as an outcome of human action clashing with the plasticity of physicochemical reality. It is instead the root of the lived contradiction of human existence (see section 1.4) and its consequence (Sartre 1978, 112). As such, it represents the condition of possibility for self-recognition.

Through their actions, human beings exteriorize and objectify themselves in the world. Although this is mostly evident in the larger effects of human actions—the things they built and the structures they form—it is also present in the smaller, more intricate traces humans leave through their actions, such as footsteps, grind marks, and wear and tear. In that human beings re-interiorize their effects and traces as objectified in matter, they discover themselves as *"Other* in the world of objectivity" (Sartre 1978, 227, emphasis in original). According to Sartre, human beings may only recognize themselves through detours. This means that they assess how they affect the world through the effects they cause through their actions. Their interiority becomes tangible to them in an oscillating process by which it is translated into exteriority and hence must be re-interiorized as Other. This can be through the *look*, i.e. the reactions and judgments of others (Sartre 2021, 401–408), or through the spotting of differences between intended and realized ends (Sartre 2021, 249–250), among other ways. Sartre summarizes this paradoxical fact in a rather poetic way: "All of us spend our lives engraving our maleficent image on things, and it fascinates and bewilders us if we try to understand ourselves *through it,* although we are ourselves the totalising movement which results in *this* particular objectification" (Sartre 1978, 227, emphasis in original).

Alienation, however, is a result of specific forms of societal interrelations in which individuals are forced to transform their exigencies according to the exigencies of another material sector without necessarily realizing this to be the case (Sartre 1978, 164).[6] Consequently, Sartre's notion of alienation is not limited to capitalist modes of production but can be applied to all forms of constellations that exhibit the characteristics mentioned above.

Historical Constellations as Ge-Stell

Sartre's description of the situation of individuals in practical ensembles with predominantly serial structures resembles Heidegger's understanding of *Ge-Stell*. This

---

6   For a more thorough discussion of Sartre's conception of alienation, see Birt (1986) and Collamati (2016).

is evident not only in Sartre's conception of scarcity and people's demands for securing potential goods, services, and other options for action; it also appears in how individuals are challenged, for instance, to respond to the demands of the instrumental means they use. In *Die Frage nach der Technik*, Heidegger analyzes the nature of technology by contrasting the way human-world relations are mediated by ancient and more modern technologies. He states that the actual essence of technology is nothing technological at all (Heidegger 2000, 7–8). Rather, technology must be understood as the very mode of disclosing and securing options for action regarding the world (Luckner 2012, 61). Technology must thus be comprehended as a mode of being that Heidegger calls *Ge-Stell*. In this mode of being, entities can appear as *Bestand*, i.e. as mere standing reserves and means to ends. The problematic aspect of this process is the threatening commitment to particular options for action and the obscuring of other modes of being (Luckner 2012, 63).

Against the background of Sartre's philosophy, it could be said that when constellations of human and non-human elements are understood through the lens of practical ensembles, they can be revealed to represent instantiations of *Ge-Stell*. Any such constellations represent material and sociocultural settings that dispose the actions of individuals by providing them with fixed options (or opportunities) for action. While this form of commitment allows for increased efficiency and effectiveness in the satisfaction and generation of needs, desires, and demands, it also obscures other options for action. Furthermore, the fixation on specific forms of conduct challenges individuals and physicochemical reality alike, as both become *standing reserve* (German *Bestand*). In the case of individuals, this is evident in apersonal structures of seriality, where each individual ultimately represents a competitor for the means of subsistence (see above). However, according to Sartre, these individuals can organize themselves and attempt to rise above the structures of their ensembles (see 4.4). How physicochemical reality becomes *standing reserve* is similar to the way instrumental means become *interest*. Because individuals satisfy their needs and desires by instrumentalizing physicochemical reality (see section 4.2), specific goods and resources become critical as they are associated with the continuation of certain constellations. This may lead to excessive demands and an overload of ecosystems and other constellations alike. Eventually, this overload can trigger *counter-finalities*, through which the very structures of practical ensembles are threatened at their core (see section 4.6).

4.4 Transformation

This section aims to identify processes through which the structures of practical ensembles are transformed. This transformation occurs because agents identify a lack of services or options for action in the current structure of their practical ensemble.

An illustration is the transformations from serially structured ensembles to communally structured ensembles and back.

However, before that, it must be noted that the analysis in this work of how Sartre conceives groups to form based on series in no way claims to be complete. On the contrary, some essential aspects of Sartre's analysis must be omitted to keep the underlying dynamics of practical ensembles in view. Regarding these underlying dynamics, Sartre's line of thinking is not so much about the sociality of these groups in particular; rather, it represents a dialectical and praxeological examination of the conditions individuals generally face when organizing in historical situations. Although Sartre uses terms like *group-in-fusion*, *organized group*, and *institution*, these terms refer to more abstract forms of supraindividual responses that condition individual actions.[7]

The Transformation from Serial to Communal Ensembles

At times a practical ensemble may form in the active attempt of its human elements to eliminate or change how the conjunction of practico-inert objects and sociocultural/material conditions scaffolds their serial unity. When this happens, and when this new practical ensemble furthermore remains defined by its undertaking, this ensemble represents a preliminary group called a *group-in-fusion*. It exhibits a communal structure (Sartre 1978, 255). The initial attempt is to change either the functional requirement the practical ensemble fulfills or how the practical ensemble fulfills that requirement. It follows that any group-in-fusion presupposes structures of seriality against which the group-in-fusion defines itself (Rae 2011, 192). Although the communal structure of practical ensembles differs from that of serial structures, they still reflect both the functional requirements of their elements and the fact that communal structures define themselves against their outside (see section 4.3).

Owing to the limited field of possibilities prevalent in serially structured ensembles, individuals situated in these ensembles can be threatened by the fact that some of their needs and desires are not provided for—either because certain options for action do not exist, or because the serial structures of their ensemble actively constrain these individuals in satisfying their needs and desires. Concrete instances of this can be the identification of exploitative labor conditions, a lack of political representation, control, or governmental regulation, or an overall lack of certain options for action. In a more abstract case, this limitation appears as the non-existence of any form of organization through which individuals may exert power over themselves.

---

7   More theoretical analyses of Sartre's theory of group formation can be found in Hartmann (1966) and Rae (2011), among others.

When these individuals actively demand or promote change and transformation, their response represents an active negation of the positing givenness prevalent in their serially structured ensemble. The response can be a riot, a public outcry, or any other spontaneous outburst of individuals who unite behind a common cause. Through this active and communal response, serial, parallel, and essentially competitive existence, as a purely exterior relation between human elements resulting from a passive synthesis, is transformed into communal and synthetic coexistence. The individuals of this group-in-fusion have interior, cohesive, and reciprocal relations with each other. Therefore, contrary to a series, a group-in-fusion must be understood as the result of an active synthesis through the spontaneous yet communal and unified response of its members (Rae 2011, 193).

As long as the constraints of serial structures pose a threat to the individuals of that group, the group-in-fusion may persist. If, on the contrary, the constraints no longer threaten, either because of the spontaneous actions of the group-in-fusion or because of other reasons, one of two things will happen to the group. Either it disintegrates because its *raison d'être* has vanished, or it organizes itself, given that it identifies the potential for similar threats to reappear (Rae 2011, 195).

When the group-in-fusion disintegrates, group members disperse into seriality. However, when the group-in-fusion attempts to organize itself, it represents a *statutory group* in the process of becoming an *organized group*. An organized group can be a political party, a social movement, a workgroup, or a task force—any larger constellation of people that actively attempts to organize itself. In this organized group, the functional interrelations between the human elements are seen to be communally structured, because groups act through the active mediation of their members. A newly founded political party, for instance, represents the whole of the intersubjective relations of its party members, both within the party and with people and conditions outside the party.

In organized groups, practical interrelations are conditioned by what Sartre refers to as the *pledge* of its members. As a *"practical device"* (Sartre 1978, 420, emphasis in original), the pledge has different functions and affects group members in multiple ways. It can be any group member's explicit commitment to recognize their role and the role of others for the functioning of the organized group. The pledge generates group cohesion in that it "simply allows each individual to promise to the other that he will act in a way that cares for and affirms the other's practical freedom" (Rae 2011, 196). Furthermore, by the pledge, each member is assigned a specific function—a form of conduct—upon which the larger organization depends as a functionally differentiated constellation. This allows an organized group to be more effective. In this regard, a pledge can be an oath to abide by certain rules, a creed featuring certain norms, or even the commitment to drive on the right side of the street. Furthermore, the internal organization of groups grows over time in response to the serially structured ensemble, as the functional requirements of the organized group correlate negatively to the serial structures the group organizes itself against. Rather than dispersing like the group-in-fusion when the exigencies of the serially structured ensemble change, the organized group adapts itself to these serial structures. The action of each member is "directly conditioned by his functional relation to the other members of the group, as *already established* either by the group […] or by its representatives" (Sartre 1978, 446, emphasis in original). Like with the preliminary group-in-fusion, the human elements within organized groups have interior, reciprocal relations to each other, but they also remain as individuals, precisely because their commitment is what constitutes their group's form of organization. Therefore, no one is interchangeable in organized groups; the group continues to define itself against the exigencies of its instrumental field through the actions of the specific individuals that are its members. However, the human elements within groups do not dissolve into the larger organic unity of the group. Rather, a group is in the constant process of totalization as its unity is actively constituted through individual action (Sartre 1978, 407). According to Sartre, membership in organized groups enhances the practical freedom of each individual, as this membership is defined both by a committed response to common threats and by an affirmation of individual responsibility to protect the practical freedom of others in the group (Rae 2011, 201).

Institutionalization as (Re-)Serialization

The longer the organized group works against the serially structured practical ensemble, the stronger the group identifies itself through both its undertaking (as a negation of serial structures) and the specific way its functionally differentiated interrelations are structured. This eventually leads to an inversion of individual and group *praxis* so that the function and structure of the organized group is superimposed on the individuals who propelled the organization of the group through their functional roles in the first place. According to Sartre, "function, positing itself for itself, and producing individuals who will perpetuate it, becomes an *institution*" (Sartre 1978, 600, emphasis in original).

Members of institutionalized groups are passive function carriers rather than active promoters of the group's organizational structure. The pledge between members is replaced by a dictum stipulating functions and the details of how those functions are to be carried out. In this way, individual practical freedom is limited, whereas the overall possibilities for the institution's action may be increased. Consequently, in the transition from organized group to the institution, the ensemble transforms from a communally structured ensemble to an ensemble exhibiting serial characteristics. The members of institutions are now defined only by their functional role. Analogous to how practico-inert objects, as *interest*, designate their user and dispose the user to act in a certain way in serially structured ensembles (see section 4.3), in institutions individuals are designated to act in certain ways in virtue of adopting a functional role (Sartre 1978, 602).

Rather than actively initiating and contributing to the overall form of organization through their committed actions, members of institutions perpetuate the institutions' organizational structure. This work is also accompanied by a concentration of authority, so that the sovereign of the institution "dictates how the institution will act, what it will be directed toward, and the manner in which each member will comport himself" (Rae 2011, 203). In political parties, for instance, individuals take the positions of party leaders, speakers, treasurers, and so on, with their interrelations governed by the party program; this arrangement occurs to streamline communication and distribute competences.

Depending on the functional requirements of the institution, the direction dictated by the sovereign, and the level of specialization necessary to fulfill their functions, the members of institutions are functionally interchangeable. This implies that the human elements in these ensembles need not be replaced with other human elements, for they can also be replaced with non-human elements. Although Sartre does not engage in this discussion in his analysis of institutions, he examines such a replacement of workers in his look at Taylorism, i.e. the attempt to optimize modes of production with the help of scientific analysis (Peaucelle 2000). Sartre claims that optimizing the labor process for maximum profit entails a de-skilling of individual laborers and their eventual replacement through what he refers to as *specialized machines*. In the case of replacing workers with machines, the labor process itself must no longer be understood as *praxis* in the form of human conduct, but as a mechanical operation (Sartre 1978, 562).[8]

This replacement can take place in institutions as well. Considering the regulation of traffic to be an institutionalized response to potentially dangerous modes of traversing streets, for instance, each road user's behavior is seen to be dictated by rules delimiting individual options for action for the sake of safer travel. Traffic lights function as active ways to control traffic, and street signs function as signifiers reminding road users to abide by prescribed regulations. Speed bumps and roundabouts function as passive, inert obstacles to which road users must adapt their behavior (Rosenberger 2014). Misconduct is sanctioned by various authorities who function as sovereigns.

---

8   In this context, Sartre also imagines the characteristics necessary for an *electronic brain* to control labor processes. He states: "There is no action so complex that it cannot be decomposed, dismembered, transformed, and infinitely varied by an 'electronic brain'; it would be impossible to construct or use an 'electronic brain' except within the perspective of a dialectical *praxis* of which the operations under consideration were merely a moment" (Sartre 1978, 561–562).

Structured Interrelations as Structural Moments of Totalization

Sartre's conceptual view on the transformation of practical ensembles does not only highlight group formation as a liberating process in which human beings free themselves from serially structured conditions. It also illustrates the compromises that individuals must make to organize themselves against inertia and scarcity. For various reasons, individuals may limit their practical freedom out of practical necessity. They consolidate forms of organization, re-distribute competences, and settle down to fixed strategies through which they satisfy their needs and desires. This allows these individuals to liberate themselves again and again and practically enact their ontological freedom. When nomad people, for instance, settle down to practice agriculture, they commit to a certain way of life at a certain place. By committing in such a way, these people gain the possibility to satisfy their requirements for food through their localized mode of production. In committing to such an agricultural mode of production, however, they also make it harder to leave, because their agricultural mode of production is constrained to a fixed place. They thus have the chance to liberate themselves from this coercion by, for instance, restructuring their mode of production. Sartre's way of framing this constant inversion from serial structures to communal structures and back accounts for the larger dimensions of his claim, that the dialectical progression of history must become intelligible—not as a natural law that dictates this progression, but as the complex outcome of simple, singular human interrelations with other human beings and their surroundings (see section 1.4).

At the same time, Sartre's anthropological focus allows him to reveal the fact that human existence is inherently situated in constellations in which serial and communally structured interrelations interplay. Although people may free themselves from structures that constrain their practical freedom, they must rely on other scaffolded, serial structures to provide them with a limited but manageable instrumental field of possibilities. Although extrasubjective forms of conduct have been poured into practico-inert objects and structures (see section 3.4) by whose use serial systems of interrelations are formed (see section 4.3), Sartre states that those who intend to transform these systems "must therefore have a project with a double aim: to resolve the existing contradictions by a wider totalisation, and to diminish the hold of materiality by substituting tenuousness for opacity, and lightness for weight" (Sartre 1978, 183). In this regard, the organizational schema of practical ensembles always involves worked and processually adapted matter as a "*minimum* of synthesized passivity [...] that praxis must transcend towards the practical situation" (Sartre 1991, 128, emphasis in original).

Based on these considerations, it becomes evident that practical constellations never exhibit purely serial or communal structures. Rather, in most constellations, structures of seriality and communality can be understood to interconnect, inform, and dialectically mediate each other in the constellations' totalizing processing. The institutionalized traffic regulations mentioned above, for instance, directly refer not only to material elements (pedestrians, drivers, cars, road infrastructure) that are governed but also to the fact that these elements are the ones whose interrelations, as governed by traffic laws, enact and thus totalize those laws in the first place. However, each of these elements exhibits different forms of structuring. The actions of pedestrians are differently structured to those of drivers, simply because the practico-inert objects and structures that pedestrians and drivers interrelate with mediate their actions in different ways. In the case of pedestrians, these objects and/or structures are the shoes they wear, the pavement they walk on, and the streetlights, for instance. The actions of drivers are serially structured by their specific car models, the road, other drivers, and so on. Although both pedestrians and drivers are situated in serial structures, their structures are not the same. Both are defined as structures by their specific forms of conduct, their material elements, and other factors. However, the actions enabled through these respective modes of structuring affect each other and thus contribute to the larger form of organization again.

According to Sartre, the fundamentally totalizing activities of human action and experience represent the very conditions of possibility according to which the operations of any larger form of organization must become intelligible in the first place.

Through Sartre's practical ensemble framework, a political party, for instance, can be analyzed as a structured whole that totalizes itself through its political work. The same party can also be analyzed regarding the way its members communicate via mobile phones, as these communicative processes represent structural moments in the party's overall processual totalization. Furthermore, the political party, understood as a practical ensemble, can also be understood as a partial totality that interrelates with other parties as partial totalities. The interrelations between these parties can again be understood to represent structural moments in the larger totalizing processing of the nationwide political discourse, for instance. This is further discussed in section 4.6.

4.5 Persistence

This section examines the dynamics through which practical ensembles persist. According to Sartre, there are two essential aspects affecting the persistence of practical ensembles in the material properties of their non-human elements and the totalizing actions of their human elements. The inertia and longevity of practico-inert means represent major factors in how practical ensembles maintain themselves. In that individuals identify instrumental means as their interest, both in the sense of means of subsistence and means of liberation, these individuals keep on perpetuating the inner structure of practical ensembles. This involves the maintenance of current technological settings according to the demands and requirements of their practico-inert elements on the one hand (see section 4.3), and technological innovation and development on the other. However, Sartre does not discuss the historical becoming of technology in particular. He is much more interested in the processes involved in how people tackle scarcity or potentially adapt to it.

As mentioned before, Sartre claims that history "is born from a sudden imbalance which disrupts all levels of society" (Sartre 1978, 126) whenever individuals recognize that their exigencies are not taken care of through the practical ensembles they are situated in. However, this recognition itself can be obscured through the way human beings internally adapt to their role in practical ensembles, even if their structure does not allow individuals to tackle their own needs and desires but instead coerces them to abide by the exigencies of another material entity or collective. In this way, the perpetual disequilibrium of scarcity can be lived as an equilibrium, when it is preserved as *hexis*[9] (Sartre 1978, 126).

The concept of *hexis* has its roots in Aristotelian philosophy, where it derives from the Greek verb *echein* (English *to have*). The noun can be translated as *habit, state, disposition,* (fundamental) *attitude,* or *characteristic,* although none of these translations fully captures its Greek meaning.[10] *Hexis* represents an "entrenched psychic condition or state which develops through experience rather than congenitally" (Lockwood 2013, 22), and which disposes the actions of agents who *have* or *hold* (Greek *echein*) this condition or state.

The conceptual dimensions of *hexis* in Sartre's philosophy are hard to pinpoint. The concept itself is not clearly defined by Sartre, nor is it well developed throughout his works. Furthermore, Sartre's conception of *hexis* changes from *Being and Nothingness* to *Critique*. Sartre's *hexis*-concept combines aspects of Aristotelian philosophy, habits, Maussian *habitus* (Mauss 1934, 1973), and processes of habituation, among other sources. Sartre discusses an individual's "habits (in the Greek sense of ἕξις)" (Sartre 2021, 232) in the context of the qualities of the *Ego*[11] in *Being and Nothingness*. In *Critique* he conceptualizes *hexis* as an action disposition that agents develop by

---

9   According to Barnes, the translator of the 2003 Routledge edition of *Being and Nothingness*, Sartre seems to have ignored the rough breathing of the Greek term ἕξις (Sartre 2003, 2). In *L'être et le néant*, Sartre uses the Greek spelling ἕξις. In *Critique de la raison dialectique*, he uses the spelling *exis*. Given that ἕξις or *hexis* is not only a technical term in Greek philosophy but also has become an established term in the philosophy of habits, the spelling *hexis* is used in this work. In some quotations from Sartre's works, where the term *exis* appears, it is replaced with *hexis* in brackets.

10   These translations refer to Lockwood (2013) the German glossary provided by Wolf in Aristotle (trans. 2015), and the LSJ entry on ἔχω (n.d a).

11   In Sartre's philosophy, the *Ego* refers to a person as a psychological unity. Sartre states: "It is as an *Ego* that we are subjects *de facto* and subjects *de jure*, active and passive, voluntary agents, possible objects of evaluative judgment, or a judgment of responsibility" (Sartre 2021, 232).

interiorizing practical relations through repetition. It is here where Sartre explores the societal significance of *hexeis*.

When agents develop a *hexis* by repeating certain practical relations, the course of these relations, in combination with the instrumental means used in them as well as the structural context they are situated in, pass into and become incarnated in the agent's corporeality. There they remain as passive residuals or imprints of former actions. In this way, the practical relations themselves have become practico-inert in the agent's bodily inertia. The reason why agents repeat certain practical relations is that these practical relations allow the agents to attain desired ends under certain conditions. The action disposition developed this way disposes the agents who *hold* it to perpetuate these practical relations in similar ways under similar conditions. In this regard, *hexis* represents a condition of possibility for the persistence of practical ensembles.

Unfortunately, Sartre studies have neglected the significance of *hexis*. This might be because Sartre's later work has gained considerably less academic attention than his early works, or it could be because *hexis* has connotations of a passive and materially inert behavior that contrasts with free and creative *praxis* (Flynn 1997, 94). Another reason might be the predominance of Merleau-Ponty's *Phenomenology of Perception*, to which philosophers seem to resort to for phenomenological research on habits and embodiment.[12] However, despite this inattention, *hexis* not only represents an important aspect of Sartre's theoretical conception of practical ensembles, but an ineluctable fact of human existence and reality more broadly.

To get a more general understanding of the mechanisms and principles underlying Sartre's conception of *hexis*, it is useful to reflect upon them against the context of other philosophers who put a similar emphasis on the societal implications of a person's habituated actions.

The Societal Implications of Hexis and Habit

In *Nicomachean Ethics*, Aristotle reflects upon a person's *hexis* in the context of his thoughts on *praxis* and *poiesis*. According to Aristotle, human action can be described by the aspects of *praxis* and *poiesis*, among others. Depending on whether actions are predominantly seen under the aspect of *praxis* or *poiesis*, different guiding principles can be applied through which the course and results of these actions can be assessed (Luckner 2005, 81–82). Under the aspect of *praxis*, an action is understood as a goal-directed activity that has its end in itself. Such activities include political control and regulation, law, and music, but also other activities aiming at the development and preservation of one's capacity to act (Hubig 2013b, 23). The guiding principle of *praxis*

---

12   For a juxtaposition of Sartre's and Merleau-Ponty's conceptions of habit and embodiment, see Crossley (2010).

is *phronesis*, Greek for *prudence*. *Phronesis* can also be translated as *practical reason* or *practical wisdom*. As such, it represents a *hexis praktike*, a disposition toward action under the aspect of *praxis*, according to which agents can reflect on whether actions are good or bad regarding their success in attaining certain ends under specific circumstances (Lockwood 2013, 24; Aristotle trans. 2015, 199).

Under the aspect of *poiesis*, an action is understood as a *making* that has its end in the effect or thing it brings into being. Such activities include productive processes such as baking, tailoring, forging, writing, and so on, but also any applied sciences that aim at producing or reproducing certain effects. Similarly to *phronesis* in the case of *praxis*, *techne* serves as the guiding principle of *poiesis*. In this regard, *techne*, as a *hexis poietike* (Lockwood 2013, 24), represents a disposition toward action (under the aspect of *poiesis*) according to which agents can reflect on and act based on how things could be brought into being, especially regarding the fact that these things need not necessarily be constituted in one specific way, but could be constituted in other ways (Aristotle trans. 2015, 198). Furthermore, Aristotle not only understands *techne* as a reflective disposition but also as the right knowledge about the relation of means and ends in the course of actions (Hubig 2006, 51–52). Good *poiesis* results in the accordance of constitutive principles with the things or effects brought into being.

Agents constitute such dispositions by repeating specific actions whose course is oriented toward mediation of *praxis* and *poiesis* aspects, among others, regarding the quality of attained ends (Hubig 2006, 52). *Phronesis* and *techne* represent intertwined *hexeis* that agents develop over time as a result of internalizing constitutive principles, the interplay of means and ends, and the situation-specific adequacy regarding the quality of actions. Once developed, these *hexeis* guide the agent's actions according to internalized principles without strictly determining the actions' exact course. Lockwood mentions that the *hexis* of justice, which capacitates agents to act in a just manner, does not imply that these agents always act in the same way (Lockwood 2013, 24). In this example, the interplay of different *hexeis* and their dispositional qualities are illustrated by the fact that what is just in one instance might not be just in another but must be adequately adapted to the respective situation. This means that both *phronesis* and *techne* must inform the action.

Ultimately, the concept of *hexis* plays a significant role in Aristotle's conception of virtues. Given that *hexeis* develop over time—by repeating actions in correspondence with certain principles, according to which these actions can be assessed for their efficacy in attaining ends—agents are responsible for their *hexeis*. It is up to them to develop dispositions according to which actions may be performed in a virtuous manner (Lockwood 2013, 25). In this regard, Aristotelian *hexis* represents an active and agent-driven condition, state, or disposition that capacitates the respective agents to act in accordance with internalized principles and norms. However, since a person's practical conduct of life is always situated in a social context, the *hex-*

eis necessarily have a social function as well. They enable individuals to adapt their actions in situational dependence to the constitutive principles of their social context. Thus, already in Aristotle, *hexis* has a social-constituting function through its action-disposing function. It enables, to an extent, the harmony of action and social order.

In James' *The Principles of Psychology I*, habits—deriving from the Latin *habitus* which is the Latin equivalent of Greek *hexis*—have similar implications for the relationship between an individual and their social context. According to James, habits have immediate ethical implications, as they enable individuals to consistently perform those actions that mark their place in society. James has a wide understanding of *habits*, which he claims to exist *"due to the plasticity of the organic materials of which* [the bodies of material entities] *are composed"* (James 1890, 105, emphasis in original). In this regard, an automated action learned through repetition is as much a habit as callous hands are, caused by manual labor. According to James' understanding, habits have a certain bodily inertia through which societal dynamics are preserved and perpetuated.

James describes the mechanics of habit formation analogous to the formation of trample paths:

> [A] simple habit, like every other nervous event [...] is, mechanically, nothing but a reflex discharge; and its anatomical substratum must be a path in the system. The most complex habits, as we shall presently see more fully, are, from the same point of view, nothing but *concatenated* discharges in the nerve-centers due to the presence there of systems of reflex paths, so as to wake each other up successively. (James 1890, 107–108, emphasis in original)

According to James, once habits are formed, they have concrete practical implications. First, habits simplify *"the movements required to achieve a given result, makes them more accurate and diminishes fatigue"* (James 1890, 112, emphasis in original). Second, habits reduce "the conscious attention with which our acts are performed" (James 1890, 114, emphasis in original). Habituated actions are thus more efficient and unconscious. Most importantly, James connects agents to their material environment through their habits. He mentions that habituated actions are not preceded by conscious choice or deliberation. Rather, "[i]n action grown habitual, what instigates each new muscular contraction to take place in its appointed order is not a thought or a perception, but the *sensation occasioned by the muscular contraction just finished"* (James 1890, 115, emphasis in original).[13]

---

13   In the psychology of habit, habitual behavior is understood as an automatic and not goal-dependent response that activates by recurring context cues (Wood & Rünger 2016). Habit formation is a form of learning that takes place when actions performed to attain certain desired goals in different contexts—environmental settings, after certain other actions, in

Habits thus allow a person to cultivate a way of life that can be enacted without much conscious thought or even effort. James also mentions another aspect of habits that, although not present in Aristotle's conception of *hexis*, seems to represent an aspect of Sartre's *hexis*-concept. James states that habits allow individuals to withstand the hardships of their labor.[14] James is convinced of the conservative power of habits for society:

> Habit is thus the enormous fly-wheel of society, its most precious conservative agent. It alone is what keeps us all within the bounds of ordinance, and saves the children of fortune from the envious uprisings of the poor. It alone prevents the hardest and most repulsive walks of life from being deserted by those brought up to tread therein. It keeps the fisherman and the deck-hand at sea through the winter; it holds the miner in his darkness, and nails the countryman to his log-cabin and his lonely farm through all the months of snow [...] It dooms us all to fight out the battle of life upon the lines of our nurture or our early choice, and to make the best of a pursuit that disagrees, because there is no other for which we are fitted, and it is too late to begin again. It keeps different social strata from mixing [...] It is well for the world that in most of us, by the age of thirty, the character has set like plaster, and will never soften again. (James 1890, 121)

For both Aristotle and James, *hexeis*/habits result from how an individual agent repeatedly conducts certain forms of behavior in a social context. *Hexeis*/habits form

---

connection to a specific person or group—repeatedly reward the agents who perform these actions. Once habitual behavior is developed, the context, rather than the goal itself, triggers the respective behavior (Wood & Neal 2007). This may not involve the agent's intention to attain their goals in the exact same way prior to performing the action (Neal et al. 2012). Lastly, because habitual behavior is contextually triggered, inhibiting such behavior must involve an active decision by an agent (Quinn et al. 2009). Changing contextual cues by changing the material setting the behavior takes place in, for instance, is a major factor regarding whether a habit can be broken or not (Verplanken & Wood 2006). As a consequence, habitual behavior can persist when agents remain in the context in which the behavior is triggered, despite the fact that this might directly conflict with the agents' current motives (Neal et al. 2011). However, the persistence of habitual behavior is not necessarily a bad thing, depending on the way in which the outcome of the respective behavior is assessed. Eating habits that, for instance, lead to a more consistent or healthier nutrition can be considered positive or good habits for agents who engage in that behavior, whereas a habituated intake of high-calorie, sugary drinks instead of water may yield negative consequences and can thus be considered a bad habit (Wood & Neal 2016).

14 In behavioral psychology, the process he refers to is known as *habituation*. Habituation refers to a process in which a repeated application of a stimulus results in a decreased response by the agents subjected to that stimulus. Withholding the stimulus leads to an increase in response. The intensity of stimuli affects the rate of decrease or increase in the agent's response (Thompson 2009).

over time in accordance with the norms and rules of this social context. In this way, *hexeis* stabilize the practical interrelations between a person and their larger form of societal constellation.[15]

Sartre's Hexis as Action Disposition

The instances in which Sartre refers to *hexis*, and how he utilizes the concept, suggest it to be a combination of aspects from Aristotelian philosophy, James' habit formation, habitual behavior, and processes of habituation. With this combination, Sartrean *hexis* is closely connected to his conception of the practico-inert (see section 3.4), or, more precisely, to his thoughts surrounding the *inertia* of material entities (see section 2.3). However, as regards *hexis*, the *inertia* in which certain forms of conduct are imprinted is not provided by the materiality of artificial objects but by the human body as a material entity itself. The practico-inert in peoples' *hexis* refers to the fact that this *hexis* expresses the mode of their production, i.e. the repeated structured interrelations in certain forms of societal organization. The material inertia of *hexeis* affects the persistence of practical ensembles, as the structure of these ensembles is automatically perpetuated by internalized practical relations between human beings, instrumental means, and scarce environments. As is the case with many of his philosophical concepts, Sartre develops his outlook on the concept of *hexis* throughout his early and later works.

In *Being and Nothingness*, Sartre briefly speaks about *hexis* in the context of his description of the human psyche. He mentions that the *Ego*'s qualities (French *qualité*) "represent the set of virtualities, latencies, and potentialities that constitute our character and our habits (in the Greek sense of ἕξις)."[16] Among these qualities, Sartre mentions "to be quick-tempered, hardworking, jealous, ambitious, sensuous, etc." (Sartre 2021, 232). He also mentions qualities that originate from a human being's history, which he refers to as *habitudes*—French for *habits*—in *Being and Nothingness*:

> I may be *aged, weary, embittered, diminished,* or *making progress*; I may appear to myself as 'having grown in confidence since my success' or, on the contrary, as 'gradually developed the tastes, habits [French *habitudes*], and sexuality of a patient' (after long illness). (Sartre 2021, 232, emphasis in original; Sartre 1943, 197)

With the French term *habitude*, he thus refers to both acquired qualities and to that which is constituted by the interplay of these qualities—which Sartre calls *hexis* in the Aristotelian sense. However, it is difficult to make a clear distinction between

---

15   For a more detailed juxtaposition of Sartre's conception of *hexis* with that of Aristotle and William James, see Siegler (2022a).

16   The original quotation reads as followed : "l'ensemble des virtualités, latences, puissances qui constituent notre caractère et nos habitudes (au sens grec de ἕξις)" (Sartre 1943, 197).

Sartre's understanding of acquired properties as habits and *hexeis*. This is because these properties, in contrast to states of the *Ego*, do not exist *in actu*, i.e. in human existence as a *praxis*-process through actions. Rather, they exist *in potentia*, as possibilities of being and as innate mental dispositions (French *disposition d'esprit innée*) which qualify a person (Sartre 1943, 197; Sartre 2021, 233).

Hexeis can thus not be explicitly experienced, but are implicitly revealed in the way they condition actions. Against the background of Sartre's primacy of human action, and on account of his recourse to the Greek term *hexis* (ἕξις), the interaction of certain properties of the *Ego* can thus be understood as *hexeis* in the sense of the Aristotelian action disposition. For Sartre, a *hexis* represents an interiorized disposition according to which agents, by virtue of their corporeality, psychic constitution, and historicity, are inclined to perform their totalizing actions in a certain way. This means that they satisfy their requirements, wants, and wishes according to established strategies acquired from their age, experiences, and pathologies.

In *Critique*, Sartre illustrates his conception of *hexis* with the relation between specialized laborers and instruments. He refers to this relation as a "technical bond [French *lien technique*]" that involves both the instrument, as a practico-inert object in which meaning has been imprinted (see section 3.4), and the "becoming-instrument of the specialised agent [French *devenir-instrument de l'agent spécialisé*]" (Sartre 1978, 455; Sartre 1960, 467). Sartre explicitly mentions training and professional instruction as forms of learning through which the instrument eventually "exists as an [*hexis*] in the practical organism" (Sartre 1978, 455) of the specialized agent. This form of imprinting in the very corporeality of agents who interrelate with the instrument regularly is fundamental for instrument-agent interconnection. According to Sartre, the "[*hexis*] of the specialist must correspond to the signifying interconnections of the parts of a machine (or tool), as an inter-connection of assemblies" (Sartre 1978, 455). In this regard, the *hexis* of specialized agents forms through practice, training, and familiarization. It thus enables these agents to form assemblies with instruments to perform actions as a unit. The fact that this *hexis* is supposed to exist *in* the practical organism implies both a form of disposition these agents *hold* (in the sense of Aristotelian *hexis*), as well as a habitually internalized way of handling instruments as a human-machine hybrid (Weber 2020). However, what Sartre exactly means with *hexis* can be scrutinized by juxtaposing it with *praxis*. According to Sartre,

> *praxis* is the temporalisation of [*hexis*] in a situation which is always individual [...] action defines itself here as the simultaneous transcendence of assemblies by the tool [French *des montages par l'outil, de l'outil par les montages, et de l'ensemble par un processus orienté que des possibilités futures ont suscité du fond de l'avenir*], of the tool by assemblies, and of the whole by a directed process which future possibilities have occasioned in the distant future. There can be no [*hexis*], no *habit* without practical

vigilance [...] without a project to actualise them by specifying them. Thus [*hexis*], as an enriching limitation of the common individual, manifests itself concretely only in and through a free practical temporalisation. (Sartre 1978, 455–456, emphasis in original; Sartre 1960, 467–468)

Sartre seems to use *hexis* and *habit* synonymously and describes them as something that, although passively present in the corporeality of agents, capacitates these agents to perform actions in certain ways—as inter-connected in assemblies, for instance—while allowing them to maintain their ontological freedom to act for themselves. Consequently, Sartrean *hexis* must be understood as a structured and structuring disposition that guides the agents' actions, rather than as a mere pattern of habitual behavior that triggers in specific contexts. Although "[r]outine opposes initiative" (Sartre 1978, 456) through *hexis*, this does not pose a problem initially for the agents. Their *hexis* simply capacitates them to form assemblies with the signifying parts of instruments to perform actions as an interconnected or coupled unity. Sartre implies a dialectic between two things: an agent's *hexis*, understood as a vigilant capacitating disposition that lays dormant until it realizes a goal-directed action with certain instrumental means; and the practical inertia of those instrumental means that also lays dormant until realized in the course of totalizing action. He frames this dialectic as an instantiation of the interplay between *active passivity*, in the form of the agent's action disposition, and *passive activity*, in the form of the material disposition of the practico-inert (see section 3.4) through contextually structured action situated in practical ensembles (Sartre 1978, 449, 603). His example is a pilot steering an airplane. He mentions that, at least in itself, the power of the airplane (as a practico-inert material disposition) is not that of the pilot. However, the specialized *praxis* of the pilot, in connection with the pilot's *hexis*, capacitates them to practically realize the power of the airplane by coupling with it. In this way, the airplane's power becomes the pilot's power on the basis of the position the coupled assembly adopts in the larger structural context of a practical ensemble like an airport, in which this assembly would be situated (Sartre 1978, 454).

In their everyday lives, human beings form coupled assemblies with the implement-things of which their practical field of equipmentality and possibility consists. People sit on couches, drive cars, cook on their stoves, and swipe on their smartphones. Their *hexis* enables these human beings to adapt to and routinize the very activities through which they efficiently, effectively, and repeatedly satisfy their needs and desires. A *hexis* thus represents a way in which individuals "maintain [...] the practical reality of [their] body as that of an instrument for directing instruments" (Sartre 1991, 261); or, in another sense, *hexis* is a way for individuals to maintain and possibly adapt their status as the center of a field of equipmentality within their respective practical ensemble (see section 3.2).[17] From Sartre's statements, it is not exactly clear whether *hexis* only applies to bodily actions or whether it encompasses all forms of practical interrelations. However, Sartre's insistence on the fundamental materiality and equipmentality of human existence allows one to suggest that Sartre's *hexis* develops through all forms of practical human-world relations.

If this is the case, what Sartre refers to as the *attitude* certain groups have in virtue of their class-being (see section 4.3) represents the whole of internalized practical interrelations, as action dispositions, that have been structured through the historical situation of the respective class. Through this class-*hexis* people are disposed to act according to their class-structures. Section 4.3 mentioned that these class-structures are the result of how a person's strictly limited practical field, i.e. their practical means of subsistence, are assigned to them by means of their situation in practical ensembles. Individuals continuously act as structured by a *hexis* resulting from how they realized themselves through their historically limited and practical equipmental field of possibility in the past. Their *hexis* thus furthers the cut between their concrete individual subjectivity and the concrete subjectivities and objectivities of their surrounding elements, based on the properties of their material milieu (see section 2.4).

Consequently, human beings are adapted to their socioculturally structured material milieu through their *hexeis* in a fundamental way. A *hexis*, as *active passivity*, results from their acquired modes of satisfying their needs and desires with their *passively active* equipment at hand. This materially incarnated interplay between *active passivity* and *passive activity* scaffolds a materially inert path for their existence through which they not only agentially distinguish themselves from other people within their practical ensemble, but also from other people outside their ensembles. By enacting their concrete subjectivity, they also enact the structures of their practical ensemble, because these structures enable their concrete agential enactment in the first place. With these implications and their shared roots in Mauss' thoughts on body techniques and *habitudes*, Sartre's *hexis* comes close to Bourdieu's concept of *habitus*.

Despite similarities between Sartre's understanding of *hexis* and Bourdieu's conception of *habitus* (Latin for *hexis*, see above), however, Bourdieu himself seems to overlook Sartre's thoughts on the formation of habitual behavior. In *Outline of a Theory of Practice*, Bourdieu criticizes Sartre's apparent neglect of long-lasting action dispositions (Bourdieu 1977, 73–76), while using the term *hexis* himself in the sense of

---

17   The fact that *hexeis*, as action dispositions, form over time and depend on a specific, historically dependent practical field of equipmentality and possibility, puts them thematically close to the formation of *operational sequences of action* in the sense of Leroi-Gourhan's *chaînes opératoires*. See Leroi-Gourhan (1988) and Schlanger (2020).

body *hexis*. A body *hexis* is a "pattern of postures that is both individual and system-atic, because linked to a whole system of techniques involving the body and tools, and charged with a host of social meanings and values" (Bourdieu 1977, 87). In con-trast, Bourdieu defines *habitus* as a system of "durable, transposable *dispositions* [...] objectively adapted to their goals without presupposing a conscious aiming at ends [...] collectively orchestrated without being the product of the orchestrating action of a conductor" (Bourdieu 1977, 72). Bourdieu makes a more nuanced distinction be-tween the way agents are disposed to perform bodily actions and the way they situate themselves in larger social constellations through their actions. He states:

> The habitus is both the generative principle of objectively classifiable judgements and the system of classification (*principium divisionis*) of these practices. It is in the relationship between the two capacities which define the habitus, the capacity to produce classifiable practices and works, and the capacity to differentiate and ap-preciate these practices and products (taste), that the represented social world, i.e., the space of life-styles, is constituted. (Bourdieu 1996, 170, emphasis in origi-nal)

Whereas the sociologist Bourdieu is more aware of the social principles, structures, and classifications implied by a person's *habitus*, the philosopher Sartre seems to conceptualize a person's *hexis* as a mediating moment between their practically to-talizing existence and the consummation of their mode of societal organization. These express the fundamental attitude (French *attitude fondamentale*) of a person's class-being (Sartre 1978, 232; Sartre 1960, 289).

Transforming Needs into Desires and Perpetuating Practical Ensembles

Although the initial relation between *praxis* and *hexis*, between initiation and rou-tinization, might not pose a problem for individuals, the case is different when con-ceived in the context of practical ensembles. The development of a *hexis* is not limited to specialized agents but rather applies to all human beings that act regularly to sat-isfy their needs and desires in differently structured practical ensembles. The pro-cess through which *hexeis* form is accompanied by the transformation of abstract needs as *besoins* into concrete desires as *désirs*. Through repeated interaction with certain instrumental means, and repeated re-interiorization of the effects of the performed courses of action, agents form bodily and practically inert action dispo-sitions. These correspond to the very means that enable them to attain their ends. Thus, these agents are both predisposed to act in a specific way and also project to-ward those strategies and courses of action that have allowed them to be successful in their endeavors.

In this way, practical ensembles can establish a certain state of equilibrium in terms of how the needs, desires, and demands of their elements are covered. This

can happen through political control and regulation, social stratification and unification, technological development, and efficient use of means to ends, among other
manners, in a given mode of production or form of organization. The condition under which this equilibrium may be preserved is the practical inertia of artificial objects and the *hexis*, "both as a physiological and social determination of human organisms and as a practical project of keeping institutions and physical corporate development at the same level" (Sartre 1978, 126).

Consequently, *hexis* itself has practico-inert qualities, in that it manifests the
agential counterpart of certain forms of conduct. These forms express a certain
mode of how individuals incarnate their actions in their corporeality (Sartre 1978,
618). In the larger context of practical ensembles and their role in the struggle
against scarcity, *hexeis* can be understood as the immaterial culture, or, more
precisely, the immaterial side of strategies employed by individuals and constellations to tackle needs and desires arising as a result of their specific socioculturally
structured relation to a scarce material environment (see section 4.2)

Hexeis thus play an essential role in the persistence of practical ensembles. By
forming stable, practical relations through their position in practical ensembles, individuals can attain their ends. Given that these relations prove to be successful,
individuals tend to repeat such actions. In practical ensembles with a serial structure, individuals may even be coerced to attain their ends in very specific and limited ways. This, according to Sartre, leads to an internal adaptation in the form of
hexis through which historically situated individuals perpetuate those actions that
already reinforce the structures of practical ensembles (see section 4.3). In *Critique II*,
Sartre even refers to *hexis* as an "eternal return [French *éternel retour*] [...] the perma-
nent unity of the organism inasmuch as it is *living;* it is life itself, creating for itself
its determinations of inertia. But this *hexis* [...] rejects the dispersion of exteriority"
(Sartre 1991, 345, emphasis in original; Sartre 1985, 355).

Hexeis not only further stabilize the internal structure of practical ensembles;
they also establish norms for the way practical ensembles are supposed to be
structured. These structures can be passed on to later generations by maintenance
through practico-inert objects and routinized actions based on individuals' *hexeis*.
However, for these later generations, the structures of their practical ensemble
are not intelligible as the result of the totalizing formation and transformation
processes at first. Rather, for these individuals, the inherited practical ensembles
present themselves as totalities, as fixed structures that dispose how needs and desires are to be taken care of. According to Sartre, this "ideologically corresponds to
a decision about human 'nature'" (Sartre 1978, 126). Later generations may perceive
the structures of their practical ensemble—such as their form of government, the
modalities of their labor processes, or the unequal treatment of men and women,
for instance—as if these structures were something that is somehow irrefutably
given by default. In this way, *hexeis* make various forms of distinction, injustice,

and unfairness within a society appear to be historically legitimized. Of course, this perception is reinforced by the fact that the current way in which practical ensembles are structured indeed provides individuals with efficient and effective ways to attain their ends.

This perception may also lead to a perpetuation of conditions under which individuals perform actions that do not necessarily allow them to do so. Individuals may even perpetuate certain exigencies instead of dissolving them without realizing it. Because individuals continuously face conditions of hardship, such as chronic hunger, for instance, these conditions can become interiorized and structured. As a consequence, need no longer represents "the violent negation which leads to *praxis*: it has passed into physical generality as [*hexis*], as an inert, generalised lacuna to which the whole organism tries to adapt by degrading itself, by idling so as to curtail its exigencies" (Sartre 1978, 95, emphasis in original). The *hexeis* of historically situated individuals systematically reproduce the negative side effects of the success factors of practical ensembles, such as exploitative labor conditions and social inequality. These negative side effects thus represent complex *persistent problems* that are difficult to both grasp and manage, because they result directly from the way that the systematic provision of goods and services in these ensembles—by which individuals sustain themselves—is organized and practically realized (Schuitmaker 2012). Because such persistent problems result from the functioning of practical ensembles themselves, tackling them is possible only by transforming how these ensembles are structured (see section 4.4).

Through their *hexeis*, however, individuals adapt to these persistent problems. Rather than questioning how the machinations of their practical ensemble produce and reproduce specific modes of inequality and poverty, they accept that their historically fabricated suffering is, despite its concretized form in practical ensembles, an abstract given of the human condition. In this regard, Sartre's *hexis* has conceptual similarities to processes of habituation. He states that "[a]n integral praxis, suffered (interiorization) and repeated (exteriorization) by thousands or millions of agents [...] becomes at once the *being* (serial impotence, relapse into *hexis*, fate as a suffered future) and the *act*" (Sartre 1991, 282, emphasis in original).[18]

Contrary to James' rather optimistic understanding of habit as the fly-wheel of society, Sartre's conception of *hexis* represents much more of a feedback loop of history. Their relative success in attaining some ends in some ways, despite other exi-

---

18   There might also be a line of thought connecting Sartre's view on *hexis* with that of Maine de Biran and Ravaisson. In *Being and Nothingness*, Sartre quotes Maine de Biran's 1803 *Influence de l'habitude sur la faculté de penser* in discussing the *sensation d'effort*, i.e. the sensations of one's own action. In *De l'habitude*, Ravaisson mentions that he was influenced by the double law of habit that Maine de Biran introduced in *Influence* (Ravaisson 2008). The double law of habit connects processes of habit formation with habituation processes (Grosz 2013).

gencies, causes individuals to repeat these actions and thus reinforce the structures of practical ensembles (see section 4.3). This repetition entails the development of *hexeis* through which individuals adapt to their means of subsistence, to the strategies to employ these means, and to the other exigencies they suffer from. As a result, the practical ensembles they are situated in stabilize because individuals become desensitized to those exigencies. After all, identifying them might cause them to transform their ensembles, and individuals create even stronger associations between some of their ends and the available means and strategies provided by their ensemble.

Under the aspect of *hexis*, practical ensembles can be understood as *autopoietic* systems that organize the reproduction of their elements so as to maintain themselves through their elements (Ally 2017, 168–173). Ally shows that Sartre himself advocates such an autopoietic understanding with regard to human beings as biological organisms (Ally 2017, 444) (see section 2.4). However, as regards practical ensembles, it can be assumed that Sartre himself would ultimately refrain from tracing their autopoietic aspects back to a supposed organismal nature. Sartre's whole argument consists in showing that practical ensembles result from the *praxis* of their human elements and eventually act back on them, through material inertia, both in objects and the human body. Practical ensembles must thus be understood as cultural techniques that dynamically develop on certain paths and adapt to enable the provision of goods and services based on human *praxis*. Eventually, this generates an inner logic that overwhelms the individuals who employed those techniques, so that they become perpetuators and not initiators of practical relations.

However, even though these individuals are supposedly trapped in potentially adverse circumstances through *hexis*, they must still be understood as ontologically free. Although their *hexis* might "scarcely resemble a *praxis* [...] in fact, it is a *praxis*: habit is directed and organised, the end posited, the means chosen" (Sartre 1978, 325, emphasis in original). Without *hexis* every human action would be a creative and revolutionary endeavor, but it would not be a *praxis*, as it would ultimately lack the underlying structures qualifying it as a transcending negation of the given and as a totalization toward the future. Although individuals might be locked into their position in practical ensembles, they still can recognize that the structures of their practical ensembles do not provide for some of their needs and desires (see section 4.4). In this regard, the structures of their *hexeis* may even capacitate them to effectively change their situation.

Obscuring Existential Liberation and Necessitation

Even though *hexis* is an overlooked concept, neglected by Sartre and his scholars alike, the significance of *hexis* for understanding the larger implications of Sartre's later philosophy must not be underestimated. To make this clearer, a larger argument is formulated.

In Chapter 1, it was mentioned that Sartre's early and later works attempt to cover two aspects of human existence that seemingly exclude each other, but that overlap, inform, and mediate each other. These aspects were referred to as the internal and external dialectics of human existence. From a perspective on the internal dialectic of human existence, human beings may perceive themselves as ontologically free agents who choose how they realize themselves and thus give rise to structures of practical necessity. Practical constraints represent merely hypothetical constraints for these individuals, and the responsibility for their lives is theirs alone. This experience corresponds to the thematic focus of *Being and Nothingness*. The internal dialectic of human existence is involved in a constant process of mediation with the external dialectic.

From a perspective on the external dialectic of human existence, human beings must be understood as situated in practical ensembles that scaffold and partially necessitate how these human beings can realize themselves. Although ontologically free, practical freedom is delimited and potentially constrained in ways such that it may result in categorical coercions. This experience corresponds to the thematic foci of *Search for a Method* and *Critique of Dialectical Reason*. For Sartre, both levels of lived experience—therefore, both planes of existential reality—represent the larger existential tension in which human existence, as a lived contradiction (see section 1.4), is situated, and to which it further contributes through the situated mediation of action and experience.

Against this background, the existential tension, as an oscillation between processes of liberation and necessitation, is itself obscured by structures of *hexis*—by the fact that human beings familiarize, routinize, and naturalize what is and what works for them in some way or another so that it becomes something that *should* be the way it is. In the spirit of Sartre's *force des choses*, this process of how an *is* becomes an *ought* through familiarization and naturalization is not that problematic on its own. It allows consistency in terms of problem-solving in combination with more efficient usage of cognitive capacities, such as deliberation and reflection. Furthermore, it allows adaptation and an eventual increase in effectiveness, both in terms of utilized means and the way these means are put to use, among other things. Not only individuals but also societal constellations may benefit from these forms of relief and optimization, especially because *hexis* allows for the stability of these constellations, consistency in means-ends relations, and reproducibility of results.

However, it is precisely in combination with time that these larger constellations manifest effects that may stabilize practical ensembles beyond a point where they may easily be changed. The relatively simple practical relations, comprising the processes through which the complex structures of practical ensembles are actually formed and transformed, generate their own normativity over time through repetition and internalization. The result is that the formation and, therefore, the principal contingency of these structures is obscured. Ultimately, this obscures the underlying oscillation of liberation and necessitation that human existence consists of. This is the very core of Sartre's point in his interview with *New Left Review*, where he mentions that his view on the power of circumstances was obscured by his earlier emphasis on the internalities of human existence without his coordinating—in the sense of *mediating*—them with the externalities of historical situations (see section 1.3). Neglecting the fact that human beings, although ontologically free, create the very patterns that lock them in their daily lifeworlds until these patterns become humanized themselves, ultimately overestimates the interior self-relation while it plays down the power of exterior circumstances.

In this regard, the true power of Sartre's theory of practical ensembles lies in its de- and reconstructive potential and its focus on the underlying dialectic of human existence. Understanding a constellation of human and non-human elements as a practical ensemble is to approach its constitutive factors, i.e. the role of human agency in the formation and transformation of this ensemble, the exigencies of its elements, and their possibilities and constraints. It allows one to deconstruct totalities and reconstruct the synthetic processes through which those totalities came to be. Furthermore, this approach illustrates how the inertia of these ensembles increases over time and is preserved, both in the inert materiality of things and in the human body. Lastly, Sartre's theory shows that the changing inert structures and routines that consolidate practical ensembles must involve some form of material intervention. Because human actions *"become Being* [...] they cannot be dissolved into knowledge even if they are deciphered and known. Only matter itself, beating on matter, can break them up" (Sartre 1978, 178, emphasis in original).

4.6 Crisis and Disruption

In this section, the last aspects of practical ensembles are discussed, namely their crisis and potential disruption through what Sartre calls *counter-finalities*. In addition to *hexis*, *counter-finality* is another concept of Sartre's later philosophy that is somewhat underrepresented in Sartre studies. It observes that the overall form of organization of practical ensembles does not just affect the elements comprising these ensembles. The overall totalizing processing of practical ensembles might also generate external effects through which these ensembles act back on themselves in what can be called an action at a distance.

A counter-finality occurs when external effects threaten the finality of practical ensembles and their very mode of structural organization. The effects generated by practical ensembles act back on the ensembles by proxy of another sector of materiality. Whether this other material sector can itself be understood as a practical ensemble depends on its mode and form of constitution.

Counter-Finality and Crisis

Sartre illustrates his understanding of counter-finalities with the historical situation of Chinese farmers. As a practical ensemble, the farmers are organized around an agricultural mode of production. This mode of production means that they deforest the landscape they inhabit to prepare the soil for future agrarian use. In so doing, the farmers eventually eliminate natural boundaries that would otherwise prevent flooding. With these boundaries removed, the farmland is flooded. Eventually, the farmers and their whole form of organization are in a critical situation.

Sartre derives three conditions for the formation of counter-finalities: the given fact of a disposition of matter, the becoming-inert of human *praxis*, and the serial ubiquity regarding this *praxis* (Turner 2014, 40). Based on these conditions, the formation of counter-finalities can be reconstructed. The first and most obvious condition is that the possibility of a counter-finality "should be adumbrated by a kind of *disposition* of matter" (Sartre 1978, 162–163, emphasis in original). According to this first condition, the material sector from which counter-final effects arise must be disposed in such a way as to enable and facilitate these effects in the first place. In the case of the Chinese farmers, this first condition is given by the geological and hydrographic structure of the landscape they sustain themselves with. However, Sartre's use of the term *disposition* also implies that some forms of actualization through action are required.

This leads to the second condition, according to which "human *praxis* has to become a fatality and to be absorbed by inertia, taking *both* the strictness of physical causation *and* the obstinate precision of human labour" (Sartre 1978, 163, emphasis in original). Here, Sartre refers to instances in which the overall structure of practical ensembles necessitates individuals to attain their ends in prefabricated and limited ways (see sections 4.3 and 4.5). In Sartre's example, this condition is given by the farmer's mode of production and how the tools they use necessitate these farmers to cut down trees to prepare the soil for agriculture. He states that "[i]n the most adequate and satisfactory tool, there is a hidden violence which is the reverse of its docility. Its inertia always allows it to 'serve some other purpose', or rather, it *already* serves some other purpose; and that is how it creates a new system" (Sartre 1978, 183, emphasis in original). This means that on a relatively small scale over long periods of time, these farmers' activities may not pose a problem for the farmers themselves nor for the landscape they deforest. This might be because the farmers deforest sustainably, or the ecosystem can counteract deforestation by adapting over time. However, through their mode of production that is manifested in these farmers' tools and practices, they fulfill one condition for counter-finalities to arise.

The bare fact that historically situated individuals must attain their ends by modifying surrounding materiality that is disposed to give rise to counter-finalities is not enough. According to Sartre, this specific form of activity "must be carried on *elsewhere*" (Sartre 1978, 163, emphasis in original). This is the third and final condition. It refers to the fact that many activities, whose effects and side effects could be dealt with on a smaller scale, accumulate through "serial ubiquity" (Turner 2014, 41). In Sartre's example, this last condition is given by the fact that not only single farmers but a larger collective recognizes the strategy of cutting trees for soil to be initially beneficial for satisfying their specific desires. They begin to repeat this strategy and thus cultivate a certain *hexis* that both stabilizes the inner workings of their practical ensemble and enables it to persist through these repeated actions. In so doing, these farmers eventually rid their land of any natural boundaries that might prevent the flooding of their fields.

When flooding occurs through the geological and hydrographic structure—the material disposition—of the landscape, this flooding represents a counter-finality for these farmers. The very strategies they intentionally employed to respond to their needs and desires—in the sense of finalities—caused effects that eventually counteracted these strategies. Consequently, the practical ensemble these farmers constitute, together with their landscape based on a specific mode of production, is put into a state of exigency that necessitates action to be transformed—or else the ensemble itself might disintegrate.

This ensemble-wide state of exigency can be called a *crisis*. Koselleck et al. (1982) reconstruct the Greek origins of this concept and highlight both its revelatory and compulsive aspects. In its wider connotation, a *crisis* was a separating, distinguishing, or deciding between things. Accordingly, a *crisis* represents a crucial moment in the course of processes, such as the operations of systems, the course of surgeries and diseases, and the totalization of practical ensembles. At this moment, certain elements and structures are revealed to be substantial or *critical* for those processes. Furthermore, crisis illustrates the potential necessity for intervention so as to avoid disruption and/or collapse.

In Sartre's example, the farmland represents the central structure of equipment around which the practical ensemble of the farmers is organized. As such, it represents these farmers' *interest* (see section 4.3). In the critical moment of flooding, the farmland itself is revealed as a vulnerability of the practical ensemble. In infrastructure research, the concept of *vulnerability* is used to determine potential flaws or weaknesses of systems (Eifert et al. 2018, 21). Egan (2007) links critical moments of systems to their vulnerabilities or weak spots (J.I. Engels 2018b, 45–46). In Sartre's example, the farmland can be understood as the critical agricultural infrastructure around which an ensemble's overall form of organization is built. The structural integrity of the farmland is thus associated with the structural integrity of the very form of organization that enables these farmers to satisfy their needs and desires. A threat to the farmland represents a threat to the ensemble and, concomitantly, to the existence of the farmers situated in this ensemble. Through flooding as a counter-finality, the very practices the farmer's ensemble consists of are in danger. This gives rise to concrete needs and exigencies for transforming how their practical ensemble is structured. That, or the ensemble collapses. This is further discussed in section 5.4 with regard to the critical significance of urban mobility infrastructures for the flow of traffic.

Objective Contradictions

How Sartre describes counter-finalities along with the three conditions he mentions almost suggests a somewhat environmentalist warning about the larger effects of humanity's intervention in their physicochemical surroundings (Ally 2017, 419). Similar processes to Sartre's counter-finalities can indeed be found in the negative consequences resulting from the rectification of rivers (Blackbourn 2006, 104–119; Bernhard 2016, 506–507)[19] or from anthropogenic climate change attributable to high CO_2 emissions, among other factors (see section 5.2). Sartre even mentions that the air pollution produced during the Industrial Revolution might represent a potential counter-finality for employers, as they are not able to avoid breathing such polluted air and thus suffer from how their actions act back on them through a larger material complex (Sartre 1978, 194). Sartre claims that the existence of counter-finalities makes it possible to identify what he refers to as *objective contradictions* in the interrelations between differently structured ensembles.

As mentioned in section 4.4, Sartre's practical ensemble framework allows one to both understand practical constellations in two ways. Such constellations can be understood regarding the overall function as a result of the interrelations of their elements or regarding these interrelations themselves. In the latter case, these elements, as partial totalities, promote this overall processing through their practical relations. These interrelations can be further scrutinized regarding their various modes of structuring. According to Sartre, the interrelations of practical constellations, such as political parties, the working class, or even individuals at a bus stop, are characterized by the needs and desires of the human elements these ensembles consist of. Such interrelations between constellations can thus be understood in two ways. One way is to focus on the individual elements or partial totalities and their interrelations. Doing so might reveal these interrelations to be clashes of interest between human beings. These clashes represent contradictions that demand solutions. The atomized people at a bus stop, for instance, all initially compete with each other for a seat on the bus. Focusing on these human elements may reveal that their needs and desires initially conflict with and contradict each other. The same can be

---

19   Much appreciation to Nadja Thiessen for these insights.

said for a political debate between two parties, considered as more structured constellations.

Another way to understand these conflicts and contradictions is to conceive them as structural moments of a larger totalization. In the case of the bus stop (see section 4.3), the needs and desires of all human elements can be satisfied when everyone gets a seat on the bus. Because of the larger totalizing process at the bus stop, the initial contradictions between individuals appear not to be contradictions at all, as they are sublated through the service provision of the bus. In the case of a political debate between parties, no resolution may be found. However, in the long run, the debate might be revealed to initiate a transformation in the debating culture of the larger political complex. As such, the debate represents a structural moment in the overall totalization of the political complex as a practical ensemble. This understanding of how the interrelations between elements mediate each other at different levels, and how they can be understood either as interrelations themselves or as structural moments in larger processes, is one of the biggest advantages of Sartre's practical ensemble framework. All of these contradictions have a materially objective foundation in the corporeality of each individual as a *praxis*-process (see section 2.4), and in the sociocultural and material conditions, they are situated in. But the contradictions still result from a clash of two interests that initially cannot be reconciled.

With the idea of counter-finalities, Sartre introduces the possibility of contradictions between human elements or constellations and inert matter. Such contradictions are not the result of two conflicting parties, because worked matter "produces a necessity for change *of itself*" (Sartre 1978, 183, emphasis in original). Sartre states that

> at the level of technical ensembles of the *activity/inertia* type, contradiction is the counter-finality which develops within an ensemble, insofar as it opposes the process which produces it and insofar as it is experienced as negated exigency and as the negation of an exigency by the totalised ensemble of practico-inert Beings in the field. (Sartre 1978, 193, emphasis in original)

Again, whether such contradictions are predominantly understood and analyzed as contradictions between elements or as structural moments of a larger totalizing process, different conclusions can be drawn about the historicity of these processes and the exact intricacies of finalities and counter-finalities. A counter-finality can, for instance, be understood as benefiting some while disadvantaging others. Sartre mentions that the over-industrialization of a country, for instance, might represent a counter-finality for rural classes, as these classes "become proletarianised to precisely the extent that is is [sic] a finality for the richest landowners because it enables them to increase their own productivity" (Sartre 1978, 193). However, in the larger totalizing process of the nation-state, understood as a practical ensemble, over-industrialization might itself become a counter-finality "as the country is now further away from its new rural bases" (Sartre 1978, 193).

With this conception, Sartre somewhat weakens the strict focus on materiality in relation to counter-finalities. In the rest of *Critique*, he uses the concept of counter-finality rather liberally to refer to instances in which the finalities and effects of one practical ensemble negatively affect another practical ensemble or material sector, and then eventually itself. This is because of his processual understanding of practical ensembles. Although any objective contradictions might result from inert material processes, they are all fundamentally attributable to human actions.

Totalization-of-Envelopment

The specific way in which Sartre frames the interrelations between practical ensembles is attributable to his larger conception of history. Section 1.3 mentioned Sartre's attempt to understand history according to his regressive-progressive method. His method essentially represents a de-reconstruction of the formation of historical situations. Section 1.4 outlined Sartre's claim that these situations must be understood as moments in transformative processes that only become dialectically intelligible as such from the inside, based on human action and experience. Sartre's theory of practical ensembles mirrors this understanding.

Any constellation, whether an individual in relation to the world, a family, a city, or a nation-state, represents both a totalization in and of itself and a partial totality that interplays with other partial totalities and thus contributes to larger totalizations. Through the practical ensemble framework, any of these totalizations can become intelligible based on *praxis*-processes directed to sublate the lacks and contradictions of human existence. However, in the course of any of these totalizations, structural moments can be identified in which objective contradictions necessitate human actions, without there being an individual subject or larger grouping that can be held accountable for those contradictions. Of course, individual and suprain-dividual responses to these contradictions can themselves be understood as contradictions or structural moments in larger totalizations. Eventually, after many iterations, history itself becomes intelligible as what Sartre calls a *totalization-of-envelopment* that incarnates the individual and ultimately progresses through itself without a totalizer (Sartre 1991). Many Sartre scholars, such as Flynn (1997) and Catalano (2007), have analyzed and criticized this understanding of history; it is not the objective of this work to provide a satisfying answer to this debate.

Anyway, Sartre's conception of historical totalizations allows for a nuanced understanding of the role of the individual in larger processes. Human existence is indeed situated within historical constellations, which necessitate certain actions while delimiting other options. Nevertheless, human beings are simultaneously free from these constellations, as it is their action that ultimately drives their transformation. Although human beings might not necessarily control their *mobiles* or *motifs*, their actions fundamentally represent an expression of their ontological freedom. In this regard, every action is a fundamentally free endeavor, even despite the fact that it represents a re-actualization of the situation within a practical constellation (see section 2.3). Ultimately, this means that human existence is intrinsically meaningful—not only in a general way but also on a concrete, individual level. It is precisely the actions of individuals, despite being inherently situated, prefabricated, and constrained through inert matter, that constitute meaning and historical momentum, whether intentional or not. Sartre incorporates both the dynamics of human existence and action as well as the forces of technology into a single endeavor to which human beings are subject. This view brings him close to Heidegger's ideas about the *Seins-Geschick* (Heidegger 2000) and to the role of human elements in *technospheres*, i.e. complex autonomous systems of human and non-human elements in the Anthropocene (Haff 2014; Heßler 2019).

One of the advantages of Sartre's theory of practical ensembles is that it allows one to understand any constellation between human and non-human elements in terms of their interrelations. The examples in this chapter exemplify this. In an abstract way, the general relation between individuals and their concrete material conditions can be understood as a practical ensemble. Such an understanding discloses the inherent structures of need, desire, and scarcity of which the ensemble consists. In a more concrete way, this understanding can reveal the various ways in which human action is mediated through material things and structures.

4.7 Concluding Remarks

This chapter has shown how Sartre's thoughts on totalizing action and the relationship between human existence and technology interconnect in his larger theoretical conception of practical ensembles. From relatively simple practical interrelations between human beings and their surrounding materiality, both in the form of other humans, non-human entities, and even structured patterns of sociocultural meaning within a scarce milieu, complex processes of formation and reinforcement, transformation, persistence, crisis, and even disruption may ensue.

With his thoughts on the formation of serially structured ensembles and the cultivation of *hexeis* as action dispositions, Sartre captures processes in which forms of societal organization ossify in matter and, at the same time, produce the necessary scaffolding for the efficient and effective satisfaction of requirements, wants, and wishes.

Sartre's thoughts on the transformation of serially structured ensembles into communally structured ensembles, and his conception of counter-finalities, outline both human and material processes. Through them, human beings are liberated from and even robbed of the socioculturally organized, structured, and undoubtedly necessary foundations for satisfying their requirements, wants, and wishes.

All these processes must in turn be considered in a larger dialectical interplay based on totalizing action, and thus through the perspective of human needs and desires. On the one hand, humanity's structured actions and strategies to tackle their material and immaterial requirements, wants, and wishes drive the combination of technology and *hexeis* that enacts the abovementioned system effects. On the other, human action, both in its active and passive, practico-inert form, stabilizes and secures the systematic provision of the required, wanted, and wished-for goods and services in the long run. Human needfulness and the inability to tackle it in a scarce milieu thus represent the abstract, fundamental basis for all concrete forms of societal organization. The structured interrelations between human and non-human elements in practical ensembles are therefore fundamentally shaped by the needfulness of their human elements. Against Sartre's conception of the practico-inert, the structured interrelations in practical ensembles also express the inherent needfulness of historical human beings. This abstract needfulness is spatio-materially concretized in certain processes and strategies. Through them, the requirements, wants, and wishes of the human elements are satisfied—both in the technological artifacts used in these processes and strategies, as well as in the *hexeis* through which the human elements adapt. Their adaptation is to the technological artifacts and the processes and strategies and occurs through repeated interaction and education over time. By highlighting the fundamental human needfulness at the heart of all sociocultural structures, Sartre's approach allows one to deconstruct the structures' totality and reconstruct their constitutive processes as active totalizations. These structures are thus disclosed as artifacts themselves, within the oscillation of human liberation and necessitation, based on the ontological freedom of human existence. Sartre summarizes this as followed:

> [T]he history of man is an adventure of nature, not only because man is a material organism with material needs, but also because worked matter, as an exteriorisation of interiority, produces man, who produces or uses this worked matter in so far as he is forced to re-interiorise the exteriority of his product, in the totalising movement of the multiplicity which totalises it. The *external* unification of the inert, whether by the seal or by law, and the introduction of inertia at the heart of *praxis* both result, as we have seen, in producing necessity as a strict determination at the heart of human relations. And the totalisation which controls me, in so far as I discover it within my free lived totalisation, only takes the form of necessity for two fundamental reasons: first, the totalisation which totalises me has to make use of the mediation of inert products of labour; second, a practical multiplicity must *always* confront its own external inertia, that is to say, its character as a discrete quantity. (Sartre 1978, 71–72, emphasis in original)

La force des choses, the power of things and circumstances in practical ensembles, arises from the fact that the abstract structures of human need are socialized and given shape in concrete, socioculturally mediated structures of desire. This shaping also occurs in the technological processes and artifacts that manifest the satisfaction of these desires as potential means to thusly manifested ends. However, *la force des choses* arises only because there exists the ontological freedom of human beings as the abstract condition for the determination of oneself by and for oneself, through concrete action, in dialectical interrelation with concrete materiality. Needfulness, both in the abstract structure of human existence and in the concrete structures of forms of societal organization, expresses the dialectical tension of liberation and the necessitation of human history.

The perspective on this dialectical understanding of needfulness allows one to disclose forms of societal organization as entangled simultaneities of mutually mediating fields of possibility. This understanding considers practical constellations to be enacted through goal-directed human actions. It also deconstructs every form of organization and reveals structured interrelations at multiple levels, while emphasizing that this form of organization can itself be reconstructed through these interlocking levels of interrelation.

Sections 4.4 and 4.6 mentioned that practical ensembles can be understood either by their overall totalizing processing or by the interrelations of their elements at different levels. According to the praxeological, dialectical, and de-reconstructive nature of Sartre's approach, human constellations are revealed as graduated interrelations that structure, inform, and mediate each other. All of these interrelations have their basis in human action. Owing to its inherent historicity, the practical ensemble framework presupposes a certain bottom-up modality in terms of how enabling and constraining processes interlock and may become intelligible through each other in human constellations. A top-down modality can be identified in terms of how larger forms of organization represent enabling factors of the structures those forms consist of. To better grasp this layered modality, a multilevel conception is used to refer to interrelations at the micro-, meso-, and macro-levels.

The micro-level represents the goal-oriented, totalizing interrelations between human and non-human elements. Depending on the nature of the constellations in question, the exact status of these interrelations might differ, but all are understood to be serially or communally structured so as to enable the satisfaction of human requirements, wants, and wishes. Furthermore, these interrelations are understood as mediated by practico-inert objects and structures. Eventually, this reveals more complex modes of structuring that mediate human actions in different ways. Depending on the granularity, the meso-level either represents the actual individual agents or, when considering larger systemic connections, practical ensembles. When individuals are perceived on the meso-level, the individual significance of practical interrelations is scrutinized with regard to an individual's existence as a *praxis*-process. When the practical ensembles are perceived on the meso-level, the modes of structuring of the practical interrelations that comprise the structures of the practical ensemble as a totalizing process are scrutinized. On the meso-level, individuals or ensembles represent partial totalities that totalize and are enveloped in the totalization of a practical ensemble on the macro-level. Based on this understanding, structured interrelations between several partial totalities can be identified, and these further mediate the interrelations on the micro-level and contribute to the macro-level processing of the constellations in question. Lastly, the macro-level represents overall forms of practical ensembles and even history as a practical ensemble itself. In these ensembles, the interrelations between partial totalities can be understood as structural moments of an overall totalizing process that again affects interrelations on the meso- and micro-level.

Based on this deconstruction of practical constellations, the interlocking levels of totalizing interrelations can be reconstructed in more abstract or concrete ways. A more abstract form of reconstruction is to outline how these interrelations themselves mediate each other. A more concrete form of reconstruction is to scrutinize individual interrelations between human and non-human elements in terms of how these interrelations mediate human action in various ways. This reconstruction can take place by focusing on either how instrumental means enable people to realize their intended ends, or how human-technology relations mediate other planes of human reality.

In section 4.5, it was shown that Sartre's practical ensemble framework also illustrates the significance of practical inertia, both in the form of practico-inert objects and structures and of human *hexeis*. The practical inertia of objects and structures plays a central role in all the processes involved in the totalization of practical ensembles. Emphasizing the role of material inertia in these processes allows for a closer, more nuanced assessment of path dependencies, practical constraints, and spaces of possibility. The same is true for bodily inertia. The analysis has shown that *hexis* does not just play a significant role in the persisting of practical constellations. It also accounts for the fact that human beings naturalize their form of organization and thus conceive it to be the normative default mode for how their interrelations are structured per se. Scrutinizing the role of *hexis* reveals the practical inertia of human elements and also shows potential ways to transform the supposedly ineluctable structures of human reality.

Furthermore, the practical ensemble framework allows one to conceive of potential contradictions and conflicts of interest between the elements of ensembles as conflicting finalities at different levels of analysis (see section 4.6). The forms of conflict may or may not represent actual conflicts when seen against the background of higher-level totalizations. This allows retracing the clashes between elements as potential drivers or disturbances on the micro-level, which may grow into driving forces or disruptions for the larger totalizing processing on the macro-level. In going beyond the internal effects of the totalizing processing of practical constellations, potential counter-finalities can be identified. These may act back on the constellations' structure, thus putting them into crisis.

To give this needfulness and the multilevel modality of practical ensembles a more concrete shape, and to ground the significance of Sartre's thoughts on practical ensembles in the contemporary challenges of the human condition, the next chapter explores how the theory can be applied to urban mobility systems in *praxis*.

5. Praxis of Practical Ensembles: Bodies in Motion

5.1 Introduction

The principal goal of this chapter is to explore some of the ways that Sartre's investigation into the dialectics of action, technology, and society, which culminate in his view on practical ensembles, can be applied to contemporary challenges of the human condition. The chapter, therefore, applies Sartre's thoughts on practical ensembles to urban mobility to illustrate some of the underlying dynamics and effects of people's spatial, technologically mediated, and organized movement through their built environment.

In this chapter, *urban mobility* systems are those that enable the movement of people, goods, and information within, as well as in and out, of urban spaces (Sheller & Urry 2006; Urry 2007). Urban mobility systems consist of people, artifacts, rules, regulations, expectations, habits, institutions, structures, infrastructures, and networks that interplay in various ways to contribute to an overall urban flow. Such systems can be found in one form or another in all cities and settlements. This ubiquity is apparent in the way the very fabrics of cities and larger settlements throughout history reflect the dominant modes used by their inhabitants to move between places (Newman & Kenworthy 2015).

5.2 Urban Mobility as Practical Ensemble

This section outlines an understanding of urban mobility as a practical ensemble. In accordance with the findings from the previous chapter, needfulness represents the entry point for this outline. Human needs and desires, as well as material demands and requirements, permeate every level of societal constellations. According to Sartre, it is always through a goal-oriented human agency that structured interrelations form and prefabricated options for action eventually become realized. Understanding the foundational role of needs, desires, and action allows one to accentuate interrelations between human and non-human elements on the micro-level. It also makes it possible to scrutinize them for the way the interrelations are structured as well as for how their specific mode of structuring affects how and why not only people but also goods and information, move through urban spaces the way they do.

Eventually, this multilevel analysis discloses other structures that equally affect, inform, and mediate such structured interrelations. In this way, structured interrelations on the micro-level reveal more modes of structuring at the meso-level. The interrelations between these modes of structuring can again be scrutinized regarding the way they mediate interrelations on the macro-level. Another possibility is to conceive of these meso-level modes of structuring as partial totalities themselves. The interrelations of these partial totalities represent structural moments in a larger totalization on the macro-level. The overall totalization represents the form of organization of urban mobility as a complex process. This process is represented by the overall flow of elements and thus affects the interrelations of structures and elements on the meso- and micro-levels.

Structural Moments of Urban Mobility

Following Sartre's thoughts about practical ensembles, the complex machinations of urban mobility systems can be understood in a more abstract way, namely as an overall totalization, reconstructed as an interplay of certain structures enabling the flow of goods and people to move through urban spaces. Through this perspective, the dynamic micro-level interrelations of road users at individual road segments must be understood as being serially structured and not communally so. These structured interrelations form through isolated practical relations between road users and other people, things, structures, and rules, or a combination of all of them. Furthermore, the interrelations mediate the various movements of all road users based on their motion-relevant requirements. In an optimal case, the controlled and safe movement of all road users is the outcome of this structuring. For instance, crosswalks and pedestrian lights make it likely for pedestrians to safely cross streets. Traffic-calming measures, such as road diets and speed bumps, slow down car traffic to mitigate accident risk (Lee et al. 2013; Kim et al. 2019). Each of these traffic-governing systems represents a mode of structuring between elements, and each of these modes of structuring contributes to the whole form of organization at the road segment.

When two or more road segments meet, like at intersections or highways, other modes of structuring mediate the interrelations between those coupled segments. In this regard, the structured interrelations between road segments can be understood as a practical ensemble that represents a partial totality on the meso-level. The structuring of these interrelations causes some road users to stop their movements and yield to others, all to enable an overall flow of traffic between the segments. Eventually, this interplay affects individual road users at road segments and enables their movement. The interplay of structured interrelations between human and non-human elements is thus both an outcome of balancing strategies to tackle needs and desires, and also a complex yet abstract need itself, which must be taken care of and concretized so as not to affect this delicate balancing.

The overall macro-level form of organization for urban mobility can thus be understood as permeated by needs and desires at every level. From the perspective of human elements, the organizational form reflects people's requirements, wants, and wishes to move from one place to another. These may be the abstract need for movement in general, or concrete desires to move to do something else, such as reach a destination.

From the perspective of non-human elements, the enabling function and the services provided by these elements are related to the needs and desires of the human elements. Traffic lights, speed bumps, and speed controls are in place simply because the ends of individuals must be attained, and because the various strategies of how this can be done must be balanced and reconciled so as not to inhibit each other. Material demands and requirements then arise, because the proper function and service provision of non-human elements is critical for managing the interrelations of human elements. Consequently, there emerges a further desire to maintain and protect these elements from damage.

From the perspective of the ensemble's macro-level, the overall provision of flow through interconnected structurings of human and non-human elements eventually affects individual road segments at the meso-level, and also enables the individual micro-level movements of road users at those segments.

Mediated Interrelations

Sartre's practical ensemble framework can be applied by foregrounding specific forms of human action and examining how these actions are mediated by technology in the form of practico-inert instrumental means. Again, the goal-directed actions of human beings, as well as their needs and desires, represent the entry point of this analysis. Here, Sartre's philosophy of technology comes into play (see section 3.2).

The movement of pedestrians, for instance, can be understood as the result of a serial structuring based on human needs and desires, which concretize abstract structures of need and thus transforms them into desires by manifesting their potential satisfaction through instrumental means. These means are the pedestrians' shoes, the pavement, traffic lights, and other items. The connected employment of these instrumental means represents an equipmental field that corresponds to the practical field of possibilities for these pedestrians (see sections 2.3 and 3.2). This equipmental field thus enables pedestrians to realize their movements by mediating between their abstract and concrete ends. This movement is governed by institutionalized traffic laws and conventions, which pedestrians either follow consciously or due to certain *hexeis*. The path pedestrians use is simultaneously chosen and prefabricated in accordance with the established ways in which pedestrians can or must satisfy their needs and desires through the larger material settings and formations of their urban environment. Depending on the pedestrians' needs and desires, and their concomitant ends, their movement through urban environments represents a self-realization (see section 2.3).

The movements of car drivers also represent outcomes of a serial structuring enabled by cars and road infrastructures alike, one which is eventually realized by the goal-directed actions of those drivers. In the case of cars, the role of technology in the form of practico-inert objects becomes even more apparent for the specific mode of structuring and the form of mediation. A car not only enables drivers to realize their ends in specific ways by supporting and accelerating their spatial movements; depending on whether it is a sports car or a vehicle specifically designed for urban spaces, a car also mediates and thus shapes the spatial experience of its drivers as well as their perceptive relation to the road in different ways (Ihde 1990, 74).

It is not just the concrete movements of people and their perceptions of how they are *on the move* that are mediated by various things, structures, and modes of transportation. Their relation to space and time is inherently mediated as well (Ebert 2020). From a perspective toward the dimension of space, the distribution of bus stations at which people might serially gather is revealed to be mediated by the positions of other bus stations throughout urban areas. The positions of these bus stations again depend on the density of the population in certain areas, and on other factors. The bus stations are connected by bus lanes, and enacted by the totalizing actions of bus drivers and passengers alike. All these interrelations result from the overall form of organization of urban mobility while simultaneously contributing to it (see section 4.3). The concrete sociospatial relations within cities are thus both constituted by and constitutive of the nature of urban mobility (Jessop et al. 2008). This applies even more to large, interconnected networks of streetcars and tracks, which link various points of interest. However, the dimension of space is also inextricably linked to the dimension of time. Schivelbusch (2018) has demonstrated this by showing how traveling by railroad mediates the perception of space and time. Handel (2017) argues that a decrease in travel time between places can cause distant areas to be perceived as closer, whereas areas that are spatially closer but less connected may be perceived as further away (Müller 2021).

Focusing on other, more obscured interrelations between human and non-human elements reveals even more profound modes of structuring. In his article *Do Artifacts Have Politics?*, Winner (1980) claims that a focus on simple use contexts of technologies might obscure the larger, potentially harmful effects those technologies can generate. Winner states that the low-hanging bridges designed by architect Robert Moses to allow cars to travel in and out of Long Island exceeded their supposed use context. Their height had a discouraging effect on buses that had to run on parkways underneath them. The result was a form of racial segregation in people's ability to reach remoter areas. The fact that black people and other marginalized groups had to rely on buses as an affordable means of transportation, on account of their socioeconomic situation, meant that they could not reach the areas past the bridges. White people who could afford cars had fewer problems going past the bridges. Winner's conclusions have seen some criticisms. He illustrates, however, the fact that material properties of technological artifacts, in combination with other factors and an overall mode of societal organization, can affect the ways people may practically realize themselves.[1]

Edwards (2017) shows a similar situation in the racial coding of public transport in pre- and post-Apartheid South Africa. Although public buses and a railway line used to bring segregated black laborers into white areas, the unreliability of these means of transport forced these laborers to walk. Consequently, the experience of racial inequality is still present in the possible provision of public transportation and its lack in some areas (Müller 2021). In these examples, the serial structuring of people's movements is a direct result of how their historical situation forces them to rely on limited modes of transportation. In doing so, people enact and reinforce the current structures. They totalize the structures that enable them to do so because they posit these structures as their practical field of equipmentality and possibility (see section 4.3).

Paths of Freedom and Necessity

The examples presented above give instances of predominantly serial modes of structuring that enable the harmonized interplay of various modes of transportation in the flow of urban traffic. However, there are examples in which serial, materially prefabricated, and rigid options of travel disturb people's preferred way of movement. For these people, it may be necessary to break out of serial structures and spontaneously form communal structures.

When pedestrians walk through a park, for instance, the deliberately designed paths that link points of interest, such as landmarks and entry points, afford to be used. Signs might even tell pedestrians not to enter certain lawn areas, which further encourages pedestrians to use the path network.

In a Sartrean sense, this path network can be understood as a practical ensemble in which a practical field of equipmentality and possibility is predominantly structured in a serial mode. The ensemble enables pedestrians to stroll or to quickly move through the park without obstacles. Depending on the needs and desires of these

---

1   For a more thorough analysis of Winner's theses and their academic reception, see Joerges (1999).

pedestrians, however, this field of equipmentality and possibility can be more or less restrictive, such as when the path network itself does not directly link two points of interest in a straight line, or when it prohibits access to certain areas. It is common, for instance, in almost all areas in which people walk between two places, to see the formation of *desire paths* or *desire lines* (Furman 2012), also sometimes called *sunken lanes* or *hollow ways*. These paths form when people break free from the restrictive field of equipmentality and possibility given to them through the larger organization of their practical ensemble, choosing instead to form their field of possibility in space through their actions across time. Every desire path initially begins as the attempt to counteract a certain lack of options for action. The term *desire path* even refers to the fact that these paths are perceived to satisfy certain requirements, wants, and wishes that are not satisfied otherwise. The processes that Sartre claims to be in effect in the formation history of practical ensembles can be used to illustrate how such desire paths form as alternative options for human action, re-serialize into roads, and thus generate the need for another transformation. If the processes and mechanics Sartre develops in the context of his practical ensembles are taken as a basis, human need and the totalizing actions to tackle it must provide the entry point for this analysis (see section 4.7).

Everything begins with people's need for movement. This need is somewhat universal, given the constitution of the human body and the human condition in general. People move from one place to another for various reasons. This can be because their scarce environment does not provide them with what they require. By moving from one place to another, these people change how their ensemble scaffolds their options for action. This is the beginning of the formation of a communal ensemble.

Through their actions, these people inscribe themselves both positively and negatively into the material world. They produce positive outcomes for themselves while also producing potentially negative effects (Sartre 1978, 162). In the case of walking, positive outcomes can be, for instance, basic and complex movements through material friction, as well as the general closing of distances. These positive results are necessarily accompanied by certain negating effects in that these positive results, "in so far as they are inscribed in the object, are turned against and into it in the form of objective, negative exigencies" (Sartre 1978, 159). The act of walking also entails various material processes in which humans and instrumental means consume each other. In the spirit of Marx, every production must thus also be understood as a consumption, i.e. a *prosumption* (Marx 1983, 25; Schivelbusch 2016, 15). Inasmuch as humans wear down their shoes in the act of walking, these shoes wear down human feet, so that the skin becomes more callous to withstand pressure. Only after time, when shoes and feet have adapted to each other, will these worn and torn shoes feel like a second skin. This is a concrete, material instantiation of a *hexis* (see section 4.5).

Walking not only wears down shoes and the human body; it also imprints itself into the material conditions it takes place in. When people move from one place to another as a result of certain needs and desires, they leave traces—such as footprints—of the strategies they employed to tackle these needs and desires. These traces deepen when people repeatedly walk from one place to another, like from their home to a well and back. Eventually, these traces amount to the aforementioned desire paths, sunken lanes, and hollow ways. They link two or more places of interest and usually represent the shortest way to travel between those places; they also reflect some of the concrete needs and desires of those who trampled the paths before. As material cues, such visible connectors may represent practico-inert, material signifiers in a Sartrean sense, as these lines refer to the goal-oriented actions of others (see section 3.3). If one meets a desire path, its very existence usually means that something is interesting in one or the other direction.

Through repeated use, such desire paths become more solid and even broader. In Sartrean terms, this means that their practical inertia increases through repeated action over time. This not only represents the beginning of a *path creation* in the sense of a *path dependence* (see section 3.4); it also represents a re-serialization and thus the transformation from a communal into a serial ensemble (see section 4.4). In some instances, desire paths might have been early predecessors of modern road infrastructures. Paving these lines gives them certain material properties, through which these newly paved roads become useful for some use contexts but harmful for others. Their accessibility and utility might be increased. But changing the course of a paved road involves effort. By paving the road, people commit to a concrete course of the road. This entails even more forms of path dependences. Most importantly, the current material form and shape of these roads represent the passive remainder of the concrete strategies of past generations. The specific width of central European roads, for instance, goes back to Roman attempts to build roads wide enough so that two carriages were able to move past each other (Frey 2018, 14).

Paved road segments can connect to other road segments, which are paved in return to increase flow. When the interrelations between these road segments are structured through things, people, or rules, modes of travel are institutionalized. At this stage, road networks represent serial modes of structuring that afford people the chance to satisfy their requirements, wants, and wishes through the materialized action possibilities these roads provide. This is one way in which ontologically free, yet inherently goal-directed actions of individuals accumulate inertia over time, and eventually form practical ensembles that act back on those individuals in return.

5.3 Disturbances, Disruptions, and Crises

This section focuses on the various grades of disturbances, disruptions, and crises in urban mobility. The practical ensemble framework does not just provide principles to scrutinize the concrete relations between people and the material conditions they are situated in. It also provides tools to analyze how certain structured interrelations may influence each other, and how this might affect the structuring of these interrelations in return (see section 4.6).

Disturbances and Disruptions

Against the larger context in which the interrelations between road users and transport users take place, it becomes apparent that they affect each other's movements. For instance, depending on how the respective actions of pedestrians and car drivers are structured, how these modes of structuring interconnect, and how agents relate to this overall structuring, the interrelations between pedestrians and car drivers are more or less balanced and reconciled. Given, for instance, that pedestrians use pedestrian lights or crossings, and given that road users tend to obey the rules of traffic, their interrelations can be understood as balanced. However, such ideal cases of balanced and functioning safety and prevention measures in traffic do not necessarily represent reality.

In the case of jaywalking, the interrelations between road users are not reconciled despite possibly being otherwise balanced by certain modes of structuring. Jaywalking occurs when pedestrians cross busy streets while disobeying the established rules that regulate this crossing. Pedestrians might do this either because they do not know the traffic rules, they do not care, or they have a habit of doing it (Zhuang & Wu 2011; Xu et al. 2013). They can also jaywalk because it is faster. In Sartrean terms, they form a practical ensemble with the road that has a communal structure, to increase their options for action (see section 4.4).

However, by jaywalking, pedestrians materially intrude into the structured interrelations of other road users, such as car drivers and bicyclists. These road users must again deviate from their otherwise structured interrelations to avoid an accident. Eventually, this causes a disturbance in traffic flow, which can be transformed through proper responses to avoid accidents and by resuming structured and balanced interrelations. If accidents happen and pedestrians get injured for jaywalking, their injury can be understood as a counter-finality. Their action returns to them through the effects they caused in the structured interrelations between themselves, the road, and other road users (see section 4.6).

Although such accidents might initially represent disturbances for local flows of traffic at individual road segments, these disturbances can amount to a larger disruption in the overall flow of urban traffic. This might be the case, for instance, when critical road segments are blocked or when traffic jams occur. Such disruptions can even be caused by exogenous events, such as natural disasters or system-wide infrastructure failures. Especially regarding networked urban infrastructures, these disruptions may lead to cascading events—events with the potential to cause further problems at all levels of constellations that rely on the service provision and the proper functionality of the infrastructures (Little 2002). Cascading effects happen because of the inherent interdependency of infrastructure systems and their critical role as lifelines of society (Rinaldi et al. 2001; BMI 2009). These systems not only enable flows of traffic and access to concomitant options for actions; the services they provide are also associated with the continued existence of societal forms of organization.

Counter-Finality and Crisis

Beyond the internal effects that a larger form of urban mobility might have on its elements and structures, there may also be greater external effects that potentially act back on the current state of urban mobility in the form of counter-finalities (see section 4.6). Undoubtedly, anthropogenic climate change represents a global counter-finality that affects not only those who are predominantly responsible for it but also all life on earth. The first condition for counter-finality—the disposition of matter—is given by the dynamic changeability of weather. Low- and high-pressure areas alternate constantly, and solar radiation is reflected by ice surfaces or warms up large land masses during the day, which then release the heat overnight. Even the confluence of cold and warm water masses in the Atlantic and Pacific Oceans affects distant weather events.

The second condition of counter-finality—the becoming-inert of human *praxis*—is given by the fact that contemporary national economies have grown to rely on international flows of goods and individualized traffic, both mainly accomplished by cars, trucks, ships, planes, and other technologies with combustion engines. The historical development of global market flows, traffic, and transport is complex and itself situated in interlocking constellations of economic interests, industrialization, narratives of modernization, and a technological push and pull among many factors. The car, for instance, developed from a luxury object for tinkerers to a fast and reliable means of transport for the middle class, until it became a given that one is supposed to own a car in modern western societies (Heßler 2012, 103–107). In this context, Merki (2008) stresses the fact that it is almost impossible to disentangle the forward and backward linkages between the economy, industry, technology, and society (22–25). Nowadays, the core modes of production and mobility in modern economies are inextricably linked to large technological systems. These widely branched and networked systems of roads, highways, tracks, fuel stops, cars, storage buildings, and other elements represent the inert and long-lasting infrastructures of modern economies. They are the material foundations around which most contemporary societies are structured. According to Rogers Gibson (2017), paved roads have an average lifetime of around 10 to 20 years, whereas bridges last around 50 to 100 years (6). In the historical becoming of these systems, multiple developmental paths crossed, blocked and reinforced each other up until the present time (Hughes 1987; Mayntz & Hughes 1988). During this process, some forms of individual and supraindividual needs and desires could be satisfied, whereas others were created and even promoted. The contemporary constitution of modern societies is thus the materially inert product of path-dependent processes. These processes are themselves permeated by human needs and desires, material demands and requirements, and the materialized strategies to harmonize them.

Following Sartre's thoughts on the persistence of practical constellations, people's *hexeis* also play an essential role in these path-dependent processes. In section 4.5, it was mentioned that Sartre's conception of *hexis* combines aspects of Aristotelian *hexis*, habitual behavior, and habituation. As an action disposition, *hexeis* may even represent attitudes in the sense of a *habitus*. Especially with regard to private traffic, travel habits and familiarity with certain means of transportation seem to play a major role in travel-mode choice (Møller & Thøgersen 2008; Middleton 2011). In the case of car driving habits, Brette et al. (2014) argue that behavioral inertia not only reduces stress and anxiety; it even contributes to the perception that driving is itself a pleasant activity. Following the findings of section 4.5, those authors further emphasize the role of contextual cues that trigger certain patterns of behavior. When the car is taken as the means of transportation for reaching the workplace, the car will most likely remain the primary mode of transportation, given the same context. Because transportation habits intermingle with various other patterns of behavior—such as buying groceries after work in the same area, visiting friends, or going to the gym—travel habits are hard to change (415–417). Although habituated behavior might not necessarily yield negative consequences on its own, the same behavior can yield such consequences when performed by a group of people on a larger scale. The habit of using a car to get to work, for instance, does not just potentially obscure other more sustainable travel options for individuals. Usually, it is also more carbon-intensive than other modes of transportation (Schwanen et al. 2012, 527). This circumstance already points toward the third condition of counter-finalities.

The third condition of counter-finality—serial ubiquity—is given by the fact that global market flows and motorized traffic have indeed promoted both national economies and modern ways of life, especially in the northern hemisphere. This makes them attractive strategies for promoting a nation's wealth. Furthermore, this entails that other aspects accompanying these strategies—such as the presence of roads or owning a car—are associated with modernity and wealth. In the case of Peru, Harvey and Knox (2012) argue that road infrastructure has become associated with speed, connection, and other promises of emancipatory modernity (523). Edwards (2003) even claims that the building of infrastructures has been constitutive of the modern condition (191). Larkin (2013) refers to the conceptual roots of infrastructures in the Enlightenment and the fantastical evocations and fantasies that seem to accompany infrastructure projects (332–334). Consequently, global market flows and individualized traffic become attractive for nation-states and individuals alike. Because the dominant technologies around which globalization and individualized traffic are structured also emit large quantities of CO_2 during normal operation, global CO_2 rises. In 2014, transport as a whole was responsible for 23% of all CO_2 emissions worldwide (Santos 2017).

If all three factors come together, the basic conditions for climate change as a counter-finality are met. Owing to the material and bodily inertia of infrastructure systems, and promises of economic progress and connection, the reliance on combustion engines becomes *serially ubiquitous*. The global rising of CO_2 emissions contributes to the greenhouse effect, which, in combination with dynamic weather conditions, results in global climate change and potentially catastrophic weather events (Gesang 2011, 16–18). These events may put systems into crisis, cause potential disruption, or even create global disasters. To avoid such catastrophes, the core structures around which modern economies and individual transport are structured must be transformed.

Although these examples represent simplified representations of urban mobility, global economics, transportation infrastructures, and anthropogenic climate change, they illustrate the potential of the practical ensemble framework to deconstruct structured interrelations in complex constellations, such as cities, from multiple levels, and even to analyze the contribution of individuals for system-wide effects.

5.4 Infrastructures as Needful Structures

This section offers a more focused analysis of urban infrastructures in general, and urban mobility infrastructures in particular, through Sartre's practical ensemble framework. Again, the perspective on human needs and desires is central.

Urban Infrastructures

Urban infrastructures are remarkable constellations of practico-inert things, structures, and practices that organize societal interrelations in fundamental ways. In modern cities, infrastructures and their concomitant structuring are omnipresent, although often unnoticed. Drainpipes and power cables stretch under widespread street networks and enable a constant flow of water, electricity, information, and power, and send those things across the borders of human settlements, nation-states, and even continents. Some of these structures, like streets, water supplies, and sanitation, date back to ancient civilizations. Compared with these old constants of human settlements, electric power, and digital information technologies are relatively new. However, these modern systems have had profound impacts on the constitution of the modern condition. In most countries, even rural areas are connected to some sort of infrastructure systems, such as roads, electricity, or information systems.

Owing to their ubiquity, historicity, and practical inertia, infrastructures do more than their basic functional roles would suggest (see section 5.3). These structures not only support and manifest forms of societal organization; they also store power relations (Engels & Schenk 2014), and produce complex intermittent fluctuations of temporalities (Engels 2020). However, in most cases, especially given proper functionality, infrastructure systems are usually obscured by everyday routine and intentional design decisions. In modern societies, infrastructures represent instantiations of background technologies. Most people relate to them without noticing it (Ihde 1990, 109–111). However, for experts and maintainers, and when everyday users are affected by infrastructure disruption, infrastructures shift to the foreground and can generate the immediate need for preparatory and preventive measures.

This illustrates the challenging manner of appearing of infrastructures (Müller 2021). On the one hand, material infrastructures provide the ever-present "artificial environment" (Edwards 2003, 189) of urban life. On the other, these technological systems become somewhat opaque in cases of emergency, catastrophe, or disruption. Five out of nine properties that Star (1999) identifies regarding infrastructures relate directly to their manner of appearing. These are *embeddedness, transparency, learned as part of membership, embodiment of standards,* and *becomes visible upon breakdown.* According to Star, these properties are essential to infrastructures. From a technical perspective, a certain infrastructure transparency is intentional. These systems are supposed to be unobtrusive for everyday users while still allowing technicians and engineers to maintain critical elements (Müller 2021). Edwards (2017, 2019) approaches the challenging manner of appearing of infrastructures differently, by focusing on habituation processes as well as on the habits and skills of their users—which potentially render infrastructures transparent or invisible throughout their use context. Edwards points out that people may become habituated to the service provision of infrastructures, given that this service provision is somewhat reliable:

> Evolution designed human attention first and foremost to detect immediate danger, so our brains always focus most urgently on things that change, rather than those that remain constant. You cannot avoid noticing a fast-moving object that

enters your field of vision, but you must work rather hard to see the end of your own nose, even though it is always visible. You notice the refrigerator's hum when it starts up, but after a few seconds it fades entirely from your consciousness—until it stops and you briefly notice it again. The same phenomenon makes infrastructures you use every day unnoticeable: they are always there, and they always do the same thing, so your mind has better things to do than focus on them. (Edwards 2019, 358)

Furthermore, users interiorize the social norms and routines of urban mobility through repeated and even daily practical interrelation with things and structures. In so doing, they cultivate a *hexis* that allows them to satisfy their material or immaterial needs and desires efficiently and effectively (see section 4.5). Despite being an acquired practical interrelation between a person's *hexis* as an action disposition and a practico-inert technological artifact or structure as material disposition, the routinized realization of this interconnection in everyday activities becomes normalized as an integral part of how the practical ensembles work. As "[h]uman attention naturally focuses on what changes, rather than what remains constant" (Edwards 2017, 329), infrastructures seem to shift in and out of everyday awareness, depending on both whether experts or laypeople interrelate with them and what extent these people routinize this interrelation and habituate it (Müller 2021).

The core characteristic that seems to constitute the very concept of infrastructure is illustrated by the fact that these systems and institutions, which are usually considered to be infrastructures, provide specific services, knowledge, or other items that other sometimes more complex services, structures, institutions, individuals, and the general public depend on (Müller 2021). This explains not only their fundamental role in the structuring of modern societies but also their manner of appearing. Furthermore, it underlines the fact that things, structures, and even institutions derive their significance from the place they adopt in larger constellations. Sartre's practical ensemble framework comes into play here. In rather abstract ways, what constitutes an infrastructure is its relative importance as a result of the barely substitutable services it provides in a practical constellation. This conception can apply to almost every element in such constellations.

However, the material focus of Sartre's practical ensemble framework, as well as the needfulness understood to pervade all levels of practical constellations, allow one to ground the concept of infrastructure in the practically inert systems that serially structure, support, and prefabricate societal forms of organization based on human needs and desires. Larkin (2013) describes this conjunction as follows: "Infrastructures are matter that enable the movement of other matter. Their peculiar ontology lies in the facts that they are things and also the relation between things" (329).

Infrastructural Inertia and Resilience

Section 5.3 already indicated the critical role of infrastructures. With regard to urban mobility, that role can be further scrutinized regarding the way material infrastructures support and structure the formation and consolidation of urban mobility cultures through the interplay of their inert elements. Urban mobility cultures describe dominant modes of transport in connection to predominant socioeconomic conditions in cities. Klinger et al. (2013) identify these dominant modes according to certain indicators, such as spatial arrangement, density, population size, available transport infrastructure and supply, travel habits, attitudes of citizens and commuters, and so on. They cluster German cities, for instance, into cycling cities, auto-oriented cities, walking cities, and transit cities, among other types. Cycling cities, like Bremen or Leverkusen, are characterized by having a below-average population size and settlement density. Generally, cycling cities are smaller than auto-oriented cities such as Aachen and Wiesbaden, which, in return, have greater than average car-related businesses and fewer travel options besides cars. Transit cities, such as Augsburg or Dresden, are characterized by lower-priced tickets for public transport as well as a generally lower household income.

A similar concept to urban mobility cultures is that of urban fabrics. Newman and Kenworthy (2015) develop this concept to consider ways in which patterns of land use change and react to the transport infrastructures and to what they call the *priorities of cities*. The authors use a clustering similar to that in Klinger et al. (2013) and distinguish between walking cities, transit cities, and automobile cities to illustrate the interplay between material arrangements of urban spaces and the population's basic and more complex requirements, wants, and wishes. The authors use Marchetti's constant as a basis for their research. According to Marchetti's constant, humans have a somewhat fixed travel-time budget of around one hour, on average, per day that they are willing to commute. Based on this constant, the authors conclude that cities grow in relation to the speed with which people can commute through them. According to the authors, walking cities have represented the most common urban form for 8,000 years, and most city cores still retain the characteristics of walking cities.

Through the lens of the practical ensemble framework, this fact can be interpreted according to the needs, desires, and capabilities of a city's human elements as well as the composition of their practical field of equipmentality. Walking cities generally have narrow streets and shorter block sizes for optimal walkability and reachability of places in less time. Given that walking, riding, or traveling by cart or carriage were the dominant modes of transportation for the majority of human history until the industrial era (Merki 2008, 16), the material arrangement of cities represents the technological possibilities of those times. Automobile cities, on the other hand, oblige their inhabitants to own cars or to switch to other modes of transportation, as streets are generally wider and blocks further apart (Newman & Kenworthy 2015).

The interplay of the inert elements of urban mobility can be further scrutinized through the concept of *resilience*, a key idea in critical infrastructure research (J.I. Engels 2018a). Resilience is understood as the "capacity of a system to absorb and cope with perturbations" (Elsner et al. 2018, 31). The concept can be understood in terms of a *bouncing back* to its initial mode of operation, or in terms of a *bouncing forward*, an adaptation, to another mode of operation. According to Sartre's view on practical ensembles, both aspects of resilience can and even must be understood through the practical interrelations between their human and non-human elements.

The material side of infrastructures is usually built to last from 10 to 20 years, in the case of paved roads, to up to 100 years in the case of water distribution and sewage systems (Rogers Gibson 2017). Their relative durability renders these material infrastructures fairly resistant to change. Moreover, given that their specific properties provide a wide range of options for action, these material infrastructures can even be used throughout changing societal and political transformations. Roads, bridges, and sewage systems scaffold fundamental practical fields of equipmentality and possibility. They represent modes of serial structuring that enable the processing and consummation of various forms of societal organization. Simultaneously, in being continuously used, these material infrastructures are totalized as the necessary conditions of possibility for the practical ensembles that build on them. In this regard, such material infrastructures also represent the necessary conditions of possibility for a *bouncing forward* in the form of an adaptation of the larger practical ensemble. The previous chapter mentioned that serial and communal modes of structuring overlap and mutually enable the other modes to be realized through human action. Throughout history, the same roads have been used for needy and desiring people, tanks and soldiers, military parades, and freedom marches. The material foundations remain and enable different forms of societal constellation.

The human counterpart of material infrastructures is human *hexis*, in the sense of the routinized action dispositions cultivated by the repeated use of these infrastructures. Section 4.5 mentioned that practical ensembles persist through the *hexeis* of their human elements because it is those elements that enact the conditions of possibility of their actions by performing them. Because human elements rely on the goods and services their infrastructures provide or enable them to produce and perform, these elements stabilize the predominant modes of structuring for their respective practical ensembles. Such *hexeis* exhibit a high inertia themselves.

Criticality and Vulnerability

The criticality of infrastructures lies in the fact that the services they provide are directly linked to the satisfaction of individual and societal requirements, wants, and wishes. Movement has already been noted as an essential part of the human condition (see section 5.2). Owing to how serial modes structure flows of people, goods, and information, urban mobility infrastructures represent the concrete *interests* of urban dwellers. This is because of the positions both urban dwellers and infrastructures adopt in the larger form of organization for urban mobility (see section 4.3).

The practical inertia of urban mobility infrastructures, as well as the serial structuring that these infrastructures manifest, prefabricates a field of possibility that urban dwellers have to make use of to satisfy their needs and desires. In this way, urban mobility infrastructures are associated and even equated with continued human existence. This, in turn, leads to a concatenation of human and non-human elements, which together amount to a mutual functional criticality (Lukitsch et al. 2018, 16).

In critical infrastructure research, the concept of *criticality* is used to assess and analyze the dynamics of how infrastructures derive their societal significance. Criticality has its roots in the Greek *crisis* as discussed in section 4.6.

In the context of urban infrastructures, the concept of criticality has a long history. Folkers (2017, 2018) dates the concept to the idea of *Daseinsvorsorge*, or *existential provision* developed in Nazi Germany in the 1930s. This idea, like other structures and institutions from that time, found its way into the Federal Republic of Germany's welfare state paradigm. *Existential provision* refers to the idea that modern conditions and urban environments challenge pre-modern ideals of self-sustenance, which is why the state must provide for the structures and services that individuals require to live productive lives. During and after World War II, the criticality of infrastructures was reassessed in accordance with their relative importance for warfare, given the fact that some structures are vital points when attacked by the enemy. In the US, for instance, this so-called vulnerability mapping and the concomitant attribution of criticality to certain structures and systems was most prominent during the Cold War. In this way, the concept of criticality and critical infrastructure found their way into the civil sector (Collier & Lakoff 2008).

In all these contexts, criticality is used descriptively to identify and measure the relevance of certain features of society. Nowadays, the *existential provision* from the state, and the *critical vulnerabilities* of society in the case of war, have yielded to more systemic thinking about the importance of infrastructures. Technological innovation, rationalization, networking, and functional differentiation have led to a more sociotechnical conception of infrastructures that complicates a clear assessment or a clear hierarchy of which structures and systems are more critical than others and why.

The COVID-19 pandemic brought increasing difficulty in determining which parts of the population to protect, on which structures and institutions to rely, and how to fairly distribute social responsibility, workload, financial compensation, and vaccination, both on national and international levels. For instance, most protective measures taken during the pandemic were meant to avoid overstraining health infrastructure while predominantly relying on transport and information infrastructures for maintaining supply chains and social connectivity. Societies wish to avoid the collapse of their health infrastructure not just because it would mean loss of life but also because they require a large workforce to maintain other infrastructure systems. Health infrastructure is thus disclosed as a critical infrastructure, because it provides services that keep other infrastructures running in one way or another for those infrastructures, like the electrical grid, to keep health infrastructures running, and so on.

To reassess the potential of the concept of criticality, J.I. Engels (2018b) identifies three dominant perspectives on infrastructural criticality in infrastructure research. They differ regarding the strategic contexts in which criticality can be used as an analytical concept. The first perspective is concerned with systemic criticality. Systemic criticality is a bottom-up perspective that highlights single components as critical for system functionality. From a systemic perspective toward criticality, for instance, roads are understood as critical for traffic, water supply is critical for living, and wastewater disposal is critical for public health. This perspective is mostly concerned with the relation between infrastructures as individual parts of a sociotechnical totality and the general functional interplay of parts and wholes.

The second perspective is concerned with consequence-based criticality. Consequence-based criticality highlights societal consequences in the disruption of individual infrastructure systems. While the systemic perspective toward criticality also considers potential consequences via the functionality of the whole, consequence-based criticality represents a top-down perspective toward individual components. From a consequence-based perspective on criticality, infrastructures are essential because their disruption potentially threatens the well-being of individuals or even society as a whole.

The third perspective is not a strategic perspective *per se*, as it is mostly concerned with how criticality emerges in political discourse. J.I. Engels remarks that infrastructural criticality is in some sense always a product of an ascription or an attribution within a specific discourse. As such, criticality is always, in a sense, ideological. What is important for whom and why is not only a result of system features or potential harms and consequences, but also a result of political decision-making and, most importantly, ideological framing. Similar to processes of *securitization* (Balzaq 2005; Balzaq et al. 2016), J.I. Engels refers to scientific approaches that analyze processes of *criticalization*, through which societal relevance is ascribed to certain infrastructure systems. In this way, criticality can become a powerful tool for exercising power by framing specific discourses. By attributing criticality to certain infrastructures, these structures transform from *matters of fact* into *matters of concern* (Latour 2004).

Based on his reflections on the analytical perspectives for criticality, J.I. Engels does not advocate for criticality as a measure or property of infrastructures that describes their importance or relevance. Instead, he sees criticality as an expression of the degree of relationality of individual components within networked systems. According to J.I. Engels, the relevance of a component or an infrastructure is expressed in the number and significance of its relations. Criticality is thus largely an expression of the density and causal quality of networking (J.I. Engels 2018b).

In the context of Sartre's view on practical ensembles, the condition of possibility for an infrastructure's density and causal quality of networking, which may be called their *sociotechnical relationality*, is grounded in two things. One is the intricate and practical interrelation between the goal-directed actions through which human beings satisfy their requirements, wants, and wishes. The second is the things they instrumentalize and thus associate as the stable means to meet their ends. The conditions of possibility for infrastructural criticality are thus inherent in the systematic provision of essential goods and services both in and through practical ensembles.

Against the background of Sartre on practical ensembles, the concept of criticality is closely connected to vulnerability, another key concept of critical infrastructure research (J.I. Engels 2018a). The concept itself evokes images of open wounds and inherent vices. Because the criticality of specific infrastructure systems is expressed through the high sociotechnical relationality of individual components and systems, this criticality also reveals the spots that may cause harm or even cascading collapse to the functionality of other systems in the case of disturbance or failure. In the continued operation of sociotechnical systems, a certain dialectic can be identified—the very conditions of possibility enabling these systems to function in accordance with their intended requirements also render these systems prone to fail when those conditions are harmed. Through this dialectic in the operation of urban mobility infrastructures as practical ensembles, certain structured interrelations are revealed as weak spots that are therefore in need of protection (Kröger & Zio 2011, 5).

There is an inherent interconnectedness in urban mobility, understood as a strategic constellation to satisfy individual and supraindividual needs and desires. The integrity and functionality of those structures support this form of organization and enable this satisfaction, and is thus equated with people's continued existence. Consequently, people experience their own vulnerability through the susceptibility of urban infrastructures to disturbances, disruptions, and crises. The inherent needfulness of human beings is thus expressed in the needfulness of their infrastructures, and vice versa.

5.5 Concluding Remarks

This chapter explored how Sartre's view on practical ensembles can be applied to deconstruct and better understand some of the challenges of the human condition in modern societies. In this view, urban mobility represents a multilayered system of structured interrelations as well as a complex network of people, things, structures, and regulations. The material rigidity of urban mobility infrastructures enables the flow of goods and people through space. This flow is itself a complex product of how the actions of individuals are mediated by and for each other. Despite this rigidity, however, people, especially pedestrians, have the opportunity to blaze their paths where the current practical field does not suit their needs and desires.

The most important aspect of urban mobility infrastructures is their criticality and vulnerability. The inherent needfulness of the human condition works its way into the structures that were produced to tackle this needfulness in the first place. From the complex entanglement between humans and non-human things in the consummation of practical ensembles, the needful structures act back on the human elements again by exposing them to more complex requirements and material demands. The oscillation of liberation and necessitation can thus be found on all planes of human reality and history—in the complex sociotechnical relationality of modern societies, and the fundamental structure of human existence.

Conclusion

The goal of this work was threefold: to explore and systematize the theoretical foundations of practical ensembles in Sartre's philosophy; to outline a theoretical framework for practical ensembles; and to apply that framework for an understanding of societal constellations. Part I laid down the theoretical context and development of Sartre's ideas (Chapter 1), the totalizing character of human action and the processual character of human existence as a material endeavor (Chapter 2), and the significance of technology and body techniques for human action (Chapter 3). Part II then reconstructed how these dialectical foundations interplay in historical contexts and between individuals, which interactions result in a dialectic of practical ensembles. Within this dialectic, forms of societal constellation emerge and reinforce, transform, persist, and potentially collapse (Chapter 4). These principles were then applied to urban mobility systems to scrutinize some of the contemporary challenges of the human condition (Chapter 5).

This work has foregrounded the inherent needfulness—in the full meaning of the term—of both human existence and the structures produced in space through time to tackle it. This needfulness can be engaged in two ways: through human requirements, wants, wishes, and material demands, and through the socialization of *besoins* into *désir*—including their long-lasting concretization by material manifestation in the form of material inertia.

Practical ensembles are permeated by needs and desires, as well as by material demands and requirements, at every level. Human beings exteriorize themselves by relating to and engaging with their surroundings based on those needs and desires. By looking for food, water, shelter, or other things they require, want, or wish for themselves, human beings totalize themselves and their material surroundings against the background of their needfulness as material beings in a scarce environment. Their concrete form of subjectivity and the concrete objectivity of their world arise within and throughout this totalizing interrelation. As these humans then construct tools and structures, and as they adapt to using these tools and structures to secure access to their needs, they socialize and concretize their needfulness in material inertia. They form a practical ensemble and relate to it as the necessary foundation for how their specific form of societal organization is structured.

In doing so, their need, in an understanding of *besoin* as an abstract and initially undirected mode of relating to their requirements, wants, and wishes is manifested in practico-inert things and incarnated in practico-inert *hexeis*. In this way, their need becomes a concretized, directed, socioculturally shaped, and mediated desire, understood as *désir*, for the continued operation of their practical ensemble. Basic and more complex human requirements, wants, and wishes, together with the various strategies these humans employ to tackle them, arise in the continued existence of these ensembles.

Through the conceptual lens of practical ensembles, any larger constellation in which human beings unite with other humans, things, and structures is revealed to be permeated by actions and action schemes. These tackle needs and desires and attempt to meet material demands and requirements. The processes of formation and transformation in practical ensembles already reflect this in remarkable ways. According to Sartre, the formation and transformation of any forms of organization throughout human history can be traced back to the fact that certain practico-inert things, structures, and *hexeis* enable individuals to satisfy their requirements, wants, and wishes—or to the fact that they, for one reason or another, do not.

When individuals satisfy their needs and desires through modes of serial structuring, and when they continue to rely on the instrumental means they are structured with, these individuals reinforce the structures binding them. In this way, they continuously enact certain strategies to tackle their needs and desires and thus associate their possibility for self-reproduction with the means they use in this process. The fundamental needfulness of these serial structures becomes apparent in the various attempts to provide continuous access to certain resources or services through which needs and desires can be satisfied in the long run. Furthermore, inasmuch as individuals become reliant on instrumental means to transform their exigencies—especially owing to the various positions these individuals may adopt in practical ensembles—the structural integrity and continued functioning of these means are disclosed, along with their susceptibility to damage and disruption. Furthermore, this susceptibility may be equated with the impossibility of continued existence.

When individuals are not enabled to attain their ends with the means at hand, or when they become aware that some but not all of their exigencies might be taken care of by the larger form of organization they are embedded in, these individuals have the chance to transform their structures. They may employ different means or use established means differently. In doing so, their whole undertaking is defined as a partial totality by their very needfulness and their lack of real-life satisfaction. These communal structures become institutionalized and serialized, which not only allows people to tackle some requirements, wants, and wishes more efficiently and effectively—it also generates rigid structures that again entail other exigencies. Thus the cycle continues.

In agreement with Hegel, Sartre is convinced that human existence is inherently an *unhappy consciousness* without the chance to surpass this unhappy state. This means that, according to Sartre, it is difficult to analyze history with categories like progress or development. Needs and desires are fundamental, and will always render physicochemical reality a scarce milieu in which only needful structures may emerge. The whole of material culture bears witness to this constant struggle at the heart of the human condition. However, although these structures are inherently pervaded by needfulness, they are not determined by it. They merely provide possibilities to transform and satisfy what humans need to live in specific ways.

The reasons for individuals to perpetuate these structures or to initiate structural transformations are manifold, but all can be fundamentally traced back to the ability or inability to attain their ends in the long run. This becomes apparent in the role of *hexis* in the persistence of practical ensembles. In Sartre's understanding of human existence and history, *hexeis* represent organic counterparts to the material cultures of societies. They store the dynamic forces of societies and perpetuate structured interrelations. The reason for their cultivation is, again, past repeated success in tackling the needfulness of human existence. Whether in the structural foundations of human society or in the structure of human existence itself, needfulness, as the motor of human reality and history, remains a constant of the human condition.

References

Ally, M. C. (2012). Ecologizing Sartre's Ontology: Nature, Science, and Dialectics. *Environmental Philosophy*, 9(2), 95–121.

Ally, M. C. (2017). *Ecology and Existence. Bringing Sartre to the Water's Edge.* Lexington Books.

Anderson, T. C. (2013). Sartre's Second or Dialectical Ethics. In S. Churchill & J. Reynolds (Eds.), *Jean-Paul Sartre: Key Concepts* (195–205). Taylor & Francis.

Aristotle. (2015). *Nikomachische Ethik* (U. Wolf, Trans.). Rowohlt.

Aronson, R. (2019). Revisiting Existential Marxism: A Reply to Alfred Betschart. *Sartre Studies International*, 25(2), 92–98.

Ashby, W. R. (1957). *An introduction to Cybernetics.* Chapman & Hall LTD.

Balzacq, T. (2005). The Three Faces of Securitization: Political Agency, Audience and Context. *European Journal of International Relations*, 11(2), 171–201.

Balzacq, T., Léonard, S., & Ruzicka, J. (2016). 'Securitization' Revisited: Theory and Cases. *International Relations*, 30(4), 494–531.

Barad, K. (2007). *Meeting the Universe Halfway. Quantum Physics and the Entanglement of Matter and Meaning.* Duke University Press.

Barata, A. (2018). Towards a theory of action in Sartre's philosophy. From action to ethics. *Philonsorbonne*, 12, 125–137.

Bernhard, C. (2016). *Im Spiegel des Wassers. Eine transnationale Geschichte des Oberrheins (1800–2000).* Böhlau.

Bernstein, R. J. (1980). *Praxis and Action. Contemporary Philosophies of Human Activity.* University of Pennsylvania Press.

Betschart, A. (2019). Sartre was not a Marxist. *Sartre Studies International*, 25(2), 77–91.

Birt, R. E. (1986). Alienation in the Later Philosophy of Jean-Paul Sartre. *Man and World*, 19(3), 293–309.

Blackbourn, D. (2006). *The Conquest of Nature. Water, Landscape, and the Making of Modern Germany.* W. W. Norton & Company.

Blättler, C. (2012). Serial Sixties auf Französisch. Zur Ambivalenz der Serie. *Zeitschrift für Medienwissenschaft*, 7(2), 70–79.

Bonnemann, J. (2009). Sartre und die Macht der Dinge. Überlegungen zum Wechselverhältnis zwischen Handlung und Welt. In K.-H. Lembeck, K. Mertens, & E. W. Orth (Eds.), *Phänomenologische Forschungen* (5–36). Meiner.

Boria, D. (2015). *Creating the Anthropocene: Existential Social Philosophy and Our Bleak Future.* 14.

Bourdieu, P. (1977). *Outline of a Theory of Practice.* University Press.

Bourdieu, P. (1996). *Distinction: A social critique of the judgement of taste* (R. Nice, Trans.). Harvard Univ. Press.

Bowman, B., & Stone, B. (2004). The End as Present in the Means in Sartre's Morality and History: Birth and Re-inventions of an Existential Moral Standard. *Sartre Studies International,* 10(2), 1–27.

Bowman, E. A., & Stone, R. V. (1992). Socialist Morality in Sartre's Unpublished 1964 Rome Lecture: A Summary and Commentary. *Journal of French and Francophone Philosophy,* 4(2–3), 166–200.

Boyle, M. (2005). Sartre's Circular Dialectic and the Empires of Abstract Space: A History of Space and Place in Ballymun, Dublin. *Annals of the Association of American Geographers,* 95(1), 181–201.

Brette, O., Buhler, T., Lazaric, N., & Marechal, K. (2014). Reconsidering the nature and effects of habits in urban transportation behavior. *Journal of Institutional Economics,* 10(3), 399–426.

Bundesministerium des Inneren. (2009). *Nationale Strategie zum Schutz Kritischer Infrastrukturen.* Bundesministerium des Innern.

Burman, A. (2018). Back to Hegel! Georg Lukács, Dialectics, and Hegelian Marxism. In A. Bartonek & A. Burman (Hrsg.), *Hegelian Marxism. The Uses of Hegel's Philosophy in Marxist Theory from Georg Lukács to Slavoj Žižek* (17–34). Södertörns högskola.

Cannon, B. (1991). *Sartre and psychoanalysis: An existentialist challenge to clinical metatheory.* University Press of Kansas.

Cannon, B. (1992). Praxis, need, and desire in Sartre's later philosophy: An addendum to existential psychoanalysis. *Bulletin de La Société Américaine de Philosophie de Langue Française,* 4(2–3), 131–141.

Catalano, J. S. (2007). The Meaning and Truth of History: A Note on Sartre's Critique of Dialectical Reason. *Sartre Studies International,* 13(2), 47–64.

Collamati, C. (2016). Alienation Between the *Critique of Dialectical Reason* and the *Critique of Economic Reason.* Sketch of a Materialist Ethics. *Sartre Studies International,* 22(1), 83–98.

Collier, S., & Lakoff, A. (2008). The Vulnerability of Vital Systems: How Critical Infrastructure Became a Security Problem. In M. Dunn & K.S. Kristensen (Eds.) *Securing the Homeland. Critical Infrastructure, Risk and (In)Security* (40–62).

Crespo, A., Dombois, M., & Henning, J. (2018). Preparedness & Prevention. In J. I. Engels (Ed.), *Key Concepts for Critical Infrastructure Research* (39–44). Springer VS.

Crossley, N. (2010). Body, Technique and Reflexivity: Sartre in Sociological Perspective. In K. J. Morris (Eds.), *Sartre on the Body* (215–230). Palgrave Macmillan.

Dahlmann, M. (2013). *Freiheit und Souveränität. Kritik der Existenzphilosophie Jean- Paul Sartres*. ça ira.

DeLanda, M. (2006). *A New Philosophy of Society. Assemblage Theory and Social Complexity*. Continuum.

Deleuze, G., & Guattari, F. (2005). *A Thousand Plateaus: Capitalism and Schizophrenia* (B. Massumi, Trans.). University of Minnesota Press.

Dings, R. (2018). Understanding phenomenological differences in how affordances solicit action. An exploration. *Phenomenology and the Cognitive Sciences, 17*(4), 681–699.

Ebert, A.-K. (2020). Mobilität. In M. Heßler & K. Liggieri (Eds.), *Technikanthropologie: Handbuch für Wissenschaft und Studium*. Edition Sigma.

Edwards, P. N. (2003). Infrastructure and Modernity: Force, Time, and Social Organization in the History of Sociotechnical Systems. In *Modernity and technology*.

Edwards, P. N. (2017). The Mechanics of Invisibility: On Habit and Routine as Elements of Infrastructure. In I. Ruby & A. Ruby (Eds.), *Infrastructure Space* (327–336). Ruby Press.

Edwards, P. N. (2019). Infrastructuration: On Habits, Norms and Routines as Elements of Infrastructure. In M. Kornberger, G. C. Bowker, J. Elyachar, A. Mennicken, P. Miller, J. Nucho, & N. Pollock (Eds.), *Thinking infrastructures* (355–366). Emerald Publishing.

Egan, M. J. (2007). Anticipating Future Vulnerability: Defining Characteristics of Increasingly Critical Infrastructure-like Systems. *Journal of Contingencies and Crisis Management, 15*(1), 4–17.

Eifert, S., Knauf, A., & Thiessen, N. (2018). Vulnerability. In J. I. Engels (Eds.), *Key Concepts for Critical Infrastructure Research* (21–30). Springer VS.

Elsner, I., Huck, A., & Marathe, M. (2018). Resilience. In J. I. Engels (Eds.), *Key Concepts for Critical Infrastructure Research* (31–38). Springer VS.

Engels, F. (1975). *Anti-Dühring; Dialektik der Natur* (MEW 20). Dietz.

Engels, J. I. (2018a). *Key Concepts for Critical Infrastructure Research* (J. I. Engels, Eds.). Springer VS.

Engels, J. I. (2018b). Relevante Beziehungen. Vom Nutzen des Kritikalitätskonzepts für Geisteswissenschaftler. In J. I. Engels & A. Nordmann (Eds.), *Was heißt Kritikalität? Zu einem Schlüsselbegriff der Debatte um Kritische Infrastrukturen* (17–45). transcript.

Engels, J. I. (2020). Infrastrukturen als Produkte und Produzenten von Zeit. *NTM Zeitschrift für Geschichte der Wissenschaften, Technik und Medizin, 28*, 69–90.

Engels, J. I., & Schenk, G. J. (2014). Infrastrukturen der Macht—Macht der Infrastrukturen. Überlegungen zu einem Forschungsfeld. *Historische Zeitschrift, 63*, 22–58.

Engels, J. I., Frank, S., Gurevych, I., Heßler, M., Knodt, M., Monstadt, J., Nordmann, A., Oetting, A., Rudolph-Cleff, A., Rüppel, U., Schenk, G. J., & Steinke, F. (2021). *Transformation, Zirkulation, System of Systems: Für ein dynamisches Verständnis netzgebundener Infrastrukturen* (1–20). KRITIS TU Darmstadt.

Engels, K. S. (2018). From In-Itself to Practico-Inert. Freedom, Subjectivity, and Progress. *Sartre Studies International*, 24(1), 48–69.

Flynn, T. R. (1997). *Sartre, Foucault, and Historical Reason. Volume One. Toward an Existentialist Theory of History.* The University of Chicago Press.

Flynn, T. R. (2005). *Sartre, Foucault, and Historical Reason. Volume Two. A Poststructuralist Mapping of History.* The University of Chicago Press.

Flynn, T. R. (2014). *Sartre: A Philosophical Biography.* University Press.

Folkers, A. (2017). Existential provisions: The technopolitics of public infrastructure. *Environment and Planning D: Society and Space*, 35(5), 855–874.

Folkers, A. (2018). Was ist kritisch an Kritischer Infrastruktur? Kriegswichtigkeit, Lebenswichtigkeit, Systemwichtigkeit und die Infrastrukturen der Kritik. In *Was heißt Kritikalität? Zu einem Schlüsselbegriff der Debatte um Kritische Infrastrukturen* (123–154).

Føllesdal, D. (2010). The Lebenswelt in Husserl. In D. Hyder & H.-J. Rheinberger (Eds.), *Science and the Life-World. Essays on Husserl's Crisis of European Sciences* (27–45). Stanford University Press.

Frey, M. (2018). Wege zu Macht und Wohlstand. Das Straßensystem der Römerzeit. In K. Andermann & N. Gallion (Eds.), *Weg und Steg. Aspekte des Verkehrswesens von der Spätantike bis zum Ende des Alten Reiches* (11–28). Jan Thorbecke Verlag.

Furman, A. (2012). Desire Lines: Determining pathways through the city. In M. Pacetti & G. Passerini (Eds.), *Sustainable City VII* (Vol. 155, pp. 23–33). WIT Press.

Garud, R., Kumaraswamy, A., & Karnøe, P. (2010). Path Dependence or Path Creation?: Path Dependence or Path Creation? *Journal of Management Studies*, 47(4), 760–774.

Gehlen, A. (2007). *Die Seele im technischen Zeitalter. Sozialpsychologische Probleme in der industriellen Gesellschaft.* Vittorio Klostermann.

Gesang, B. (2011). *Klimaethik.* Suhrkamp.

Gibson, J. J. (1966). *The Senses Considered as Perceptual Systems.* George Allen & Unwin Limited.

Giddens, A. (1986). *The Constitution of Society.* Polity Press.

Graham, S. (2010). When Infrastructures Fail. In S. Graham (Eds.), *Disrupted Cities: When Infrastructure Fails* (1–26). Routledge.

Grosz, E. (2013). Habit Today: Ravaisson, Bergson, Deleuze and Us. *Body & Society*, 19(2–3), 217–239.

Haff, P. (2014). Humans and technology in the Anthropocene: Six rules. *The Anthropocene Review*, 1(2), 126–136.

Handel, A. (2017). Distance matters: mobilities and the politics of distance. *Mobilities*.

Hartmann, K. (1966). *Sartres Sozialphilosophie. Eine Untersuchung zur Critique de la Raison Dialectique I*. De Gruyter.

Harvey, P., & Knox, H. (2012). The Enchantments of Infrastructure. *Mobilities, 7*(4), 521–536.

Hegel, G. W. F. (1986). *Phänomenologie des Geistes*. Suhrkamp.

Heidegger, M. (2000). Die Frage nach der Technik. In *Vorträge und Aufsätze* (7–36). Vittorio Klostermann.

Heidegger, M. (2005). *Die Grundprobleme der Phänomenologie*. Vittorio Klostermann.

Heidegger, M. (2006). *Sein und Zeit*. Max Niemeyer.

Heßler, M. (2012). *Kulturgeschichte der Technik*. Campus.

Heßler, M. (2019). Technik und Autonomie Kulturhistorische Bemerkungen zu einem komplexen Verhältnis. In H. Hirsch-Kreinsen & A. Karacic (Eds.), *Autonome Systeme und Arbeit: Perspektiven, Herausforderungen und Grenzen der Künstlichen Intelligenz in der Arbeitswelt* (247–274). transcript.

Hubig, C. (1978). *Dialektik und Wissenschaftslogik: Eine sprachphilosophisch-handlungstheoretische Analyse*. De Gruyter.

Hubig, C. (2006). *Die Kunst des Möglichen I, Grundlinien einer dialektischen Philosophie der Technik Band 1: Technikphilosophie als Reflexion der Medialität*. transcript.

Hubig, C. (2007). *Die Kunst des Möglichen II, Grundlinien einer dialektischen Philosophie der Technik Band 2: Ethik der Technik als provisorische Moral*. transcript.

Hubig, C. (2010). Kulturbegriff – Abgrenzungen, Leitdifferenzen, Perspektiven. In G. Banse & A. Grunwald (Eds.), *Technik und Kultur. Bedingungs- und Beeinflussungsverhältnisse* (55–72). KIT Scientific Publishing.

Hubig, C. (2013a). Arnold Gehlen: Die Seele im technischen Zeitalter. Sozialpsychologische Probleme der Industriellen Gesellschaft. In *Nachdenken über Technik* (150–153). Edition Sigma.

Hubig, C. (2013b). Historische Wurzeln der Technikphilosophie. In *Nachdenken über Technik. Die Klassiker der Technikphilosophie und neuere Entwicklungen* (19–40). Edition Sigma.

Hubig, C. (2015). *Die Kunst des Möglichen III, Grundlinien einer dialektischen Philosophie der Technik Band 3: Macht der Technik* (1. Aufl.). transcript.

Hubig, C. (2016). Dialektik. In P. Richter (Ed.), *Professionell Ethik und Philosophie unterrichten. Ein Arbeitsbuch* (133–144). Kohlhammer.

Hughes, T. P. (1987). The Evolution of Large Technological Systems. In W. E. Bijker, T. P. Hughes, & T. Pinch (Eds.), *The Social Construction of Large Technological Systems. New Directions in the Sociology and History of Technology* (51–82). MIT Press.

Huning, A. (2013). Ernst Kapp: Grundlinien einer Philosophie der Technik. In C. Hubig & G. Ropohl (Eds.), *Nachdenken über Technik* (214–217). Edition Sigma.

Ihde, D. (1990). *Technology and the Lifeworld. From Garden to Earth*. University Press.

James, W. (1890). *The Principles of Psychology Vol I.* Henry Holt and Company.

Jay, M. (1984). *Marxism and Totality. The Adventures of a Concept from Lukács to Habermas.* Polity Press.

Jessop, B., Brenner, N., & Jones, M. (2008). Theorizing Sociospatial Relations. *Environment and Planning D: Society and Space, 26,* 389–401.

Joerges, B. (1999). Die Brücken des Robert Moses. Stille Post in der Stadt- und Techniksoziologie. *Leviathan, 27*(1), 43–63.

Kant, I. (1974). *Kritik der Urteilskraft.* Suhrkamp.

Kapp, E. (2015). *Grundlinien einer Philosophie der Technik.* Meiner.

Karafyllis, N. C. (2019). Soziotechnisches System. In K. Liggieri & O. Müller (Eds.), *Mensch-Maschine-Interaktion: Handbuch zu Geschichte – Kultur – Ethik* (300–303). J.B. Metzler.

Kim, S., Park, J., Abdel-Aty, M., Lee, S., & Kim, S. (2019). Influence of road lane reductions on motorised and non-motorised traffic safety. *Proceedings of the Institution of Civil Engineers – Municipal Engineer, 172*(4), 233–238.

Kleinherenbrink, A., & Gusman, S. (2018). The Ontology of Social Objects: Harman's Immaterialism and Sartre's Practico-Inert. *Open Philosophy, 1*(1), 79–93.

Klinger, T., Kenworthy, J. R., & Lanzendorf, M. (2013). Dimensions of urban mobility cultures. A comparison of German cities. *Journal of Transport Geography, 31,* 18–29.

Koselleck, R., Brunner, O., & Conze, W. (Eds.). (1982). Krise und Kritik. In *Geschichtliche Grundbegriffe. Historisches Lexikon zur politisch-sozialen Sprache in Deutschland* (617–675). Klett-Cotta.

Kröger, W., & Zio, E. (2011). *Vulnerable Systems.* Springer London.

Larkin, B. (2013). The Politics and Poetics of Infrastructure. *Annual Review of Anthropology, 42*(1), 327–343.

Latour, B. (2004). Why has Critique Run Out of Steam? From Matters of Fact to Matters of Concern. *Critical Inquiry, 30*(2), 225–248.

Lee, G., Joo, S., Oh, C., & Choi, K. (2013). An evaluation framework for traffic calming measures in residential areas. *Transportation Research Part D: Transport and Environment, 25,* 68–76.

Leroi-Gourhan, A. (1988). *Hand und Wort.* Suhrkamp.

Little, R. G. (2002). Controlling Cascading Failure: Understanding the Vulnerabilities of Interconnected Infrastructures. *Journal of Urban Technology, 9*(1), 109–123.

Lockwood, T. C. (2013). Habituation, Habit, and Character in Aristotle's Nicomachean Ethics. In T. Sparrow & A. Hutchinson (Eds.), *A History of Habit. From Aristotle to Bourdieu* (19–36). Lexington Books.

LSJ-Ancient Greek dictionaries (no date a): ἔχω. Retrieved from https://lsj.gr/wiki/%E1%BC%94%CF%87%CF%89

LSJ-Ancient Greek dictionaries (no date b): τέχνη. Retrieved from https://lsj.gr/wiki/%CF%84%CE%AD%CF%87%CE%BD%CE%B7

Luckner, A. (2005). *Klugheit.* De Gruyter.

Luckner, A. (2012). Gestellte Möglichkeiten. Heidegger über die technische Seins-weise. In P. Fischer, A. Luckner, & U. Ramming (Eds.), *Die Reflexion des Möglichen. Zur Dialektik von Handeln, Erkennen und Werten* (51–64). LIT.

Lukács, G. (1923). *Geschichte und Klassenbewusstsein. Studien über marxistische Dialektik.* Luchterhand.

Lukitsch, K., Müller, M., & Stahlhut, C. (2018). Critiality. In J. I. Engels (Ed.), *Key Concepts for Critical Infrastructure Research* (11–20). Springer VS.

Marx, K. (1983). *Grundrisse der Kritik der Politischen Ökonomie* (MEW 42). Dietz.

Marx, K., & Engels, F. (1962). *Das Kapital. Kritik der politischen Ökonomie. Erster Band Buch I. Der Produktionsprozeß des Kapitals* (MEW 23). Dietz.

Mauss, M. (1934). Les techniques du corps. *Journal de Psychologie, 32*(3–4).

Mauss, M. (1973). Techniques of the Body. *Economy and Society, 2*(1), 70–88.

Mayntz, R. (2002). Zur Theoriefähigkeit makro-sozialer Analysen. In R. Mayntz (Ed.), *Akteure, Mechanismen, Modelle: Zur Theoriefähigkeit makro-sozialer Analysen* (7–43). Campus.

Mayntz, R., & Hughes, T. P. (Eds.). (1988). *The Development of Large Technical Systems.* Campus.

Merker, Barbara (2015): Die Sorge als Sein des Daseins (§§ 39–44). In Rentsch, T. (Ed.), *Martin Heidegger: Sein und Zeit* (109–124). De Gruyter.

Merki, C. M. (2008). *Verkehrsgeschichte und Mobilität.* Verlag Eugen Ulmer.

Middleton, J. (2011). I'm on Autopilot, I Just Follow the Route: Exploring the Habits, Routines, and Decision-Making Practices of Everyday Urban Mobilities. *Environment and Planning A: Economy and Space, 43*(12), 2857–2877.

Møller, B., & Thøgersen, J. (2008). Car Use Habits: An Obstacle to the Use of Public Transportation? In C. Jensen-Butler, B. Sloth, M. M. Larsen, B. Madsen, & O. A. Nielsen (Eds.), *Road Pricing, the Economy and the Environment* (301–313). Springer.

Monahan, M. J. (2008). Sartre's Critique of Dialectical Reason and the Inevitability of Violence: Human Freedom in the Milieu of Scarcity. *Sartre Studies International, 14*(2), 48–70.

Müller, M. (2017). The Urban Disposition. A Sartrean Framework for the Analysis of Urban Life. *Filosofia. Revista Da Faculdade de Letras Segunda Série, 34,* 187–203.

Müller, M. (2021). Structure and Background. The Influence of Infrastructures on Human Action. In M. Nagenborg, T. W. Stone, M. González Woge, & P. E. Vermaas (Eds.), *Technology and the City. Towards a Philosophy of Urban Technologies* (121–136). Springer International Publishing.

Neal, D. T., Wood, W., Labrecque, J. S., & Lally, P. (2012). How do habits guide behavior? Perceived and actual triggers of habits in daily life. *Journal of Experimental Social Psychology, 48,* 492–498.

Neal, D. T., Wood, W., Wu, M., & Kurlander, D. (2011). The Pull of the Past: When Do Habits Persist Despite Conflict With Motives? *Personality and Social Psychology Bulletin, 37*(11), 1428–1437.

Newman, P., & Kenworthy, J. (2015). *The End of Automobile Dependence. How Cities are Moving Beyond Car-Based Planning*. Island Press.

Norman, D. A. (2013). *The Design of Everyday Things*. Basic Books.

Orlikowski, W. J., & Scott, S. V. (2008). Sociomateriality: Challenging the Separation of Technology, Work and Organization. *The Academy of Management Annals, 2*(1), 433–474.

Peaucelle, J. (2000). From Taylorism to Post-Taylorism. Simultaneously Pursuing Several Management Objectives. *Journal of Organizational Change Management, 13*(5), 452–467.

Peirce, C. S. (1878). How to Make Our Ideas Clear. *Popular Science Monthly, 12,* 286–302.

Petit, V., & Guillaume, B. (2018). We Have Never Been Wild: Towards an Ecology of the Technical Milieu. In S. Loeve, X. Guchet, & B. Bensaude Vincent (Eds.), *French Philosophy of Technology. Classical Readings and Contemporary Approaches* (81–100). Springer.

Pickering, A. (1995). *The Mangle of Practice: Time, Agency, and Science*. Univ. of Chicago Press.

Quinn, J. M., Pascoe, A., Wood, W., & Neal, D. T. (2010). Can't Control Yourself? Monitor Those Bad Habits. *Personality and Social Psychology Bulletin, 36*(4), 499–511.

Rae, G. (2011). Sartre, Group Formations, and Practical Freedom: The Other in the Critique of Dialectical Reason. *Comparative and Continental Philosophy, 3*(2), 183–206.

Ravaisson, F. (2008). *Of Habit*. Continuum International Publishing Group.

Remley, W. L. (2012). Sartre and Engels. The Critique of Dialectical Reason and the Confrontation on the Dialectics of Nature. *Sartre Studies International, 18*(2), 19–48.

Richter, M. (2011). *Freiheit und Macht. Perspektiven kritischer Gesellschaftstheorie—Der Humanismusstreit zwischen Sartre und Foucault*. transcript.

Rietveld, E., & Kiverstein, J. (2014). A Rich Landscape of Affordances. *Ecological Psychology, 26,* 325–352.

Rinaldi, S. M., Peerenboom, J. P., & Kelly, T. K. (2001). Identifying, understanding, and analyzing critical infrastructure independencies. *IEEE Control Systems Magazine, 21*(6), 11–25.

Rogers Gibson, J. (2017). *Built to Last. Challenges and Opportunities for Climate-Smart Infrastructure in California*. Union of Concerned Scientists.

Ropohl, G. (2009). *Allgemeine Technologie: Eine Systemtheorie der Technik* (3., überarbeitete Auflage). Universitätsverlag Karlsruhe.

Rosenberger, R. (2014). Multistability and the Agency of Mundane Artifacts: From Speed Bumps to Subway Benches. *Human Studies, 37,* 369–392.

Rosenberger, R., & Verbeek, P.-P. (Eds.). (2015). *Postphenomenological Investigations. Essays on Human-Technology Relations*. Lexington Books.

Santos, G. (2017). Road transport and CO2 emissions: What are the challenges? *Transport Policy*, *59*, 71–74.

Sartre, J.-P. (1943). *L'être et le néant. Essai d'ontologie phénoménologique*. Gallimard.

Sartre, J.-P. (1960). *Critique de la raison dialectique I. Théorie des ensembles pratiques*. Gallimard.

Sartre, J.-P. (1963). *Search for a Method* (H. E. Barnes, Trans.). Alfred A. Knopf, Inc.

Sartre, J.-P. (1969). Itinerary of a Thought. *New Left Review*, *58*, 43–66.

Sartre, J.-P. (1978). *Critique of Dialectical Reason I. Theory of Practical Ensembles* (A. Sheridan-Smith, Trans.). NLB.

Sartre, J.-P. (1985). *Critique de la raison dialectique II. L'Intelligibilité de l'histoire*. Gallimard.

Sartre, J.-P. (1991). *Critique of Dialectical Reason II. The Intelligibility of History* (Q. Hoare, Trans.). Verso.

Sartre, J.-P. (2001). To Be Hungry Already Means That You Want To Be Free. *Sartre Studies International*, *7*(2).

Sartre, J.-P. (2003). *Being and Nothingness. An Essay on Phenomenological Ontology* (H. E. Barnes, Trans.). Routledge.

Sartre, J.-P. (2005). Der Existentialismus ist ein Humanismus. In *Der Existentialismus ist ein Humanismus und andere philosophische Essays 1943–1948* (145–192). Rowohlt.

Sartre, J.-P. (2021). *Being and Nothingness. An Essay on Phenomenological Ontology* (S. Richmond, Trans.). Washington Square Press/Atria.

Schatzki, T. (2010). Materiality and Social Life. *ResearchGate*, *5*(2), 123–149.

Schivelbusch, W. (2016). *Das verzehrende Leben der Dinge. Versuch über die Konsumption*. Fischer.

Schivelbusch, W. (2018). *Geschichte der Eisenbahnreise. Zur Industrialisierung von Raum und Zeit im 19. Jahrhundert*. Fischer.

Schlanger, N. (2020). André Leroi-Gourhan (1911–1986). In M. Heßler & K. Liggieri (Eds.), *Technikanthropologie: Handbuch für Wissenschaft und Studium* (22–130). Nomos Verlagsgesellschaft mbH & Co. KG.

Schuitmaker, T. J. (2012). Identifying and unravelling persistent problems. *Technological Forecasting and Social Change*, *79*(6), 1021–1031.

Schwanen, T., Banister, D., & Anable, J. (2012). Rethinking habits and their role in behaviour change: The case of low-carbon mobility. *Journal of Transport Geography*, *24*, 522–532.

Sheller, M., & Urry, J. (2006). The New Mobilities Paradigm. *Environment and Planning A: Economy and Space*, *38*(2), 207–226.

Shove, E. (2016). Infrastructures and practices: Networks beyond the city. In J. Rutherford & O. Coutard (Eds.), *Beyond the Networked City: Infrastructure Reconfigurations and Urban Change in the North and South* (242–258). Routledge.

Shove, E., & Trentmann, F. (Eds.). (2019). *Infrastructures in Practice. The Dynamics of Demand in Networked Societies*. Routledge.

Siegler, M. (2022a). Der Regelkreis der Geschichte. Sartres Überlegungen zur Gewohnheit im Spannungsfeld von Aristoteles und William James. In A. Betschart (Ed.), *Pragmatismus und Existentialismus. William James und Jean-Paul Sartre* (121–148). Schwabe Verlag.

Siegler, M. (2022b). The Dialectics of Action and Technology in the Philosophy of Jean-Paul Sartre. *Philosophy & Technology, 35*(2), 1–28.

Simont, J., & Trezise, T. (1985). The Critique of Dialectical Reason: From Need to Need, Circularly. *Yale French Studies, 68*, 108–123.

Smith, Q. (1979). Sartre's theory of the progressive and regressive methods of phenomenology. *Man and World, 12*(4), 433–444.

Sparrow, T., & Hutchinson, A. (Eds.). (2013). *A History of Habit. From Aristotle to Bourdieu.* Lexington Books.

Star, S. L. (1999). The Ethnography of Infrastructure. *American Behavioral Scientist, 43*(3), 377–391.

Stone, R. V., Bowman, E. A. (1986). Dialectical Ethics: A First Look at Sartre's Unpublished 1964 Rome Lecture Notes. *Social Text, 13/14*, 195–215.

Sydow, J., Windeler, A., Müller-Seitz, G., & Lange, K. (2012). Path Constitution Analysis: A Methodology for Understanding Path Dependence and Path Creation. *Business Research, 5*(2), 155–176.

Thompson, R. F. (2009). Habituation: A History. *Neurobiology of Learning and Memory, 92*, 127–134.

Tomlinson, G. (2014). Totalization, Temporalization and History: Marx and Sartre. In L. Jeschke & A. May (Eds.), *Matters of Time. Material Temporalities in Twentieth-Century French Culture* (87–102). Peter Lang.

Turner, C. (2014). The Return of Stolen Praxis. Counter-Finality in Sartre's Critique of Dialectical Reason. *Sartre Studies International, 20*(1), 36–44.

Urry, J. (2007). *Mobilities.* Polity Press.

Verplanken, B., & Wood, W. (2006). Interventions to Break and Create Consumer Habits. *Journal of Public Policy & Marketing, 25*(1), 90–103.

Weber, J. (2020). MenschMaschine. In M. Heßler & K. Liggieri (Eds.), *Technikanthropologie: Handbuch für Wissenschaft und Studium* (318–322). Nomos Verlagsgesellschaft mbH & Co. KG.

Weismüller, C. (1999). *Jean-Paul Sartres Philosophie der Dinge. Zur Wende von Jean-Paul Sartres Kritik der dialektischen Vernunft sowie zu einer Psychoanalyse der Dinge.* Psychoanalyse & Philosophie.

Winner, L. (1980). Do Artifacts Have Politics? *Daedalus, 109*(1), 121–136.

Wood, W., & Neal, D. T. (2007). A new look at habits and the habit-goal interface. *Psychological Review, 114*(4).

Wood, W., & Neal, D. T. (2016). Healthy through habit: Interventions for Initiating & maintaining health behavior change. *Behavioral Science & Policy, 2*(1), 71–83.

Wood, W., & Rünger, D. (2016). Psychology of Habit. *Annual Review of Psychology*, 67(1), 289–314.

Xu, Y., Li, Y., & Zhang, F. (2013). Pedestrians' intention to jaywalk: Automatic or planned? A study based on a dual-process model in China. *Accident Analysis and Prevention*, 50, 811–819.

Young, I. M. (1994). Gender as Seriality: Thinking about Women as a Social Collective. *Signs: Journal of Women in Culture and Society*, 19(3), 713–738.

Zhuang, X., & Wu, C. (2011). Pedestrians' crossing behaviors and safety at unmarked roadway in China. *Accident Analysis and Prevention*, 43(6), 1927–1936.

Essay

João Costa
Health as a Social System
Luhmann's Theory Applied to Health Systems.
An Introduction

January 2023, 198 p., pb.
30,00 € (DE), 978-3-8376-6693-9
E-Book: available as free open access publication

PDF: ISBN 978-3-8394-6693-3

Markus Gabriel, Christoph Horn, Anna Katsman, Wilhelm Krull,

Anna Luisa Lippold, Corine Pelluchon, Ingo Venzke
Towards a New Enlightenment –
The Case for Future-Oriented Humanities

2022, 80 p., pb.
18,00 € (DE), 978-3-8376-6570-3
E-Book: available as free open access publication
PDF: ISBN 978-3-8394-6570-7
ISBN 978-3-7328-6570-3

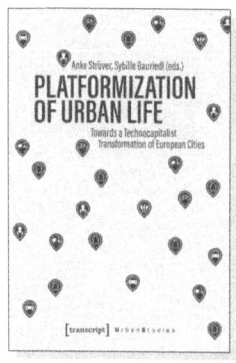

Anke Strüver, Sybille Bauriedl (eds.)
Platformization of Urban Life
Towards a Technocapitalist Transformation
of European Cities

2022, 304 p., pb.
29,50 € (DE), 978-3-8376-5964-1
E-Book: available as free open access publication

PDF: ISBN 978-3-8394-5964-5

**All print, e-book and open access versions of the titles in our list
are available in our online shop www.transcript-publishing.com**

Essay

Frank Adloff, Alain Caillé (eds.)
Convivial Futures
Views from a Post-Growth Tomorrow

2022, 212 p., pb.
25,00 € (DE), 978-3-8376-5664-0
E-Book: available as free open access publication
PDF: ISBN 978-3-8394-5664-4
 ISBN 978-3-7328-5664-0

Sven Quadflieg, Klaus Neuburg, Simon Nestler (eds.)
(Dis)Obedience in Digital Societies
Perspectives on the Power of Algorithms and Data

2022, 380 p., pb., ill.
29,00 € (DE), 978-3-8376-5763-0
E-Book: available as free open access publication
PDF: ISBN 978-3-8394-5763-4
 ISBN 978-3-7328-5763-0

Sabine Pfeiffer
Digital Capitalism and Distributive Forces

2022, 282 p., pb., ill.
59,00 € (DE), 978-3-8376-5893-4
E-Book: available as free open access publication
PDF: ISBN 978-3-8394-5893-8
 ISBN 978-3-7328-5893-4

GPSR Authorized Representative: Easy Access System Europe, Mustamäe tee 50, 10621 Tallinn, Estonia, gpsr.requests@easproject.com

www.ingramcontent.com/pod-product-compliance
Lightning Source LLC
Chambersburg PA
CBHW061742120626
46550CB00005B/1865

9 783837 662825